ALEKSANDER PLATER-ZYBERK

The Last Barons
of Weyssensee

(Novel in the autobiographical vein)

Dui Sun Jin Publishing

ISBN: 978-0-615-25397-8

Library of Congress Control Number: 2008938722

In this book, I did not want to reproduce the exact history of the real characters. These have instead served as a backdrop to a tale that claims to be a sociological study of our epoch.

I especially would like to thank here Master Paul Blagny, advocate to the Court of Appeal of Dijon, for his invaluable collaboration in the editing of this work.

I also express my great gratitude to Mademoiselle Mahaut de Cordon, master of arts, and Mr. Gonzague Saint-Bris, brilliant writer, for the suggestions and the encouragement that he brought to me.

A. de Plater

This translation is dedicated to
Marietta Czacka née Plater-Zyberk,
My grandmother.

Her encouragement guided me
through an enjoyment of French.
I wish I could have worked on
the translation with you.

Table of Contents

FIRST PART   : In a World That Self-Destructs 1

    CHAPTER 1   : The Baptism of Philibert 2

    CHAPTER 2   : The House of the Steward 5

    CHAPTER 3   : An Evening in Weyssensee 9

    CHAPTER 4   : The Curate and the Baroness 12

    CHAPTER 5   : A Hunting Party 15

    CHAPTER 6   : The Zeelu Ball 19

    CHAPTER 7   : The Archbishop and the Governor 22

    CHAPTER 8   : The Cousin the Bishop at Weyssensee 26

    CHAPTER 9   : Voyage to Saint Petersburg 31

    CHAPTER 10   : The Bartzels Across Europe 37

    CHAPTER 11   : The Seasons 43

    CHAPTER 12   : 1914 46

    CHAPTER 13   : The Departure from Weyssensee 49

    CHAPTER 14   : Life in Exile 53

    CHAPTER 15   : The Great Revolution 57

    CHAPTER 16   : The Return to Weyssensee 61

    CHAPTER 17   : A New Turning Point 66

    CHAPTER 18   : The Liberation of Wilno 70

    CHAPTER 19   : Perspectives of Sobierzyce 76

    CHAPTER 20   : The Fate of Weyssensee 80

SECOND PART: Towards New Ruins 85

    CHAPTER 1   : Ball at Otwocko 86

    CHAPTER 2   : The Bartzels in Sobierzyce 90

    CHAPTER 3   : Lord and Lady Beechforest in Sobierzyce 93

    CHAPTER 4   : A Grand Reception at the Bristol Hotel 97

    CHAPTER 5   : Wolodia and Philibert 102

    CHAPTER 6   : At the Beechforests' Home in America 106

    CHAPTER 7   : The Decision of Philibert 111

    CHAPTER 8   : The Death of the Old Baron 115

    CHAPTER 9   : A Reunion of Young Bartzels 117

    CHAPTER 10   : Beginnings of the War of 1939 119

CHAPTER 11   : The Gestapo 122

CHAPTER 12   : The Germans At Otwocko 125

CHAPTER 13   : The Warsaw Ghetto 127

CHAPTER 14   : The Warsaw Uprising 133

CHAPTER 15   : Decision at Otwocko.. 142

CHAPTER 16   : Through Germany.. 146

CHAPTER 17   : The Arrival of the Americans.............................. 153

THIRD PART   : In a World That Changes 161

CHAPTER 1   : Abbot Philibert's Problems 162

CHAPTER 2   : In the United States 172

CHAPTER 3   : The Czerski Family 180

CHAPTER 4   : The Last Years of Ermelyne............................... 185

CHAPTER 5   : The Last Will and Testament of Ermelyne 192

CHAPTER 6   : Rendezvous at the Hotel Crillon 197

CHAPTER 7   : At the Vatican 208

CHAPTER 8   : Grand Kermesse in Bourg-sur-Landarge 212

FIRST PART

IN A WORLD THAT SELF-DESTRUCTS

CHAPTER I

THE BAPTISM OF PHILIBERT

Philibert, the only son of Baron Sigmund Bartzel von Hohenwaitzen and of the princess Ermelyne of Caramanlys, was born at the dawn of the XXth century, in the vast castle near the waters of the immense lakes of the same name.

Imperceptibly, moved with the light lapping waves, some small sailing boats moored to the foot of the steps leading to the mansion, so much of the day was calm and hot. Imperturbable, with immense forests of black firs of thousands and thousands of hectares, framed the blue waters like the blue of the sky where swim some rare puffs of clouds. In the park, a solitary bird would weakly chirp always the same refrain.

In a room, all white and all gilded, scented with roses that the gardener had just brought, the birth giver in a bathrobe and her spouse together discussed the list of people invited to the baptism of their son. The Baron – he was the twenty-fifth descendant of the name – belonged to one of the oldest, the most powerful and the richest families of this region, seated on the coasts of the Baltic Sea, intersection of the nations where since the XIIIth century, native Latvians, Germans, Swedes, Poles and Russians squabbled for domination. The Baron Bartzel had some relatives as well in Poland as in Russia, in Germany, in France and in Italy; the Baroness descended from the loftiest Austrian nobility; she was related to almost all the reigning houses of Europe. To all their invited guests – dukes, princes, counts and barons – it would be necessary to assign the rooms in the castle according to their rank and their age.

The Baron, a small man, fine and slender, remained standing near a large open window facing the lake, upon which he gazed with dreamy eyes. An agreeable breeze was blowing over the waters. Visibly, the theme of the conversation bored him to the highest level. He was thinking, in that instant, to an ancient Latin book in which he projected to enrich his magnificent library.

The baroness, a little annoyed by the distracted attitude of her spouse, said finally, "But we need to decide, my poor Syg, this is due to the archduke that our "royal chamber" returns but to the cardinal-archbishop; in Rome, in Vienna, the cardinals always take precedence over the princes of royal blood." She had pronounced these words in a calm and soft voice because she was always brought up well and although a deep-down snob, she was above all profoundly pious.

"Go for the cardinal," exclaimed her husband, who above all loved peace. The baroness of Bartzel, born princess of Caramanlys, decided then (as it was close to habit) that the cardinal-archbishop would occupy the chamber so named "royal." For the baron, it was an indifferent thing; he was a believer, little conformist, and was attaching only a weak importance to the protocol, above all to the ecclesiastic protocol. Moreover, he did not love very much the clergy, which he rarely found up to the level of its task. From another side, plunged into his books and his problems, he cared very little for all the archdukes of the world that he considered otherwise vain, at least superficial.

Some days later, the baptism of the little Philibert came and went as planned, to the point that it was no longer a question of precedence between the cardinal and the archduke; the last had begged to excuse his absence because of the precarious political situation where his country found itself. In effect, the Hapsburg monarchy was already feeling the first swirls that had to soon precipitate Europe into the world war.

The family flag of the Barons of Bartzel, in the black and yellow colors splashed with Polish white and amaranth, floated already on the highest tower of the castle when started to arrive the numerous cars, carriages and calashes, filled with invited guests coming from the closest station of Weyssensee. A crowd of livery lackeys were welcoming them on their arrival. After having freshened up and put on their formal dress – ladies in long and low-cut dresses, gentlemen in immaculate tailcoat and polished shoes – the guests, dignified and calm, came down the stairs of honor, covered with a thick, crimson rug and reunited in the grand salon, where their hosts were waiting for them.

Under the portraits of the ancestors of the Barons Bartzel von Hohenwaitzen, small circles form, perfuming discreetly the atmosphere with an eau de Cologne; then they move to the dining room where immense and illuminated splendors "a giorno" would reflect from a thousand fires the table silverware and the jewels of the ladies. On the side, a discreet orchestra played the deafening airs of Lehar and Strauss. Prepared by the best cooks of the capital and from which each guest could read the menu in golden letters on a small place card present on the side of his place setting, the dinner was a veritable treat. Numerous domestics were silently changing the plates and pouring, into rich crystal, prestigious wines, red or white. Around the table, they barely hear the rustling of a conversation nevertheless animated.

For the steward, the tutors, the secretaries, the ladies of honor and the high staff, a second table was dressed in the "red salon," while the lower staff had to be content with taking its meal in the outer buildings of the castle. If from the "red salon," the notes of the orchestra were barely audible, they would absolutely no longer hear them at the third table and even more, the plates there were less refined than those served at the second, in order to not speak of the first. But the quantity replaced the quality. Nevertheless, the ambiance was everywhere distinguished and each rose finally happy to have attended a dinner of such grand class.

The next morning, in the lordly chapel of the castle, Philibert-Stanisław-Aleksander-Jerzy-Zygmunt-Jozafat of the high Barons of Bartzel von Hohenwaitzen was baptized by His Eminence the Cardinal-Archbishop of Saint Petersburg, the high Baron Edward von Hoffisch-Buxwolden, relative of his father. The baptismal registers were signed by the godfather, the Marquis of Tamerlan des Etoiles, himself also a relative of the father, and of his Highness Serenissimo the Princess Osterwelden-Campini, née Archduchess Austria first cousin of the mother of the baby. The entire staff attended, on the sides of the family, this ceremony. The enormous chapeaus decorated with fantastic ostrich plumage, worn by the grandest and most elegant of Europe, were next to the white aprons of the chamber maids and the grey hoods of the "muiziniks."[1]

The baroness, who regulated discreetly the protocol, was fully satisfied with the ceremony.

---

[1] Muiziniks: Latvian peasants.

CHAPTER II

THE HOUSE OF THE STEWARD

Three hundred meters from the caste, at the periphery of the great forest, under the century-old oaks, lived the steward and his family. The house of two stories was the ancient home of the owners of Weyssensee. Very comfortable, his furnishings and his settlement kept a rustic character almost peasant.

With his two stories, the house dominated the principal farm where among the muliple buildings, homes, stables, sheds, castle courtesans and workers bustled about. From morning to evening, in the suitable seasons, a large sawmill would cut into symmetric planks, the immense trunks of firs that they would bring non stop from the neighboring forest. The air was filled with the monotonous chant of the sawmill and with the fresh and vigorous perfume of the resin that flows from the cut trees.

At the other end of the farm, in the garden of the Management, innumerable bees would flutter about around their hives that furnished honey well. Although it was absolutely nothing like a castle, the house of the steward was not any less very agreeable and moreover, easier to live in than the latter. "If I could," sighed sometimes the lord of the manor, "exchange the castle for this home, I would be even more tranquil."

Because the poor baron would often arrive only with difficulty at coping with all the disturbances and with the multiple expenses that the maintenance and the continual reparations, which his immense domicile required, caused him.

The house under the oaks was inhabited by Kurt Buchenwald, the steward, and by his wife, his two children and his mother. In addition, they had a domestic for the cooking and another for the housework. Kurt Buchenwald was of Jewish origin, but – although not believing neither in God nor in Devil – he was made to be baptized in order to be able to marry a young girl of the neighborhood, of ancient Polish nobility impoverished. He had had with her two children, a boy and a girl, and looked after his old mother, Ryffka, née Meyerholz. This one looked always after the ancient Israelite traditions, lighting the Sabbath candles and eating the hard and crunchy "matzo."[1] Kurt Buchenwald tolerated these habits. On the other hand, he detested the travels of his grandfather, always in a life that was perceived too often to his liking through the village, wearing a "mytzka,"[2] his patched-up "tallit"[3] fluttering around his body and an old sack on his back from where he pulled out his merchandise in order to sell to the peasants.

"Stop turning always to Weyssensee," Kurt would say to his old grandfather Levi, you make me ashamed; you will come to live with me and you will no longer need to haggle..."

"No," responded the elderly man, "you are no longer Jewish; myself, I want to stay what I am and I will not come to live with you." They loved each other however, well in the Buchenwald family, but too much distance separated now one from the other.

Kurt Buchenwald was a very intelligent man. With a tenacious work ethic, he was a social climber to climb out of the misery. He was even a graduate from foreign schools where he had studied all that concerns agriculture and forests. Without being unethical, he knew how to skillfully profit from the events that offered him his situation at the estate of the Baron of Weyssensee and constituted a significant fortune. However he had not a bad heart, and while the Baron, always short of cash, would ask him for a loan, he would easily accord it to him, not so much in order to lose sight of his own interests, taking some mortgages on the properties of his lord.

"You have no shame," to him said the old Ryffka once, "to cut the branch of the tree on which you sat," because the old Jewish woman loved the patrons well and did not want that they were ruined.

"Anyway, Mama," responded the son, "they are lost, not only the brave Baron and his wife of whom no one can say something bad and who are full of kindness and of good will, but all their caste. All of them live only in the past and have no practical notion about the future. Likewise, I was better from understanding what is waiting for us; the war with Japan, the revolution, were not only from weak premises, sisters of the

---

[1] Matzo: kosher grilled bread.
[2] Mytzka: Polish variant for yarmulke, skullcap that Jews wear.
[3] Tallit: prayer shawl.

immense catastrophe into which will self-destruct the old world and all its values."

The old Ryffka was not consoled, but she understood that well-ordered charity begins through one's self and did no longer ever recapture the former conversation with her son. And she would continue her excellent relations with the Baroness; this one would come to see her and would discuss with her for a long while. The pious Baroness did not like the Steward, who never ceased to complain of the Curate, of his endless pretensions and demands – he had always a need, be it for firewood, be it vegetables for cooking, be it pasture for his two cows; the Steward would go on to accuse him of entertaining a mistress, which was the last straw to the antipathy that the Baroness felt towards the Jewish social climber. On the other hand, the lady of the manor very much loved Ryffka, not only for the delicious "matzo" that she knew how to prepare so well, but most of all, because she judged within this Jewish woman a profound faith and thought to convert her to the true religion. Notwithstanding, at the termination of long discussions, the two ladies each stayed with her initial position and the Jewish woman would not let go of her traditional beliefs.

Never had Ryffka dreamed of harming in her faith the Baroness, but she could not admit neither that Jesus of Nazareth was a God descended from heaven ; because this one had known only how to teach to men how to die on the cross while the Jews themselves were waiting for a triumphant Messiah. It is in vain that the Baroness responded to her that Jesus had proved his divine power since he arose from the dead, Ryffka nodded only the head, she had however not been up to say – like her son had recently done – that a resurrection was scientifically impossible.

While leaving Ryffka, the Baroness said to her, "I will pray for you." But she had not asked for the reciprocal action because she was not fully sure that the prayer of a "hardened heretic" could be of great usefulness.

And however something very profound continued to attract her to this Israelite. The proletarian Jew, coming from the depths of the ghetto, and the aristocrat, raised in the Court of Austria, had something in common: a grounded honesty, an unwavering attachment to what they both believed to be their God; an ideal of heroism confining to the fanaticism. Despite the divergence of their religious opinions, they continued no less to mutually respect and help each other. Ryffka and the Baroness understood each other maybe often better than many others among them, who however have the same convictions.

CHAPTER III

AN EVENING IN WEYSSENSEE

Once after the evening meal, the sleeping children in their room on the second floor, the baronial couple retired to the grand library on the ground floor where in front of a small glass of fragrant cognac, the Baron would read to his spouse the latest novels appearing on the scene. He was himself an author known in his country – they called him the "Polish Turgenev" – and he would read very well, making the situations and the characters in the book come to life. Always in admiration before the immense culture of his husband, the Baroness would listen to him religiously, accomplishing at the time some her prodigious and skillful knitting; they would barely arrive at following the maneuvers of that one among the fine and distinguished hands. As she was still a child, the Austrian aunts would repeat to her, "Ermelyne, never remain in laziness."

On the fourth stage of the castle, in the apartments situated under the gables, from where from the windows to the bull's eye, extended a splendid view on the infinite ocean of black forests of the Duna[5], the masters and teachers, before going to sleep, would go, be one or the other. The little pretty Luxembourgeoise woman with blond hair, the tall Belgian with chestnut hair who taught mathematics, would furtively throw tender glances. Everyone were aware of them for awhile, the children the first. That would be able to lead even farther if it had not been the sever look of Madame Irene Drozdowska, a Pole from Warsaw, lady of a certain age, who would rejoice from the full confidence of the Baroness and who had her room on the same floor. This one had quickly reported to the lady of the manor who was not amused by this chapter.

In the dining room in the basement, where a petrol lamp hanging from the ceiling arch made huge shadows flutter, the domestics were reunited at a long oak table where the remains of the supper were lying around. The old head waiter, Andrzej Karp, his shirt front completely covered with grease stains, had already retired to a large straw armchair, from which, while digesting his

---

[5] Duna: Daugava, river in Latvia.

9

meal, he would listen to the conversation continuing at the table. The domestics spoke amongst themselves, in Latvian, the native language, even though they also knew Polish, Russian and German and could even make a mockery of some French or English words, that they had heard pronounced by their patrons and by the teaching body.

At the end of the table spoke at length a tall boy, young and blond, with a rather heavy and massive beauty, very sure of himself. It was the hunter for the Baron, Anton Wajdewis, whose precocious intelligence had attracted the attention of this one who had made him do his studies and employed him now as his "factotum." The handsome Anton accompanied his master in all his voyages abroad and in the capitals and believed now to know all and better than anyone else.

Anton was the idol of all the chamber maids of the castle. They drank his words with rapture, most of all the pretty Ewcia. "All this must change," enunciated Anton emphatically, "the time of the barons is obsolete, it is necessary to look forward to the future!"

"And what is this future?" interrogated the old Karp, buried in his armchair. Karp was old, but his dignity, his rugged and honest behavior, had conferred to him a certain authority with the rest of the domestic staff.

"The future, Mr. Karp," retorted Anton, "it is the abolition of all the castles and the lands to everyone."

"But what is it that our Baron has then done to you," continued the old domestic, "did he not take you from the mud, did he make from you what you have become? Without him, you would be nothing. And you forget also all that the Bartzels and their equals did for the region: the schools, the asylums, the hospitals, the factories, and even the co-ops that they founded… If our region is one of the most civilized of all the Russian provinces, is it not above all thanks to our barons…?"

"It could well be that they had accomplished something, but it is only their most strict duty and that to the excess, they did it only partly. The land belongs to everyone and all that is found on the land must benefit all and not only some privileged few. Moreover, who are these privileged? Some strangers, some noble Poles or Germans who took over territories that did not belong to them and who ensconced themselves by force on the Latvian lands!

All these barons, be they Polish or German, have only to leave and if they want to stay, only to work like us! Otherwise, they will worry beyond measure about their money and even their lives! The barons had their time! We no longer have a need of their civilization! The future belongs to us!"

In front of such eloquence, the entire audience including the old Karp remained silent. He rose slowly from his chair and went outside. Night had fallen and the sky sparkled with stars. The full silvery moon pulled its disk from the clouds, it seemed to Karp to notice on his face a mocking smile in front of these incessant whirlpools of men.

CHAPTER IV

THE CURATE AND THE BARONESS

Three times a day, across the great lake, one would hear the Angelus ringing out. Depending on the thickness of the air, the pealing seemed more or less to come nearer. A triple serious chiming calling out, into the far surroundings, the heroic death of the young Jagiellon prince, Ladislas of Warna, who in the XVIth century, had fallen in an unfortunate charge against the Turks at Mohacz in Hungary, at the head of his army.

From the other side of the lake, the great parish church raises its visible white towers of several versts.[1] It had been founded by the great grandfather of the present lord of Weyssensee, the Baron Sygbert Engelfahrt, third Palatine of Livonia and enclosed the tombs of the family of the Bartzel barons. Four evangelists, greater than nature, decorated the façade of the church.

Its incumbent was the Abbot Mikhail Latlajtys, half-Latvian, half-Polish, who gave his sermons in these two languages. He was young, dynamic and intelligent and the Baroness regarded him with great esteem, what moreover would come from him because she had a neat fondness for those, who served the Holy God.

In a sailing vessel, she went often to the church alone or even in the company of her children, the two twin daughters at the beginning and later, the little Philibert when he had grown up a little. The children loved very much these escapades because the Curate offered them always some jams and if the mother permitted it, a little of very sweetened wine   The children exited from the parish with the hands completely sticky.

That time, the Baroness went alone because she had a case of a heavy conscience. Entering into the state room that moreover she had known so well – where a Christ on an ivory cross sat enthroned among a clutter of small red armchairs and baskets full of plants – the Baroness felt suddenly very embarrassed. "Excuse me, Father Curate," said she while sitting down face to face with the young pastor, "if it pleases you that I am very indiscreet, impolite even... But it is a matter of the good of the Church and of

---

[1] Verst: obsolete Russian unit of length equal to 3500 feet.

yours."

"Speak, speak, Baroness."

"It is that, Father Curate, one accuses you of having a mistress."

The priest blushed all the way to the neck, then controlled his emotions and burst out laughing. "I know, Madam, it is surely that Buchenwald, that free mason who cannot stand the priests and who looks to harm me each time he can. No, Madam, I do not have any mistress. I am surely not better than another but how do you want that a priest worthy of this name, who has the faith and must teach it during his existence, active in a permanent manner against his teaching. It would be the highest level of falsehood, of hypocrisy and of imposture. Have I the air of being such a hypocrite?"

"No, surely not, Father Curate, but you are young and all the girls of the village run after you. Watch out..."

"Thank you, Baroness, I will take heed of it," responded the Curate half-reassured.

At present, another thing, Father Curate," replied the lady after a pause, "Do you believe that we, my husband and I, do our duty in regard to the community? From the point of view of the Church, are we in order?

"You pose to me a question to which it is very difficult for me to respond," said the priest. "God alone is the judge of our actions. It would seem that both of you do all that is possible. Notwithstanding, since you asked me, I say it to you," and the Curate had a little forced laughter, "I strongly doubt that you could satisfy everyone. No one speaks poorly of you, you are, in general, appreciated, but you also wear a great weight that you could never remove."

"Which one?" worried the Baroness.

"In this nation, you will always remain foreigners, aristocrats, the people who are not from 'our home.' Wherever you go, it will always feel like that. You will eternally suffer the weight of your superiority and you will never get rid of it. You will always be happy ones who had done nothing in order to merit their privileges. And that is only pardoned difficultly."

It was late when the Baroness left the rectory in order to return to her home. A sun of a fine September declined at the horizon, making glitter from a thousand lights the waters of the lake gilding the wilted leaves of the birches, which appear in the distance at the foot of the black mass of firs. The air is filled with a great calm. The Baroness was very tired, never had she felt so alone. "Even though we have given the best of ourselves, we will always be misunderstood," she tells herself in her interior conscience. And however, there was in her soul no bitterness; to the contrary, it seemed to her that God was still closer, more present across all and despite all, God always comforting, God above everything.

And thereafter, despite this conversation rather disagreeable, the relations between the pastor and the lady of the manor did not deteriorate at all.

CHAPTER V

A HUNTING PARTY

Weyssensee, with its huge forests and its innumerable lakes, was a place reputed for its hunts. With nothing comparable on the plains of Posnania or of Pomerania – where one would make a bloodbath of jackrabbits, of black grouse and of partridge – its impenetrable forests hid the rare species of antediluvian elk and of the large blue grouse, which are only accessible in the epoch of its vernal love. During the rigorous and long winters, there one would hear even the howling of famished wolves, and he even happened to encounter a bear come by chance from northern Russia. On the great lakes congregated all sorts of savage birds – teal ducks – which soar in the dense swarms with the loud flapping of wings.

Numerous were the friends, relatives and neighbors, who came in all seasons, to hunt at Weyssensee. Polish relatives and Baltic neighbors were the most assiduous. The great hall of the castle smelt then the powder and the rifles of every caliber stacked up on the table in front of the entrance at the side of the cartridge belts. Long lines of carts, called "bryczki" or according to the season, sleighs, waited in front of the steps to the entrance.

The hunters came back late into the evening after a brief supper of with sauerkraut – the "bigosse" – and large drafts of "vodka," they joined together in the grand library on the second floor in order to terminate the day after their weariness. One would still serve cognac and the conversation would regularly take a political turn.

"These Latvian peasants have become quite impudent," would cry the Ritter von und zu Winkelkopf, a close neighbor of Weyssensee, standing with his glass of cognac in one hand, with a giant of a monocle. "Yesterday even, one of my workers addressed me – imagine – with German words. Do you know what I replied to him? 'Myself, I speak German with the lords and with the Germans, but to the dogs, to the peasants, to the Latvians, I address them only in Latvian.' I put him back in his place, didn't I?" With these words, he burst out with enormous laughter.

Even though half of the guests were German, this joke of the Ritter von und zu Winkelkopf, known for his Prussian sentiments, did not raise the enthusiasm to which this one was waiting for. Some smiled, but most received these words with an embarrassed silence. The Baron and his two brothers-in-law, the Marquis Edelfred and Arthur Bardzopolski, even seemed profoundly shocked. "You do not measure the consequences of your words," said the Baron, with a voice that he strived to render calm. "Your attitude renders the worst services to the same cause that you want to defend. This manner of treating your inferiors is no longer acceptable in our times. Let alone a pagan, but not even a Christian could speak like that."

Ritter von und zu Winkelkopf became furious. He controlled his emotions and said in a voice filled with muted anger, "Everyone knows your liberalism, dear Baron. But it is justly this liberalism that made us let go of the rudder and thanks to which everything is now going adrift. Alexander II abolished the servitude. Nicholas II established a Parliament; now we perceive only too late where that is driving us. We descend always from a march, and finally, it is the ruin of the Empire that is waiting for us at the bottom of the ladder. What is necessary," and then the Ritter von und zu Winkelkopf lifted his voice, "is to reestablish the methods of the ancient Teutonic knights, who conquered this country by the sword and the fire, it is to introduce the manner of the Iron Chancellor Bismarck; look at Prussia at this moment. It is the greatest power of the world! And it has not yet shown all of which she is capable."

"He who laughs last laughs the best," the Baron made the remark, "I am not, in principle, against the powerful manner and I love that one knows what one wants. However, this does not exclude the sense of justice and of humanity, which are totally lacking in your own conception. The situation does not degrade because of liberalism – the western countries are all liberal, what does not impede them from achieving the results that Prussia could often envy from them. It is not the liberalism that is bad in itself, but the lack of decision, the laziness, the corruption at the heart of our government that will be the channel for losing this country. We give from one hand, and we take with the other. It is that which is detrimental. The first condition of all politics is the logic…"

As the conversation deviated towards the critique of the government, the two young Polish marquis use fatigue, the late hour as a pretext. They stood up in order to go make another visit to their sister who, slightly indisposed had remained lying down in her boudoir on the third floor. In their internal conscience, they gave enough of a reason to their brother-in-law, but he preferred to remain prudent. Edelfred occupied an important post of Jägermeister[1] to the Imperial Court while Arthur was captain and "fliegel-adjutant"[2] in the regiment of the Cavalry Guard of Tsarskoye Selo of which the emperor assumed personally the command. Both did not care to compromise needlessly.

The family of the Bardzopolski marquis was, since several generations, at the head of the Polish party that had spoken out for a cooperation with Russia; according to their opinion, the total independence of Poland was inconceivable at this time and collaboration with the German occupiers impossible ; they had then chosen the solution that seemed to them the most reasonable: an understanding with the Russians. Evidently, the parties in Poland treated the Bardzopolskis as evil politicians, otherwise as traitors and as sell-outs. But those of grand lords convinced of being right responded with total contempt.

Ermelyne loved her two half-brothers very much. They were all of the same race, tall and handsome. She radiated joy when they entered into her salon that a fire from wood heated comfortably at this start of autumn, though a large petrol lamp illuminated, through a lampshade decorated with Chinese landscapes, the elegant furniture of the room. "Are you satisfied with your occupations in Saint Petersburg?" she asked them when the two younger siblings had unfolded their long bodies in their armchairs.

"Certainly, we are content," responded Edelfred, "but do not make any illusions of our career. We will never go very far. To me, they will never entrust a post of minister responsible and Arthur always remains a captain even though almost all his comrades of the Page Corps have been for some time colonels; there are even some general-majors."

"And why then?" worried Ermelyne. "For what do they reproach you?"

"But nothing! On the contrary," continued her brother. "Everyone recognizes that there are no subjects more loyal and more honest to His Majesty than the both of us. But our great

---

[1] Jägermeister: hunter for His Majesty.
[2] Fliegel-Adjutant: military aide.

shortcoming is wanting to remain Catholic. The Baltic Germans succeed better than us – such as the von Bärenkampfs, the von Waldriesens – but they are all of the "prawoslawnïje."[3] There is nothing to do. Obviously, that arranges well the Russian government of having at its sides, in the Court or in the Army, representatives of the highest Polish aristocracy, related to the royal families. They are completely read to give us situations in name only where it needs people well bred and of good stock. But we will never go further, the career in Russia will always be closed to us."

The Baroness grew somber a little. And nevertheless, she could not miss being proud of her two brothers who carried so high the banner of their Catholicism. She did not delude herself for so much and knew that the attachment of those to religion explains less their profound convictions than rather by the sense of respect, of loyalty, of honesty towards the family traditions.

The sister fully comprehended her brothers; they were of the same caliber and of the same race of grand faithful lords until the sacrifice to what they regarded as their duty.

---

[3] Prawoslawnïje: of the Orthodox religion.

CHAPTER VI

THE "ZEELU BALL"

Each year after the conclusion of the field work, the lady and lord of Weyssensee would organize a grand ball for the workers, the neighboring peasants would equally participate. Since the morning, the grand school – work of the Baroness – was the object of all sorts of works and plans. Once the classroom emptied of its benches, of its chairs and its desks having become useless, a crowd of "meitini"[1] of the village set about during several hours to scrub and to wash the rough floorboards; afterwards, they placed on the walls and the ceiling numerous multicolored Venetian lanterns; finally, two tables came to be piled up with pyramids of plates and glasses, countless rolls of sausages and balls of country bread. With all that, some large pitchers full of beer brewed on site were added.

Slightly before the ball, one illuminated the Venetian lanterns, while the orchestra, that included a violin, a harmonica and two flutes, settled into a corner of the hall.

Even before the Venetian lanterns were lit, the hall, already supervised by the Steward, filled up with children and women bundled up in grey shawls. The women stood along the wall while the children were waiting with impatience the lighting of the hall and above all the arrival of the Baroness who came to distribute to them large sacks of bonbons and caramels. The air became thick and heavy without the persons present being bothered by it.

It was already night when the large carriages stopped in front of the entrance. Everyone pricked up his ears while the Steward welcomed at the door the lord and lady surrounded by their two twins, Amaldyne and Cathaline, those were flanked by their governess while the little Philibert walked along by the side of his tutor who held his hand. The hall saluted with deference the couple, Baron and Baroness; that couple, after some amicable words of assistance, opened the ball with a rhythmic and majestic polka. To the sounds of the violin, the harmonica and flutes, several notable couples from the village followed the movement, dancing a sophisticated polka, during which the dancers do not

---

[1] Meitini: young girls.

stomp on the floor but drag the feet.

After having finished several turns at dancing, the masters of the places stopped and with a very amicable smile, the Baroness offered to the children enormous sacks of bonbons; then followed by her spouse, her children and the people, who accompanied them, she left the hall in the middle of a crowd, which respectfully ceded passage to them. It was, in effect, preferable to leave the place in time, in order to averting the children from the sight of a spectacle, which became easily savage, coarse, even indecent.

After the departure of the lord and lady and their children, there were sighs of relief in the hall. "Voilà, they have finally left, the "lieuskungs"[2]said some voices.

Immediately afterwards, in the door-frame of the door appeared the chubby and smiling face of the Curate, the Abbot Latlajtys, saluted by the acclamations of joy. He went to the middle of the hall exchanging the jokes with the men and giving the amicable taps on the head of the children and teasing the women. "Eh, you, mother Zakis, will you dance with me?" asked he to the eldest of the village, edental, wrinkled, hunched and shriveled in her old armchair of straw.

"Alright," responded maliciously the old Zakis, "If you want to marry me; my old man died just twenty years ago!" The crowd burst out laughing.

The curate sat astride of a seat, his hands fixed on the back of the chair and observed the dancers. He found that the things went very slowly and that there was not enough energy. "Eh! The musicians!" he cried. "Eh! The dancers! Go faster!" And he clapped his hand and stomped his feet in order to arouse more enthusiasm.

And there the hall started to truly whirl. Even the "very dignified" Anton Wajdewis, the hunter for the Baron who held in his arms his "fiancée" Ewka, pretty, little, brunette chamber maid for the children in the castle, went from the polka "with dragging feet" to the polka "with stomping feet;" the gendarme with the cook, the teacher with the most beautiful daughter of the village, the buxom Wercia, who with a single slap, dispersed some too enterprising candidates, all the boys started to tap their feet and to took frenzied turns with the dancers. Through this noise, they

---

[2] Lieukungs: illustrissimo lords.

almost no longer heard the music, and in the swirl of dust lifter by the boots, they perceived only barely the whirling couples. Afterwards, tired dripping with sweat, boys and girls approach the tables in order to consume sausages and beer. A little sad and worried, Ewka remained near Anton because she had noticed the looks too insistent that her fiancé threw at the beautiful Wercia. Meanwhile, the curate had left, he had not even finished his breviary. However, the ball continued.

After having drunk beer in abundance, the men initiated a style of dance that the Baroness, with reason, feared for her children. This style was called the "marriage of the bear." The men set out on four paws and imitated the loves of the bears. That was very vulgar, sometimes even obscene, but aroused thunders of laughter in the crowd of spectators.

After that, one started anew the classic dances, polkas, waltzes, but all were exhausted, men women, children left in great numbers. There remained however several die-hards who wanted to continue until dawn. The orchestra could no longer continue and stopped. Then, in order to replace the music, the Steward beat the measure with his cane. Some girls and boys, completely drenched in sweat, danced until dawn which already started to whiten the nocturnal sky.

"Enough! Each one to his home," screeched the Steward. Then the boys and the girls went out into the pure and fresh air of the morning, meeting here and there on the return route of the men dead drunk stretched on the lawn along the inverted beer bottles. That festival was a success.

The next day, the people of the village, in speaking of it, concluded, "Not so mean at heart are the Barons."

"Only," Anton grumbled, "do not delude yourselves! The balls that they organize in their milieu are infinitely better than our ball of yesterday!"

"But they do not dance there the "marriage of the bear," intervened with dignity Madam Irena Drozdowska, the right hand of the Baroness.

"They do worse there in secret," replied Anton.

"As if you do any better yourself!" the lady responded to him. Anton blushed with anger but remained silent.

CHAPTER VII

THE ARCHBISHOP AND THE GOVERNOR

One summer morning, still grey, just before the sunrise, from the bed room of the barons, on the second floor, was heard, through the half-open window, a screech of sand in the courtyard; it announced the arrival of a car at the entrance door. The Baroness jumped out of her bed, slipped on a bathrobe with large yellow and red flowers and looked discreetly between the drapes; a priest with a graying beard descended from a modest carriage, hitched up with a single horse while the coachman carried the valise to the front steps.

"But it is Eduardo!" screamed the Baroness. "What is he coming to do at this hour?" murmured the Baron barely awake. Eduardo von Hoffisch-Buxwolden, the archbishop of Saint Petersburg and first cousin to the proprietor of Weyssensee, loved very much to give surprises of this type to his friends, Without announcing himself, he embarked on the first train, got off at the closest station to his destination and took the first cab that came. Here, it was always the same, that one of Isaac Szmugel; the last dozed on his seat since morning by waiting for the train passengers.

The archbishop loved very much these escapade incognito in a car that jogged along with noise from the poorly paved streets of the little village, while the houses were still profoundly asleep; beyond the line of the forests, the horizon illuminated a long purple fringe announcing the sunrise. The fresh air of the morning recalled for him his youth, his hunts, so much now that he had become archbishop; Msgr. Edward was happy, happy also of the improvised encounters and the conversations linked with the people that he did not know and who on their side, knew nothing of him.

But this impromptu visit did not serve the purpose of the lord and lady of Weyssensee. However, on the same day, these waited the visit of the Governor with the representatives of the government. How did he come to pass by today?

"What a surprise, Edward!" screamed the Baroness while descending the steps of the grand staircase to the meeting with the episcopal cousin, "we were not expecting you at all! Your room, the 'royal chamber,' had been made up for the Governor, the

22

Prince Myssiourkine Razanski, who is coming to dinner. But you will have the blue room. And if, notwithstanding, you preferred not to come down for the meal, we would bring it to you in your apartments."

"That will not do! That will not do!" repeated the Prelate, caressing his cross next to his chest, "My Master would not even have had the 'grand blue chamber...' The Prince Myssiourkine, you say? But I just met him, several days ago in Petersburg! He is a perfect gentleman... No, no, I will take my meal with everyone."

The Governor had just arrived before the meal, in a grand carriage decorated with the imperial eagle. He was accompanied by his military aide and a peloton of Cossacks, who surrounded his car. The cars of the district chief and of the Commander of the Military Police followed behind. I.P. Nekralow, wiezdnyjnachalnik [1] and the Lieutenant-Colonel Kobylkine were accompanied by their spouses.

Having beside them their steward, the head waiters and several domestics, the Baron and Baroness were waiting in front of the entrance way, while the archbishop found himself already in the salon, leafing through foreign reviews. The Baron whispered in the ear of his wife, "Watch out, the Governor is a great chaser of skirts."

In the uniform of a general, Prince Myssiourkine descended nimbly from his car, accompanied by his military aide. He was a very handsome man. An extreme man of the world, he kissed the hand of the Baroness while the other cars emptied their occupants. A great commotion was made in front of the entrance door. It was only an exchange of compliments and clinking of spurs. "Your castle is so magnificent!" declared loudly in French, Mrs. Nekralow and Kobyline.

They directed the governor and his entourage into the grand salon, where standing, the Cardinal waited for him. "Old acquaintance! Old acquaintance!" repeated the prince while cordially shaking the hand of the Prelate, "the Governor is always delighted to meet the representatives of the Church of Rome, church which defends so well the order in the world."

"The order and the justice do not forget it, prince" replied

---

[1] Wiezdnyjnachalnik: district chief.

the archbishop.

"Of course! Of course!" agreed the governor, who did not wish to proceed with this chapter.

The door opened and the governess brought the children of the manor in order to present them to the Governor. "They are so cute! They are so cute!" always in French exclaimed the two Russian ladies. In view of the children, the Prince-Governor rose with a bounce and went to meet them.

"What are you doing" interjected the Baroness a little frightened.

"Russia always and everywhere salutes the imperial blood!" responded very loudly the Governor who wanted at the time to do a favor for the mother, descendant of the emperors, and to give a little lesson to the Archbishop; even though descended from ancient Baltic Barons, this one did not have a drop of royal blood in his veins. The Baroness blushed with delight while the Prelate smiled maliciously.

The Baroness presented her children to the Prince: the brunette Amaldyne, the blond Cathalyne and the little Philibert who hid his head in the dress of his governess. "Your children are truly superb, Baroness," affirmed the Prince, "quite the portrait of their mother. As one would find from imperial blood!"

The Baron grew somber, the compliment was not destined for him, it was as if they had pulled a curtain between his wife and him. But, too bad, there was still an affair very important to regulate with the Governor: to obtain from him the authorization to construct a great paper mill.

After the domestics had brought two rolling carts with the "zakuski"[2] – vodka, caviar sandwiches, Finnish fish, marinated chanterelles – and that the guests had largely benefited from them. Karp, the head waiter, in an immaculate tailcoat, announced in Polish, since the door, "Madam Baroness is served."

Everyone moved to the dining room. On the request of the Governor, the Archbishop pronounced the "Benedicite" then everyone sat down, the Prelate to the right of the Baroness, the Governor to her left. When arrived the moment for the wines, Andrei Karp, obsequious towards those that seemed to him to weigh the heaviest, wanted to serve the Governor first. "No," that

---

[2] Zakuski: appetizers in Poland and Russia.

one said holding the hand of the head waiter. "Begin with His Excellency the Archbishop." That gesture of courtesy pleased everyone.

The numerous wines and the savory dishes soon delighted their taste buds. Mrs. Nekralow and Kobylkina were the most expansive. Wanting to show their knowledge of the French language, they grate on the words with a detestable accent. The Prince would make grimaces of discomfort while the Baron and his wife laughed in their inner selves and the Archbishop smiled into his beard.

Once the dinner was finished, the cognac and the coffee was digested in the salon, the proprietor slipped into his work chambers with the Governor to talk business. But the latter was not easy to convince. The Baron followed a stratagem that succeeded the most often; he placed beside the Governor a French novel in the pages of which he slid five thousand rubles. The next day, when the Governor had left, the Baron went back into those chambers. The novel and the bills had disappeared. Several days later, he received by mail the book at the same time as some thanks and some excuses, but not the bills. The Governor had understood, the Baron also; the affair of the factory was regulated.

The Archbishop even stayed several days more at the home of his cousins.

CHAPTER VIII

THE COUSIN THE BISHOP AT WEYSSENSEE

They at Weyssensee loved very much the cousin archbishop. Grand Baltic lord, he remained always proud of the seniority of his family, but deep down, he was a simple and good man; amicable with everyone, he would speak Latvian with the domestics, was interested in the members of the teaching staff of the castle and could amuse himself for hours with the children. His great defect was his perpetual spirit of contradiction. Often, that was only very annoying because the bishop was a fierce tease. That became however more serious when the prelate brought his mania of contradicting the Court of Saint Petersburg or the one of the Vatican, in front of the pope or an emperor. The Archbishop was unanimously respected for his frankness and his courage, but finally, everyone found him embarrassing and that had caused to him much harm in his existence.

While his cousin Sygmund told him, "But Edward, so be more prudent."

He responded, "What do you want, it is everywhere the same thing the flatterers always have the last word. 'Mudus vult decipi.' You will find difficultly someone who truly searches the truth, it is often disagreeable. One loves too much what pleases him, what momentarily arranges his affairs without searching farther. The truth, one makes a mockery of it!..." And he became bitter because he had suffered so much from all that. However, he recovered his serenity very quickly while ordering the events of his life to the rank of the designs unfathomable yet infallible of the divine Providence. In his conscience profoundly honest, he would always find the voice of God because Msgr. Edward was, before everyone, a priest, a man of great faith.

The private altar of the Baron Archbishop was located in the small, white salon adjoining the "royal chamber," that he had taken back after the departure of the Governor. Every morning, he would say there his mass and in order to make himself understood to the foreign instructors who accompanied the Baroness and her children there, he made short addresses in French. He knew well and spoke fluently this language but expressed it a little in his own manner, persisting to prove that the modern French was not the

26

correct French. They let him do it while laughing under their capes.

Every Sunday, he loved to replace the Curate and gave sermons in Latvian, the language of the people. A large crowd would amass in the nave, each one on tiptoe, in order to see well this "Koungs-Bischop," [1] who completed gilded and mitered, tapping the ground with his cross, proclaimed the Word of God, the white beard floating in the wind. Then he resembled a prophet of ancient times.

After the mass, the Archbishop went to lunch at the castle, in the Regency boudoir of the Baroness; the latter spread out on the table her most beautiful of an immaculate white, on which Andrei Karp placed a service of Meissen porcelain; there were toast, ham, a rabbit pâté, very strong coffee, very fresh butter, cream and the best strawberry jams from the private pantry of the Baroness. The children of the manor, who came to greet their Episcopal uncle, regarded all the marvels with an almost religious envy because their morning menu was infinitely simpler, their mother having for the principle of not spoiling her children too soon.

Once the infants left, the Baroness confided in her cousin her worries and solicited his advice. "There are some days," said she, "I had to send back our little Luxembourger maid. She was very sweet and the children loved her very much. Unfortunately, she had pushed too far her intimacy with the Belgian tutor... excellent mathematician, in addition. For a long time, Mrs. Irena Drozdowska reported to me that she often encountered them who kissed each other fervently on the landing on the third floor. I told it to Sygmund who responded to me, 'They are young, you cannot stop them from it.' But there it was that the Luxembourger comes to announce to me that she is pregnant, that she proposed the marriage to her lover and that he refused. I have already then declared to her, 'Mademoiselle, I do not have the right to condemn you, you know what you have to do but I cannot either keep you near my children, who are too young to see all this.' She started crying but she understood. Afterwards, I called the Belgian and put him against the base of the wall. He flatly refused marriage. 'You are not a man of honor, sir,' I professed, 'and I do not want that you stay near my children.' I sent them both back. It will not

---

[1] Koungs-Bichop: Monsignor Archbishop.

be easy to replace them. But could I do otherwise? What do you think of it, Edward?"

"It seems to me," said the Bishop, after reflection, "that it is very difficult for you to act differently. Your infants are still very young, and at their age, it is not recommended to give them the spectacles of this genre. Notwithstanding a moment will come where the life will show them something other than what they have usually seen at your home. I think that a certain initiation to the sexual problems will soon be useful to them and that it is already necessary to think of preparing them, little by little, to what in one way or another wait for them."

"But they see how the animals do it. Isn't that sufficient?"

"Of course! That is already something. But the love between man and woman does not stop at the animal mating between them. At what age and in what manner is it necessary to prepare the young to the sexual life? I know nothing of that. It would seem that that depends on many circumstances, temperaments. Another side, to distance the children at all cost from all that could touch upon sexuality is, in my opinion, abad thing. Many mothers do it in our milieus. But they do not understand that the sexuality, far from being detrimental in itself, is good, natural, created by God. Then, the problem must be approached always with a lot of simplicity and as the greatest natural event. And most of all, it would be necessary to inculcate in the children from the very youngest age, the sense, I will say "poetic" of the purity as a gift of the soul to God. It is like this that the fear of sin covers this character of filial affection towards a celestial Father, the love for whom we persist in keeping. 'Happy are the pure because their angels contemplate the face of God.' And I will preach to the converted by telling you finally that what will always decide the life of the child, it is the example of his parents..."

The conversations of the Archbishop with the Baron were from a completely other genre. They would remain together for long evenings in the semi-darkness of the library, by smoking the excellent Havanas that the Baron reserved for his best friends.

"Tell me, Syg," asked the Prelate, "you do not seem to be a very convinced Catholic. What hinders you?"

"Many things," replied Syg. "Not that I am an unbeliever. It seems to me even to deeply have faith. The life is a very beautiful mystery, the nature a too marvelous thing in order that one not be that, I will say almost far-fetched, to recognize a Supreme Principle, Supra-Personal Synthesis of all. It is not that aspect that worries me but the presentation that the Church gives of it. The creation of the world in seven days, a good number of miracles from the Old and even from the New Testament, all that seems sometimes so extravagant that I do not absolutely arrive at admitting it, not only the authenticity, but still the possibility. Fairytales for children, idle gossip for the good "muiziniks"[2] who will swallow everything provided that one tells them that it comes from God! This faith of coalmen, which is also that of my wife," pursued the Baron while laughing, "does not suit me at all. I do not refuse to admit the principle of miraculous interventions of God. But the interpretation that we give from those of this Holy Scripture, does not seem to me even honest. How can the Church, who asserts a single true God, force us to believe in some similar nonsense! It is to propagate the lie!"

"I know, Syg, those are not the universities of France or of Germany which prepared you to this style of faith. Do not forget, however, that the Holy Scriptures, completely by remaining the messages of God, do not cease to be the human works which reflect an epoch, a mentality, a language, a manner of seeing the things and of expressing them. The principal, it is to discover the Word of God under the human envelope. It is what can conjure within us the scandalous and shocking misunderstandings. Do not forget either that the oriental people are carried to exaggeration. Already, Saint Thomas Aquinas wrote, "In Scripture, the divine things are transmitted to us according to the mode of which the men have custom to use.' He goes from it similarly with the Church; founded by God, it remains a human enterprise, often very imperfect. But who can deny its necessity in order to show us the way of God? You will admit, without a doubt, that it is justly by the voice of the Church that we are the most certain that God spoke?"

"I will recognize this great probability. It remains from it no less than the Church must not constrain us to follow to the letter the inspired texts by the Holy Spirit!"

"Listen, Syg, the literal interpretation of the Scriptures is

---

[2] Muiziniks: Latvian peasants.

not the only possible one. There are some more liberal and this since the most ancient times of the Church. Today prevails the strictest interpretation, but tomorrow that can change. I believe that our faith in the Holy Scripture and in the Church would not have to suffer."

It was becoming late in the grand library. The Archbishop had to return to Saint Petersburg the next day before noon. And he wanted still before his departure to explore a little of the forest with gun in hand. He had asked for this authorization from the Pope, who had granted it to him. Nevertheless, what the Holy Father could no longer do was to render to the aging Prelate the eyes of bygone times and the steadfastness of his aim. The game no longer risked much. Being that it was late, the cousins would wish each other a good night.

CHAPTER IX

VOYAGE TO SAINT PETERSBURG

The children of Weyssensee were growing up. Amaldyne and Cathalyne were becoming charming little girls, long, fine, distinguished, one brunette, the other blond. Gifted with an acute and curious spirit, they learned their lessons well, much better than their young brother Philibert. That one lacked some capacities but lived instead in an imaginative world less open to the exact sciences.

"It will be necessary to present them soon," thought their mother, "to numerous relations, Polish, Austrian, Italian and French, and in order to do that, to prepare a voyage across Europe." But the first to leave on a voyage was Philibert to whom one had to make him take his first exam in a high school in Saint Petersburg because the girls were dispensed from it.

His first grand voyage was a great event for Philibert. He went there accompanied by his mother. The two chestnut steeds newly acquired by the Baron, left from the front steps with a sharp crack of the whip and pushed into the great forest. The wheels covered in rubber, glided without noise and without any jolts under the tall firs, while the perfume of resin caressed agreeably their nostrils. They emerged on to the grand highway which crossed the vast fields where here and there the rooftops of isolated houses crowned the massifs of gardens. The sand squeaked under the wheels while one could glimpse from faraway the majestic Duna rolling around the important cantonal village; in this last village, the ancestors of the Bartzel, after having governed as all-powerful Starosts of the King of Poland, must have been shot by the Russians for having defended the liberty of their homeland.

They approached the suburbs; it was truly in town that while the squeaking of the wheels in the sand stops suddenly in order to leave in place to the firm and rhythmic resonance and of the hooves on the street pavement. The car passed in great trot in front of the dirty houses, low and grey. They only catch sight of the Jews in "Tallit"[1] who gesture, cried out and argue endlessly. Several among them recognized the car of the lords of Weyssensee

---

[1] Tallit:prayer shawl.

and respectfully greeted it on its passage.

All of a sudden, they saw leaving from behind the corner of a lateral street, a group of Jews, but those carried tallits of waxed silk and of felt like otter skin. They surrounded tightly a little, old man who walked with a rapid gait, the eyes lowered and the hands crossed behind the back. Everyone was making grand gestures and each was looking to catch up as much as possible with the little old man. A crowd , numerous with children and adolescents, wearing "mycka,"[2], with hair with corkscrews on their temples, ran behind the group. "It is their grand savant, from Minsk, the Rabbi Hasserman!" said the coachman by pointing out the group with his whip, "they execute his orders as if they came from the True God."

The car approached the station. The houses became taller. Several had even two floors with balconies and a entrance decorated with a lawn and flowers. Here was the house of the chief of the gendarmerie, the Lieutenant-Colonel Kobylkine, next to it is the home of the district chief I. P. Nekralow and below, at the bottom the Central Hotel, where one eats well but where one risks finding fleas in one's bed.

And here it was finally the Grand Station with the streams of black smoke which rose from the locomotives; with some profound roars, those came and went on the railways. One heard only the metallic noise of the hammers tapping the rails and the buffers of the wagons that clanged together. Philibert was impressed.

A dozen of "nossilschiki"[3] with multicolored "rubashki"[4] with immense red beards, waited on the front steps of the station, each one had a badge furnished with a number on his chest; seeing a rich and elegant team, they bolted in order to propose their services. "Mama, I'm scared, mama, I'm scared," murmured Philibert more and more awestruck.

"Don't be afraid, my little chap," said an immense "starover"[5] all covered with red hair. He hoisted the suitcases on to his powerful shoulder in order to drop them off in the waiting room of first class. "When does the grand express from Warsaw to Petersburg arrive?" asked the Baroness in poor Russian. "In ten

---

[2] Mycka: Polish for yarmulke, skullcap worn by the Jews.
[3] Nossilschiki: porters.
[4] Rubashki: Russian shirts.
[5] Starover: old believer.

minutes, barinia," responded the porter, "you have all your time to take your 'chai.'"[6]

In effect, the mother and the son could at their complete leisure taste this hot and comforting drink and before the grand express entered into the station, making the walls tremble and the glasses on the table jingle. "Most of all, do not rush," said the Russian who was watching the lady become nervous, "wait for the signals."

"Pierwyj zwonok!" [7] rang out the first call from a public servant making the great bell sound out.

"Now it is time for you to rise," said the porter tranquilly. "Wtoroj zwonok!"[8] rang out the second signal of the bell several minutes afterwards while the voyagers aided by the "nossilschik," settled into a very comfortable first-class coach.

Generously remunerated, the Russian descended from the train and planted himself in front of the window of the compartment in to say goodbye to his passengers. Soon rang out "tretij zwonok"[9] and the train moved slowly while the Russian made friendly signs to Philibert leaning against the window.

Night fell. The conductor lit a large red lamp camouflaged over the door. After prayers, the mother prepared the beds, that of the boy on the berth on the bottom, her own on top; then the two voyagers stretched out in sheets of immaculate whiteness. The train lightly wobbled swaying sometimes by the switching. The light sighs of the mother asleep were barely heard, but the boy did not arrive at finding sleep. The voyage had excited him too much. He tossed and turned and at each instant, he threw open the window curtain and regarded outside; the streams of cinders that escaped from the locomotive into the black night seemed to him gigantic combats between the light and the shadows. The whirlpools red, blue, yellow and purple appeared and disappeared at their turn. There was something beautiful and terrible in the succession of these images. "Is it there the mystery of life?" meditated unconsciously the little boy. He bustled non stop preventing his mother from sleeping. "But just remain still!" she screamed at him from the top of her bunk.

---

[6] Chai: tea.
[7] Pierwyj zwonok: first alarm.
[8] Wtoroj zwonok: second signal.
[9] Tretij zwonok: third signal.

Philibert finally succeeded in falling asleep. When he woke up, his mother was already dressed and recited her rosary. The curtains were pulled back and the light inundated the small compartment. A sun with long and slanted rays illuminated some infinite marshes and thin forests with scrubby birches. Some wooden "dachas" aligned themselves along the course. Across the massifs of large parks, on could already catch sight of the sumptuous summer mansions of the Russian aristocracy, of the grand duchesses, of the empress-dowager. Gatchina, Peterhoff:; the train continued its march. "It is time for you to dress," said the mother, "we are approaching Petersburg."

The great capital, song by the immortal Pushkin in the "Bronze Knight," dominated by tall towers and golden domes, was already outlined on the horizon, while on the approach of the train, more and more distinctly rang out the universal droning of the bell towers of the churches. Petersburg celebrated a "prazdnik,"[10] one of the numerous birthdays with the Imperial Family.

An "izvoshchik"[11] well padded with cushions, took the voyagers to get out at "Warchawski Vokzall."[12] Its "ryssak"[13] gained momentum, the coachman cried out some "beregisses"[14] as loud as possible at each street corner and soon dropped his passengers off in front of the "Ewropeijskaja Gostinniza," the grandest hotel in the capital. Nearby consecrated in the memory of the Emperor Alexander II, assassinated in this place, stood a church of the Byzantine style richly gilded. At the hotel desk, the hotel porter, old acquaintance of the family, handed out to the Baroness a ticket on the part of the Illustrissimo Marquis Arthur Bardzopolski, fliegel-adjutant of His Imperial Majesty. The brother announced to his sister that he invited her and her son to lunch and to go afterwards on a visit to the city. "That would be nice," said the mother to her son, "anyway, it is not a question of making you take your exam today." Arrived the Marquis to the deafening sound of his spurs, clothed in a magnificent crimson tunic of horsemen for His Majesty on which was pinned the "Cross of Vladimir with Swords" that he had earned during the last war

---

[10] Prazdnik: festival, feast day.
[11] Izwochtchik: cab or carriage.
[12] Warchawski Vokzall: Warsaw Station.
[13] Ryssak: trotter.
[14] Beregisse: Watch out!

with Japan. All three climbed to the top floor in the hotel, where under enormous glass, the Tartar head waiters in white vests, served them the delicious "shashlyks;"[15] some fountains whispered nearby, the temperature agreeably refreshing. From the glass, one delighted in the splendid view over Petersburg: of Nevski Prospect until the Star of Admiralty and to the banks of the Neva which mixed here its tumultuous waves with the infinite waters of the high sea.

The next day, the Baroness drove Philibert to the grammar school of the Fontanka where the exams must have been set. They lasted three days. Some professors in long, blue frock coats, with the sign of their rank on the cuff, of whom several decorated with medals and stars, questioned the boy on different subjects; the student, put at ease by these pedagogues, showed himself to be very brilliant in history, in geography and in languages; he was, on the other hand, rather mediocre in mathematics. With the full account done, the exam result was positive and Philibert went to the higher class.

"Your 'maltchik'[16] is very nice," said the director to the mother after the exam, "but he does not have a veritable Russian accent; it would then be preferable to put him in a Russian school, for example the Page Corps or the Imperial Lyceum. Your brothers, Baroness, are, for that matter, from High Russian dignitaries, yourself are of Austrian origin; why then do you persist in raising him in a Polish ambiance? I know well that the Barons of Bartzel hold to remaining Polish, but themselves are they not either of German origin?"

"All that is perfectly true, Wache Prevoscheditelstwo"[17] (The Director had the rank of general)," admitted the Baroness, but our family attaches a high distinction to its Polish traditions, which arose in the XVIth century. In addition, if it is maybe not the principal, I find my child very much too young to put him as a lodger in a school. I am opposed absolutely to what he would be subjected to some influences that can show up harmful for his young, very impressionable character. Another thing, my husband is a man exceptionally cultivated and the child could only gain by being at his sides.

---

[15] ShaShlyks: roasts of grilled mutton.
[16] Maltchik: small boy.
[17] Wache Prevoschoditelstwo: Your Excellency.

"I know, Madam, the influence of your husband on Philibert has not escaped me at all; we were all astonished and amazed by his knowledge. If you had seen with what aplomb and what sureness he recited to us the reforms of Alexander II! With what eloquence and what sentiment, he declaimed the poetry of Pushkin and of Lermontoff! And then his knowledge of languages, German, French...! Astonishing! But you must not lose sight that his first homework is to become a good Russian cititzen, a loyal subject of His Majesty our Emperor... It is necessary that he learns to speak Russian as a Russian... Notwithstanding, as an escape from this impasse, I propose to you another solution; since you refuse to confide your child to a school in Saint Petersburg and that you desire to keep him, you could have a Russian come into your castle, a young professor, who speaks Russian perfectly and with whom your son would be in permanent contact; he would learn in that case to speak perfectly our language. But a true Russian is needed... an Orthodox... I emphasize it."

The Baroness did not like to introduce the heterodoxies in the capacity of teachers to her children, but as he had posed on her this condition for the continuation of the studies of her son at home, she promised the Director that it would be done. In fact, in order to compensate her son for the good results from his exam, she took him again in the afternoon on the banks of the Neva to the Winter Palace and to the Hermitage; spectacular and grandiose visions by their severity, menacing even with fortified prison of Petropovlosk situated on the other bank of the Neva, that carries its metallic waters towards the sea. Before returning to the hotel, they listened together a "moleben."[18]

---

[18] Moleben: Russian religious service.

CHAPTER X

THE BARTZELS ACROSS EUROPE

A great commotion in Weyssensee Castle, the Bartzel family was leaving on a trip: Warsaw, Vienna, the Riviera maybe even Paris. The domestics are bringing down the large suitcases from the attic, the chamber maids arrange the linens, the outfits, the toiletries. The general atmosphere is feverish and busy. Amaldyne and Cathalyne are dancing with joy.

"What is it that has excited you girls in this manner," casts their young brother,who was playing being indifferent, "a voyage, what an affair!"

"As if you had done so many of them!" retorted to him Cathalyne while sticking out the tongue to her brother.

"I have done one of them... And you, none still!" uttered the brother while rendering the gesture to his sister.

"Ah, yes! And as you were afraid! All pale and completely trembling in front of the locomotive! As if it was going to swallow you, little snotty kid!"

Furious, Philibert threw a fist at his sister, but Cathalyne did a pirouette and dodged it. She stopped at the door, turned and stuck out her tongue again at him. "Until the floor!" she cried out bowing deeply.

Philibert burst out laughing, "Little idiot!" declared he simply.

"My children, enough!" to them cried out the mother from the adjacent room where she found herself.

The next day, two cars and two baggage cars were immobilized in front of the front steps. However, in addition to the parents and their three children, a governess and a domestic took part in the trip.

The Steward and Mrs. Irena Drozdowska came to attend the departure of their patrons. While the Baron exchanged several words with Mr. Buchenwald, the Baroness once again recommended her house and her people in surveillance of her lady in confidence.

"Don't be afraid, I will do everything necessary," assured calmly Mrs. Drozdowska.

The procession of cars shook into motion. The masters left

for an entire season.

*
* *

The Petersburg-Warsaw express where the voyagers had taken their places, was already approaching its destination. While the parents and girls conversed in their compartment, Philibert went out into the corridor and glued his nose against the window pane. They were crossing a large plain; rye fields ran until the horizon, the sandy roads furrowed into the landscape. They encountered everywhere the grand villages with houses white as snow and the flocks of geese coming to whine up to the food of the embankment. Monotonous scenery, but gay under a sun of the end of August. What a contrast with the tundra of Petersburg or the somber forests and the transparent lakes of the Baltic Sea!

Warsaw! Very different from Saint Petersburg, the immense city, with an overwhelming beauty with its monuments, its severe palaces, its long streets. Here, everywhere was much smaller, but also so much more elegant! Some charming particular hotels, surrounded by the lawns richly flowered aligned along discreet streets where silently, glided on their rubber-covered wheels with on beautiful cars. In their very fancy interior lived the Warsowians, hospitable, affable and gay people.

It is in the grand "Europejski Hotel," constructed by a cousin of the Bartzel, situated in the exact center of the city, that the lords of Weyssensee took a suite of rooms. While the Baroness took her children in the grand stores of Herse, then to the "Stare Miasto," the medieval quarter and its ancient cathedral, in order to end up in the café "Ziemianska" in front of the cup of "Wedel" chocolate and a plate of "pączek," these famous Polish fritters, the Baroness popped off to see her peers at the "Klub Mysliwski." Her numerous cousins and Polish friends, the Otwockis, the Bartzels of the Wirklany line, the Piepierzynskis, the Babakiewicz and many others still, welcomed her with bursts of joy. They recounted the extraordinary stories that sparkled with puns and everyone laughed loudly. But the theme was almost always the same: the hunt, the women, sometimes a political anecdote. The Baron entertained himself well, but he missed this atmosphere that he preferred to any other: that of the professors, of the scientists, of the thinkers, which one encounters instead in Krakow. His interlocutors realized this and said:

"He is good and knowing, this dear Syg Bartzel, sometimes maybe a little bore also!"

*
* *

After plunging themselves again for several days into the atmosphere so hot, so friendly and affectionate of their Polish relations, the Bartzel took the train for Vienna. Philibert had a new impression when he caught sight for the first time at the Austrian border of the rigid military caps and the dark blue uniforms of the bureaucrats of the Hapsburg monarchy.

Barely after arriving at the "Erzherzog Karl" Hotel, where some rooms had been reserved for them, the Bartzels received the visit from the uncle of the Baroness, the Prince Edelbert of Corvo Vecchio. He was the nephew of the emperor close to whom he fulfilled the functions of Grand Master of ceremonies. With a cold and distant approach, he was no less strongly affectionate towards his niece.

"You know, Ermelyne," he said by taking his place beside the Baroness, "How much I hold to you, the daughter of my sister, and how much I look after your well-being. Accept then a word of advice that I am going to give. By coming to my home, I encountered your husband in the hall but it would hardly be lost as speaking with him about it. I do not understand your persistence in remaining Polish. Poland does not exist and will never exist. You could be Russian, German or Austrian, but there is no longer any Pole. Besides, the Bartzels are not of Polish origin and yourself, you are of Austrian lineage. All these Poles, Czechs, Slovaks, Slovenians, Serbs are a very dangerous breed. I fear that they will precipitate us all into the war... I admit that you do not want to become Russian, but it would be easier for you to become, for example, Austrians. It is, in addition, of all the occupiers, those who are the most tolerant..."

"I am going to speak with Sigmund about it, my uncle, but I fear that there is nothing to make him listen," responded calmly Ermelyne.

The same night, she made her uncle's advice known to her

husband. "We cannot gamble on two tables at the same time," retorted the Baron to her, "we are not Russians, but we decided to play their card, it is necessary to continue on the same path. I know well that the Bartzels do not weigh heavy on the Court of Austria, but we can also do without the Hapsburgs." This conversation gave a reason furthermore to push the Baron Bartzel to avoid the meetings with the Austrian relations of her wife. Luckily, there were a great number of other things to do in the old Danubian city!

The next morning, in the "Erzherzog Karl," the Baroness was called to the telephone; it was her other uncle, the Count Karl Vitriani, chamberlain of the house of the Archduchess Walpuryna Severina, also a relative of Ermelyne, who communicated with him the desire of Her Imperial Highness to see her niece at her home. She was asked to bring her children.

As agreed, the Baroness, accompanied with the latter, arrived the next afternoon at the home of the archduchess. Uncle Karl was there, strapped in his beautiful uniform wearing a helmet with interminable ostrich feathers. They waited some time in a small salon by conversing in a soft voice until the door opened. The archduchess appeared in the doorway.

"Ach, liebe Ermelyne," said the archduchess while the Baroness kissed her hand with a profound reverence, "deiner Kinder, wie nett!"[1] she continued while the children executed the gestures that they learned the same morning.

They did not sit down because the archduchess had to take her leave. "I wanted," that woman recalled suddenly, "to propose to take your son into the service of the Court of Austria. He would be there very well and would make an elegant career." On these words, the archduchess smiled amicably at Philibert.

"I am extremely flattered by this," responded the Baroness, but it is impossible to decide anything without the consent of my husband."

"I understand very well, I will wait for your response," responded the archduchess while retreating. The Baroness could not suppress a smile because she was convinced that the response would be negative.

All that did not impede the Baltic Baroness from making

---

[1] Deine Kiner, wie nett!: It is so wonderful that you brought your children!

her children visit the tombs of the emperors, of attending the evening before battle at the Hofburg, the imperial fortress, no more than regaling in some excellent "Knackwursteln"[2] followed by a cup of coffee and of some slices of a delicious "Linzertorte."[3]

*

* *

The next day, the Bartzel family took the train for Italy. The Austrian mountain crossing was an authentic enchantment for the children: the slow reptilian march of the cars on the edge of immense precipices, the torrents of water falling from very high above in deafening cascades, the prairies of an extraordinary green and the chalets lying low in the troughs in the valleys, finally the infinite panoramas of the snow-covered mountains stampeding towards the faraway horizons, all that stirred up some exclamations of enchantment, "You do not have any need to scream so much," would say the mother. They put their feet on the ground in a station perched very high, there was even some snow on the platform. The atmosphere was of a freshness and of a strength such that they had difficulty breathing.

Around evening they crossed the Italian border. Night fell and there was an incredible gentleness in the transparent air, in the hot light of the moon, under the silent sky of the night scattered with innumerable stars. The stations passed by: Milano, Torino. In the morning, they arrived in Genova and in the Riviera. The Mediterranean Sea created its profile already in a profound blue, almost black, until the horizon. Several boats rose a little on the white foam. The shores were encumbered with tall white hotels glittering with light and surrounded by gigantic palm trees. In this privileged place, it was as if the land married with the sky; the songs accompanied by a barrel organ expressed such a joy of living in the glory of the universe! "Here they believe themselves before Original Sin," remarked the Baroness. "Scratch a little," responded her husband, "And you are going to see how your 'fata morgana'[4] is going to flow."

The Bartzels rented a villa in the vicinity of Genoa. They

---

[2] Knackwursteln: Austrian sausage.
[3] Linzertorte: cake from Linz.
[4] Fata morgana: mirage.

received there often during the entire season because there was a great affluence from all the corners of Europe: from Poland, the Princess Otwocka, sister of the Baroness, from Hungary, the Count and Countess Wysterzy and two of their daughters, from Rome, the Countess widow Callafesta, sister of the Baron and two of her sons, arrived in order to pass some days, the Count Wipperg came to encounter his king of Württemberg, finally the families of the Wisiecki counts and of the Czerski princes brought from Poland their whole offspring....

From the good morning, the young ran towards the large sunny beaches and plunged into the delicious waters of the Mediterranean Sea; every afternoon, they were the escalades in the surrounding mountains. The Baron wanted to go to Paris in order to see again the places of his life as a student, but he had to abandon it; a serious disease, a type of paralysis, seized hold of him to make him soon into a veritable cripple. Then they curtailed the stay on the Riviera and the whole family took the road of return.

CHAPTER XI

THE SEASONS

The seasons passed: golden autumns during which it was beautiful for hanging around in the forest in search of a misplaced hare; winter premises that saw, whipped by the strong icy winds, the downpours ripped from the trees the rest of their finery; then, abruptly, the imperturbable silence of the forest buries under the snow during some long months; finally the spring when the small lakes became seas where swarmed to infinity, quantity of savage birds. While the farmers benefited from a certain respite, Philibert and his sisters were leaning on their books and notebooks.

But the vacation arrived; during the short and torrid summers, everyone would spend his days on the edge of Weyssensee Lake. The shores were invaded by the crowd. All the children of the village, the youngest completely nude, exchanged insults and an immense clamor reflected its echoes into the forest under the sky of azure.

The children of the manor benefited from special cabins and did not mix with the wild children of the village. That was admissible still for Philibert, who was accompanied by his friend, the new Russian instructor, but not by his sisters; those were becoming young girls and one had to raise them with delicacy. In addition, they had companions their own age, most often the children of the steward; those were perfectly well bred. In fact, this entire small world was flanked by governesses or sometimes parents; the swimsuits hid much more than was necessary.

The son of the Buchenwald, Wladimir, Wolodia as everyone called him at school, was the oldest of the young band and his sister, Barbarka, the youngest; she was two years younger than Philibert. Wladimir and one of the sisters of Philibert, Katalinka, was the most watched because they had come out of childhood and betrayed visibly the taste that they had one for the other. Regarding Philibert and Barbarka, there was nothing to fear because those were still only infants. Philibert marked however already several feminine preferences for the sister of the beautiful Wercia, the blond Ancia, with long pigtails and sky-blue eyes; he regarded her with great pleasure crossing for one reason or other, the village.

But his attraction for Barbarka seemed more profound; he discovered in the eyes of his companion the promises that filled him with happiness. Barbarka would follow him like a small dog and it was visible that she was very attached to him. The two children never left the other, and they gladly separated from the others, navigating in the boat, swimming in the sea, following the unknown paths in the forest. That amused everyone but no one saw anything wrong in that. "We will marry together one day," confided once the boy to the girl on a solitary path.

"Do not say such silly things," responded Barbarka, "we are too young and then your parents would never accept it; imagine a baron espousing the daughter of his steward, of Jewish origin on top of that! No, it is impossible! But I will remain always your loyal friend."

"We will see," concluded the boy squeezing the arm of his companion.

The Buchenwald parents discussed on evening of the other couple : Wladimir-Katalinka. "You have seen with your gentle eyes what Katalinka has done to Wladimir?" asked the husband to his wife.

"Of course," responded the wife, "Wladimir is a very handsome boy. Tall, strong, like you and he has even your grand Bourbon nose."

"Katalinka is not a villain either: gay, intelligent, her legs and her hands so fine, she is a veritable little aristocrat. I understand that they mutually enjoy each other's company. But for the moment, it is not necessary to think of that; with my Jewish origins and my subordinate position, they will never want from us… unless the situation changes from top to bottom."

"What does that mean?" asked bitterly indignant Mrs. Zinaida Buchenwald, née Kuncwill. We have obviously not the situation and the fortune of the Bartzel barons, but… despite being of little nobility, my family values well their own. The Kuncwills carry as a coat of arms the golden fox which is better than the silver fox of the Kuncwills of Wykowice. Yet, those carry the title of baron, but it is because he bought it. If we had the fortune, we would be barons, us also, and could speak as equals to the Bartzels." Mrs. Buchenwald was a very brave person, but on the subject of nobility and of coat of arms, she had become tenacious.

"All that will have less and less importance," concluded her husband, "they are the situations that count."

Yet, the situation began effectively to change. The same evening, the barons were alone in the boudoir. Because of his malady, the Baron moved more and more difficultly; he often remained in the room of his spouse, reading the newspaper, while his spouse was doing wonders with her knitting.

"You seem very worried to me," interrogated the Baroness, "What is it?"

"The general situation is not good. I fear that we will soon have a war. It will come from the Balkans and it seems to me that the Austrians and the Germans will push towards it. They are so proud that they benefited of the slightest opportunity in order to put the Slavs, who abhor them, on their knees. You are Austrian, I have, myself, some German blood and we can very much say it without offending whoever."

"But this war of which you speak, she is faraway," remarked the Baroness, who will take the trouble to oust us from our Baltic swamplands?"

"Do not say that. Ermelyne, this war can easily be generalized and I fear, in such an occurrence, that we would lose all our fortune. As you know, I have out of principle of not putting much money aside and above all not in the foreign banks. I believed always of my duty to invest in the country where I live. For me, it is a civic duty. The new paper factory that we are building has already swallowed immense sums. If there is war, we will lose everything and we will be ruined."

"We have still my small property in Poland. And then, there are my pearls and my diamonds, which are of a rare beauty and have a great value, most of all those that came from my grandmother, the Archduchess Olgeria-Ostwalda, who was richissimo. We will know how to struggle through it and God will help us!"

"I fear also that with my malady, all the work and all the worries will fall upon your shoulders…"

"It is not necessary to worry, Zyg," said the Baroness soothing, "Kommt Zeit, kommt Rat,"[1] concluded she in her maternal tongue.

---

[1] Kommt Zeit, kommt Rat: comes time, comes advice.

CHAPTER XII

1914

The year 1914 was fatal.

A large envelope with the Austrian imperial initials in wax was laid down next to her cup of coffee; the Baroness read a letter coming from the Hofburg; her aunt, the princess of Corvo-Vecchio, wife of the Master of Ceremonies in the Court of Austria, described to her the funeral of the Archduke Franz Ferdinand and his spouse similar to Morgana, the countess von Chotek, assassinated recently in Sarajevo.

"Your uncle," wrote she, "had the terrible difficulties regarding the protocol of the funeral. He could not give the same class to two spouses and however, he needed to bury them together. Uncle Edelbert looked frantically to satisfy simultaneously the protocol, the families, the people, but he succeeded in only displeases everyone. The imperial family finds that they did extremely too much for the Choteks, the family of the latter considered themselves offended because they had not sufficiently recognized her. Her rank and the 'populo' felt insanely mocked by all of it, proclaiming to every wind that the type of ceremonies is completely outdated in our era. All the newspapers are talking about it."

At the end of her letter, the Princess added, "The political situation between Austria and Serbia seems to be very strained. It would be necessary to finish it, once and for all, with those bandits."

The events were rushing towards that since then. Feverishly, Sygmund examined the newspapers, gathered the news and then abruptly, it was an avalanche of declarations of war: Austria, Serbia, Russia, Germany, France, England... The entire continent of Europe was on fire.

At Weyssensee, however, it was always the same calm. From morning to night, the harvesters hummed pacifically, with immense wagons loaded with golden wheat, came and went. The workers in open shirts, sunburned and dripping with sweat, would drink, from time to time, gulps of curdled milk, would chomp with beautiful teeth down on fat round bread as black as coal and again would go about their business on their wagons. It was necessary to hurry because a great storm was advancing on the horizon, inundating with clouds half of the zenith.

But already, at the heart of the immense forest, they perceived the pulsating progression of the trains; they drove to the front the best dressed regiments of the Imperial Guard, cavalier-guards, guards on horseback, light cavalry, lancers... The Baroness went to the closest station in order to meet her brother Arthur, who was leaving with his regiment towards his future battlefields in Eastern Prussia. Arthur recounted to his sister that the entire people in Petersburg was enthusiastic in favor of the war and that there was this splendid declaration from the Grand Duke Nikolai-Nikolaevich in favor of Poland... One new era seemed to be opening up between the two Slavic peoples, sealed with the blood that they were going to shed together for the same cause! The first to rejoice because of it were Philibert and his new Russian instructor; their friendship, already great, could only be augmented by it. They waited. They were convinced of victory.

Each evening, Philibert went up to the room of his Russian friend in order to discuss with him the strategic situation on the front. The latest news appeared less reassuring. "It is nothing," said the Russian, "our troops are concentrating on giving the last assault and opening up the route towards Berlin."

One day, the Baroness received a telephone call which announced to her the arrival of a messenger from the government. It was the very own military aide to the Governor, the Prince Myssourkine-Razanski. He was in a grand uniform and his expression was serious. The Baroness had a bad premonition. "Madam," said the officer standing at attention, "His Excellency the Prince Serenissimo sends me in order to announce to you glorious news although sad for yourself; your brother, the Illustrissimo Captain, the Marquis Arthur Wsewolodovich Bardzopolski, commanding a squadron in the Regiment of Hussars of his Majesty our Emperor, was just killed by a bullet at the front while he led his unit into an attack at Gumbinen against the Germans. He did not suffer, he died on the spot. With a posthumous title, for reason of his heroic attitude, the High Command just named him Colonel and bestowed upon him the Officer's Cross of Saint George, the most glorious decoration for a military man."

"Here is the destiny of my poor brother," dreamed the

Baroness, "that I met barely several weeks ago, so full of youth, of joy, of hope and whom I will never ever see again…" She sagged under the shock of this news, but immediately regained control of herself and said to the officer, "Please thank the Prince for having wanted like this to soften the sad news for me. And thanks to you, Lieutenant, for your troubles."

"I will report to His Excellency how heroic you have been in your sadness," responded the officer; he kissed the lady's hand, set out again standing at attention, made his spurs jingle, executed a half-turn and disappeared.

And the weeks, the months, passed. They could not have believed, from the exterior that in the life of the habitants of Weyssensee, nothing had changed.. Certainly the military requisitions had diminished the lifestyle of the lord and lady, the sorrel horses stamping the ground had been replaced by the lazy and melancholic plow horses; without a doubt, a good number of young workers had left for the war and they heard less juvenile laughter in the countryside; the Baroness had taken up the bereavement after the death of her brother and remained dreamy and silent; it does not impede, the work, the activities continued as before and everything seemed to take of itself as through the past.

Those who know how to read plunge each evening into reading the newspapers after the Russian debacle at Soldau, the French victory on the Marne and the spectacular Russian offensive in Galicia, the situation on the fronts seemed stabilized; but the German push towards Lodz and Warsaw began to take on a worrisome allure.

Philibert continued to take his exams in Petersburg, having become Petrograd. Several noisy convoys of military transports, of dead silent wagons packed with wounded, encumbered the tracks and disturbed each and every schedule. Everyone slipped on a uniform, most of all those fleeing from trench warfare whose romanticism dissipated quickly in contact with the cruel reality. It sufficed to meet the innumerable mutilated, who decorated with medals and crosses of war, filled up more and more the elegant streets of the capital, stopping as a crowd in front of the stores and admiring their rich and beautiful storefronts.

CHAPTER XIII

THE DEPARTURE FROM WEYSSENSEE

The news from the front became worse and worse, more and more alarming even. The great battle of Lodz, where the Russians anticipated a resounding victory, was a total defeat; encircling the enemy, the Russian troops were themselves taken into a trap; leaving tens of thousands of dead and prisoners, losing almost all its equipment, the Russian army was annihilated. Warsaw fell soon after into the Germans, and one after the other, the other cities of the General Government of Poland did the same.

One morning, Buchenwald came, all afraid, into the work chambers of his master; "Baron, sir," said he, "it is the time that we should all clear off, the Germans will be here in a month or several weeks. It is true that the southern front still holds but I fear soon a recoil along the entire front, which would place us at the center of the operations. No matter what happens, I will remain here but I have already done everything to send my family and my affairs to Petrograd. I advise you to do the same and this soon as possible. When you will be settled in Petrograd, I will send you news from Weyssensee, I will liquidate everything that will be able to be sold and I will send you the money. You will need it."

It is true that the Baron will need it greatly. It remained to him so few funds in the Russian banks, above all since he had underwritten, at the beginning of the war, to a grand national loan, operation that already revealed itself as a total fiasco After consulting each other, the baron and the baroness chose the most precious objects, furniture, silverware, paintings, rugs, wrapped them up into huge crates and expedited the whole lot by express train into the capital.

They discharged almost all the personnel, among others, the hunter of the Baron, Anton Wajdewis, that his fiancée Ewcia cried warm tears and who left to an unknown destination. They were equally separated from the tutors; the Russian, the friend of Philibert, had already enrolled into the Mikhailowskoye Artillerijskoye Yuchilishche [1] in Petrograd. There must have remained only several persons in the castle, of which the

---

[1] Mikhailowskoye Artillerijskoye Yuchilishche: artillery school of the Grand Duke Mikhail.

management and the direction were confided to Mrs. Irena Drozdowska, devoted, honest and serious person.

The passages of military units across Weyssensee multiplied, some entire detachments traversed the village; they constructed everywhere in the forest and even in the park, pressure points for the infantry and the artillery; some officers stopped in the castle, overjoyed to have found a place beautiful and hospitable enough in the middle of the incessant marches and of their interminable weariness. And that thundered stronger and stronger behind the forests, the incessant noise of the canon fire enveloped the entire horizon to the east. Wilno[2], Kowno[3], must have already been occupied.

It is high time to leave. Several cars and simple carts already waited in front of the entrance steps. The curate, Father Abbot Latlajtys, Mrs. Drozdowska, the old Karp, several domestics and Mr. Buchenwald, had come to say their goodbyes. "It will not last long," proclaimed the curate, always optimistic, "you are going to come back to us soon!" Mrs. Drozdowska cried, the domestics furtively wiped their eyes while the lords hid their tears. The children had ad hoc appearances, but despite their a little saddened faces, with flashes of joy lit up on their eyes, this new voyage seemed to them rich of surprises and of novelty; it is that they also were bored several times in the beautiful castle of Weyssensee.

He had been agreed that the Bartzel family stopped provisionally in a cheap hotel in Petrograd and looked, by walking, a stabler domicile. The Bartzel had already been anticipated by their relations and friends; the first to see them was the cousin archbishop, his beard crammed under his collar, then came the brother of the Baroness, the Marquis Edelfred Bardzopolski, "jägermeister"[4] of His Majesty, who seemed very worried; some cousins and Polish friends rushed in also, overjoyed from having found again some companions who, like them, had escaped from the horrors of war; there had been even the two Russian ladies, former neighbors, Mrs. Kobylkina and Nekralowa; having learned of the arrival of the lords of Weyssensee, they went to greet them without delay, "Kak priatno, kak chechastliwo wstretitsia w

---

[2] Wilno: Polish name for Vilnius in Lithuania.
[3] Kowno: Polish name for Kaunas in Lithuania.
[4] Jägermeister: master hunter.

Petrogradie!"[5]

The Buchenwald family did not delay either to present themselves. But, to the inverse of the Bartzels, his situation was already well assured and stabilized in the heart of a charming little dacha situated in the suburbs of Petrograd. Wolodia was a great, handsome jet in his uniform of "praporshtik,"[6] whose uniform he wore in waiting awhile to leave for the front; his look pleased Katalynka very much. Barbara had become a ravishing high-schooler, she showed a great joy in meeting his former companion Philibert. Mrs. Buchenwald was very friendly towards the Baroness and said to her, while taking leave of her, with a certain air of superiority, "Madam Baroness, if I can be useful to you, I am always at your disposition."

Vaguely foreseeing that the steward's family which seemed to pull through much better than herself, could be to her very useful, the Baroness, accompanied by her daughters, did not wait long to pay her a visit. She observed, in effect, that the upkeep of the dacha of the Buchenwalds was perfect and that these people seemed to lack nothing.

After embracing as old friends, Ryffka and the Baroness conversed for a long time by recalling the past. Mrs. Buchenwald observed always an attitude very respectful towards her former lady, but the Baroness discovered quickly in her words, a little protective tone.

"I will find you a stable domicile," said she, "that will not be long." In effect, at the end of about ten days, the Baroness could move with her entire family into a little wooden villa, close to the one of the Buchenwalds; much more modest than their last home, it was without contest, more agreeable to inhabit than the anonymous room of the hotel.

The children and the two families met with each other frequently. They made excursions into the region of lakes of Finland, often made some escapade into the cinemas of Petrograd, or with great bursts of laughter on the rides of the roller coaster of Narodni Park. It was a joy to see this beautiful youth, three ravishing girls and two boys with good figures, all exuberant with life and health. However, finally, Wolodia did not leave for the

[5] Kak priatno, kak chechastliwo wsretitsia w Petrogradie: "It is so agreeable and fortunate to meet us in Petrograd."
[6] Praporshtik: officer ensign of subordinate rank.

front, they do not know how, his father had in effect found for him a situation in the Ministry of War.

The steward continued to send money from Weyssensee, but very insufficiently, account taken for the increasing degradation of the money and the vertiginous rise of life. The Baroness was very worried. Guessing her anxieties, Mrs. Buchenwald always said to her, "Madam, if you have need of something, you have only to address me."

The Baroness would not dare, but she sought the advice of the old Ryffka, "Do not fear anything," that one said, "if my son made a fortune, it is in large part, thanks to you."

"Of course," responded modestly the Baroness, "but he knew how to make do."

"Ah, that, it is another affair," concluded the old Jew showing her yellowish and chipped teeth in a large smile.

CHAPTER XIV

LIFE IN EXILE

Mrs. Buchenwald was busy in her dacha, watering the flowers, laying out the furniture while her mother-in-law prepared the evening meal. The children had not yet returned from school and the autumn sun set already behind the golden leaves of the thin birches, illuminating with its oblique rays the swamplands scattered here and there with wooden villas. One glimpses from faraway the long stretch of water from the Kronstadt estuary. Three hundred meters from there, the red roof of the Bartzel villa emerged from a massif of firs.

"You know, mother-in-law," said the daughter-in-law to Ryffka, "Wolodia would absolutely like to marry Cathalyne Bartzel."

"I wondered about that after all their promenades and escapades together. But this marriage will not give them happiness," responded meditatively the Jewish woman, "because they are not made for each other."

"And why? Are we not the equals of the Bartzels and even, at this moment, superior to them? Today, it is they who need us while before, we were almost their servants. The advances of money that we made to them! And the loans that maybe they will never reimburse us. And our advices! Our recommendations! All our kindness! Does all that not count, maybe?"

"It is not a matter of that or justly because it is a matter of that," replied the old woman, "it would be dangerous to precipitate the marriage under such circumstances. Yesterday, the Bartzels were still our masters, today it is the contrary; they are themselves our debtors and we their creditors. As they feel obligated towards us, the Bartzels would feel, to say it like that, forced to give us their daughter. I understand that that would flatter you to have for a daughter-in-law, a Bartzel, but that would not be reasonable to marry these youths. In addition, Cathalyne is not made for Wolodia."

"And why?"

"Because Cathalyne is a little aristocrat, a spoiled and capricious child, which is not the woman that Wolodia needs. Very rapidly, she will tire of the boy and will turn her back on him.

Moreover, you figure that I know nothing of what Wolodia is plotting? All these reunions, the Marxist comrades, these ultra-secret meeting... emerge towards communism. And Cathalyne will always remain an aristocrat. They will never understand one another. A passing fancy, maybe, but nothing more."

In their dacha close by, the Barons and the Baroness discussed the same subject. They are alone because the children have not yet returned.

"Before beginning reading your book," said the Baroness, "it is necessary that I confide in you that yesterday evening, on the return from her errands, burst into crying on her bed, declaring to me that she could not live without Wolodia Buchenwald and that she wanted to marry him. I am not opposed to her and him, only said to her that before marrying, she must reflect a lot, adding that she had all the time needed since was only seventeen years old."

"You believe that nothing serious has happened between them?"

"No, frankly I do not believe it. Wolodia is, in addition, an honest and serious boy."

"You have done very well," said the Baron a little relieved, "this marriage does not overly please me. Barely several months ago, we would have categorically refused... Today, the situation has changed. We depend on them and would be very embarrassed to refuse them our consent."

"I have nothing against Wolodia," said the Baroness, "he is a well raised boy, hard-working, intelligent, he has some instruction and will soon be a bearer of an engineering degree. But he is not of our milieu and they will never understand each other. Moreover, Cathalyne is not herself made to marry this boy; he is too serious and she too light. If it is a matter of Amaldyne, who always works relentlessly on her philosophy courses, I would maybe not say no although deep down, I would no more like that marriage. But Cathalyne thinks only of having fun, she will never bend to the will of another, she will always want to submit her entourage to her caprices. This whim will pass as so many others."

Fortunately, it was never a question between the parents of two families, of the eventual marriage between Wolodia and Cathalyne. The second lieutenant Wladimir Kurcewich Buchenwald suddenly received a convocation from the General's Chiefs of Staff prescribed to him to rejoin a unit on the front. The order was sealed and did not consist of an indicated destination, but it was a matter in fact of assigning this officer of firefighters to the construction of a bridge situated on the front where the majority of officers of the Engineering Corps had been killed.

Wolodia was so hurried in leaving that he said only some very rapid goodbyes to his "fiancée;" the pretty blond spilled, it is true, torrents of tears. At the beginning, they wrote to one another every day long love letters but they became spaced out little by little, Wolodia being taken by the intense occupations while Cathalyne found soon other consolation for her suffering.

The two other children, Philibert and Barbarka Buchenwald continued to see each other often. Philibert prepared for his baccalaureate while the young girl finished her secondary studies. The two young people met each other almost every day after their courses in the "Publichnaia Biblioteka;" each one prepared there his dissertations, Philibert in philosophy, Barbarka in literature.

Philibert was on an original spirit and of a rich imagination, but he was undisciplined; Barbara was very much more methodic and enjoyed an excellent memory; she was also very hard-working, quality that she retained maybe from her ancestors. In the silence of the grand work hall, they were sitting side by side and very softly exchanged their impressions and information.

It was late when they returned together by train from the suburbs in order to reach their domiciles. The little train jogged along, what made tremble the little lamp suspended from the coach's ceiling, it whistled often, its locomotive breathed hard; she deposited its passengers on a long wooden platform in front of a miniscule and dilapidated station,which was the terminus of their voyage.

Philibert took his satchel and the one of his companion and all while discussing with conviction on the theme of their works, accompanied her in the black night up till her domicile. They spoke little of their personal affairs, because it was above all their work that occupied all their attention. The boy led the young girl until her door and after having squeezed her hand, returned home.

Another time, it was that one who brought a book to her companion and if it was absent, placed it in his dacha. She was pleased very much by the barons; there were something very concentrated, very pure and serious inside this girl who was barely out of childhood.

"If that one wanted to marry Philibert, maybe I would not say no," said the Baron half-serious.

"Then think," remarked the Baroness, "they are still only children."

With the acumen of an old Jewish woman, Ryffka said between her yellow teeth, "If those will not marry one day, I would be very astonished."

CHAPTER XV

THE GREAT REVOLUTION

One day in an early spring of the year of 1917, Philibert, completely breathless, excited, and overwhelmed, rushed from the station to the villa of his parents. "The revolution has broken out in Petrograd!" he screamed from the door, "some entire regiments are joining the revolting crowd and are firing on the police that disappeared from the street and found refuge on the roofs of the houses. Immense cohorts with accents of the Internationale and of the Marseillaise, unfolded along Nevski Prospekt and other principal streets. Thanks to our uniforms as high schoolers, my comrades and I had been able to easily pass, but I have seen with my own eyes officers beaten to no end carrying through the soldiers because they had refused to remove their epaulettes. Everyone displays red badges."

"There it is, the anticipated revolution, and for how long," said the Baron in an undertone, "God alone knows where that is going to lead us!" Several days afterwards, the Bartzels received the visit from their cousin archbishop. He came on foot from the station. No one could have recognized him; with his white beard floating on a cassock without insignias, he resembled strangely to a Jewish rabbi with tallit and the Jews, at that time, were viewed very well by the revolutionaries. Incidentally, Monsignor Edward, despite his age, loved risks and willingly ran to adventure, so much so that he wanted to have the news of the Bartzels, which he had not been able to obtain otherwise.

"The Tsar was interned with family at Tsarskoye Selo," he recounted. "There is a provisional government of the Prince Lwow, but that is barely holding together. Anarchy reigns everywhere, the trains run with difficulty, provisions are more and more difficult to find and some entire regiments abandoned the front on their own accord. All those who protest are savagely beaten. The past was not pretty, but I fear the future is still reserving some surprises for us." And the Bishop left soon again in order to take his hardly enviable post in Petrograd.

Several days later, the Baroness received a ticket from her brother Edelfred Bardzopolski. He wrote how he had been recognized in the street as a old regular of the Emperor, pursued by

57

a raging crowd and in some way, finding himself by chance next to the entrance of the Embassy of Great Britain, there he found refuge and asked for asylum. Recognized by the bureaucrats, he was very generously received by the ambassador who accorded to him asylum and opened his house to him anticipating that a false passport would be delivered to him in order to go abroad. "Goodbye, Ermelyne," he finished his letter, "good fortune to Sygmund and to your children!"

Several months later, the Bartzel dacha had an unexpected visit from Kurt Buchenwald. By some means of fortunate transport, he arrived directly from the front and from Weyssensee. "My role is finished there, it is completely useless that I stay at Weyssensee," explained he to his former master. "During this entire period, Russians and Germans were battling on the frontline of the Dwina, cutting our forests. Those forests are literally devastated by the trenches and the shells, the sawmill is burned, almost all of the population has fled. The frontline is now three kilometers from the castle. That castle is still undamaged but inhabited. Mrs. Drozdowska found a shelter at the home of the curate, Father Abbot Latlajtys, on the other side of the lake. Regarding me," continued Buchenwald, "I intended to take my entire family to the United States where I have some money, some cousins and some friends." Bartzel knew some of them by name, Americanized Jews, often important personages on Wall Street. "If you want to accompany me, Baron and Baroness," concluded Buchenwald, "I would be overjoyed to be able to aid you and to arrange your voyage and your stay in the New World."

It was agreed that the two families Bartzel and Buchenwald came together the same evening for dinner at the dacha of the Buchenwalds, the Bartzels no longer having the means to offer an appropriate meal for everyone; at the Buchenwald home, on the other hand, there were more space and then they ate not only canned dried fish accompanied by potatoes half-spoiled and bread that resembled to rubber, as for a certain time, it was the habit at the Bartzels' home.

In effect, the dinner at the Buchenwalds' led everyone back to the era before the war. It made everyone forget everything, including the revolution; there were heat and light, excellent zakuskis with vodka, a thick, fragrant soup, some small lamb chops with potato croquettes, and for dessert, beautiful pears. The wines were from the best made in France. The covers were looked after and clean. In the salon, after dinner, they served cognac and cigars.

The barons were dumbstruck, their two daughters radiant from joy of having found their former ambiance, Philibert sitting in a corner, spoke softly with Barbarka. Alone, Wolodia remained somber and rigid in his chair; he had exchanged his former uniform of an officer of the Czar for the stern suit of a revolutionary Commissar. Ryffka said nothing while Kurt Buchenwald tried at all costs to make conversation. He strived to evaluate the situation in order to know above all who would leave with him for the United States.

"It is the last chance of leaving to go abroad. Still today, under the Kerenski regime, I can obtain exit visas. Tomorrow, everything could change. I would like to know the names and the number of persons who are ready to follow me. I am taking, no matter what, my wife and my daughter," – Barbarka and Philibert sadly looked at one another, – "and then my mother..."

"No," protested Ryffka, "I am not leaving with you. I want to die in my country." Buchenwald had a resigned look.

"Wolodia?"

"No," responded that man, "I am a soldier of the revolution and I want to have nothing in common with the capitalist America." While speaking, he had not even a glance towards his former "fiancée," Kathalynka, who however, observed him tenderly.

Everyone understood that it was merely wasted in discussing with him.

"You and your family? Mr. Baron?" continued Buchenwald.

"It will be difficult for us to leave with you," responded the Baroness, "my husband is sick and moves with pain. Myself, I will not abandon him and I want my family to stay with me. If we must die, we will all die together."

It was therefore decided, finally that Buchenwald would go to America with his wife and daughter, that Wolodia would remain in Petrograd, but what to do about Ryffka? "Oh!," said the old Jewish woman, "don't worry! I will join the family of the Bartzel barons, and as soon as possible, we will return to Weyssensee. I would like to die there where I was born."

Kurt Buchenwald became perplexed, "If you have," he said to the Baron, "the intention of returning to your home, do it without hesitation. Benefit from the disorder on the Russian front, I will procure for you all the papers attesting that you are a Jewish family originally from Witebsk, that will put you for the moment in the protection of the red commissars; at the beginning, try to find accommodations incognito in the surroundings of Weyssensee and... wait for the coming of the Germans, which is imminent because the front practically no longer exists. But do all that the quickest possible. If you wait, it will maybe be too late."

And like that, while the Buchenwald family embarked for America, the Bartzels disguised as Jews and accompanied by Ryffka, bundled their old clothes on to two sleighs because winter had already settled in and left for Weyssensee. Any which way, their ancient furniture, silverware, paintings and rugs, deposited at the Gorokhovaya[1] in Petrograd, everything had disappeared in the pillaging by revolutionaries. Everything went so quickly that one did not even have the time to lament the separation.

---

[1] Gorokhovaya: Little Pea Street.

CHAPTER XVI

THE RETURN TO WEYSSENSEE

Following the instructions and the counsel of Kurt Buchenwald, the two sleighs pursued their route in direction of Weyssensee.

The first, with Philibert for a coachman, was occupied by Ryffka and the Baron; in the second, had taken their places the Baroness and the two daughters who took turns steering the team of horses.

It was bitterly cold, and despite their immense reindeer pelts – the "dachas," vestiges of former splendors – the passengers shivered from cold.

They crossed the plains uniformly covered with snow on which a glacial wind lifted up whirls of white powder.

It is in the deep forests, buried under the snow, that they found a shelter against the cold. But those would be dangerous because they also served as shelters for the bands of deserters and all sorts of criminals, who lived for theft, rape and even assassinations.

Finally, after the weeks of travel, they arrived in front the prominent city of Witebsk. At the gates of that city, they were stopped by a patrol of soldiers in grey hoods, wrapped with cartridge belts. They wore no insignia, except the traditional red badge. Their welcome was harsh and fierce:

"Where are you going? Who are you?" demanded they to the travelers.

"We are a Jewish family," responded Ryffka while Bartzel presented them the documents and we want to rejoin our relatives in Witebsk."

"It is good, you can pass," said the leader of the detachment of Semite type by throwing a furtive look on the papers, "we are in search of the counter-revolutionaries and aristocrats who congregate across the region in order to rejoin the Germans and the Whites who are already on the other side of the city... Pass quickly! And bon voyage!" added he, recognizing his own. In effect, one heard the gun shots and the burst of machine-gun fire coming from the opposite side.

The "prefectorial" city of Witebsk, all covered in snow,

resembled a great village. The houses, mostly with one story, extended along the wide and never-ending streets. Everything seemed dead. Some passers-by with a quick step, which resounded on the hard pavement, reached their houses, chilled to the bone.

The two sleighs came to a stop finally in front of a tall brick house with two stories. It was the home of the richest trader of the region, Szmult Winkelmann, with whom Buchenwald and Weysenssee had a tight relationship before the war.

"Dear Baron, dear Baron, I bid you welcome," said the host as soon as he had recognized the identity of the travelers. He was accompanied by his wife, a little Jewish woman, fat and ugly, whose immense nose seemed to join her chin.

Totally numb from the cold, the arriving parties sat with a true pleasure around a table that Mrs. Winkelmann had covered with an immaculate tablecloth. A large samovar with very hot tea boiling in the middle. Some round loafs of white bread, very fresh butter, the slices of ham and jars of jam waited on the table. The travelers ate with a very apparent appetite, but Ryffka did not want to touch any non-"kosher" ham.

Winkelmann explained to the Baron the political situation; after the accession to power of Lenin and of Bolshevikism, the front between the Russians and Germans had ceased to exist; the Germans penetrated into Russia as a knife through butter, supporting the formation of all sorts of White guards, who operated in the back of the Soviets; there were many negotiations between the Russians and Germans at Brest-Litowsk, but the situation of the new Bolshevik government seemed desperate, so much more that several White generals and Ukrainians had started to operate with success into Northern and Southern Russia and even into Siberia.

"For me," continued the merchant of Witebsk, "I wait hour by hour for the arrival of the Germans, sure of being able to continue to do with them as brilliant business as those that I did, there was hardly any, with Weyssensee and our dignified friend Buchenwald under the regrettable czarist regime. Regarding you, abandon the soonest possible your Israelite getup and appear in front of the Germans in all the splendor of the high barons Bartzel von Hohenwaitzen zu Weyssensee. You will have success! For the moment, rest well, my good Malka prepared bedrooms for you."

After the long journey, the insomnia and the fatigue, it was a true delight for the voyagers to slide their painful and half-frozen limbs between clean sheets and under warm blankets prepared by Malka Winkelmann. The first to wake up was Philibert. He heard the rhythmic noise of large boots beating the pavement of the street, and through the frost-covered window, he caught sight of the first German soldiers entering into the city: true military men, those there, plus the disheveled bands of Kerenski! "Yes," confirmed Winkelmann the next day at breakfast, "the Germans occupied Witebsk during the night, without meeting any resistance. I advise you, Baroness, to go and speak to the Kommandantur as soon as possible."

Accompanied by her two daughters, the Baroness reported before the sentry who raised the barricade at the entrance gate of the new Kommandantur.

"What do you desire," asked that Kommandantur.

With her purest German, the Baroness responded, "Ich möchte gern mit dem Herrn Kommandanten sprechen."

Completely surprised to hear his maternal tongue spoken without the least accent by a lady with an appearance as distinguished, the orderly made a sign to a sergeant, who left from the courtyard, and asked politely, "Whom must I announce to Herrn Kommandanten?"

The Baroness tendered to him her name card on which one could read: Ermelyne geb. Prinzessin von Caramanlys, Reischbaronin von Bartzel zu Hohenwaïtzen auf Weyssensee.

The orderly rushed away with the card and two minutes later, appeared an aide-de-camp who stood at attention and said very kindly, "Der Herr Kommandant is waiting for you, Frau Baronin. Please go up."

The authorization to enter into Weyssensee having been delivered to them with an incredible speed and an exquisite courteousness, the Bartzels, after having thanked wholeheartedly the Winkelmanns, left immediately bringing the old Ryffka. The Germans posts that they encountered gave them no difficulty.

By arriving at Weyssensee, they had however some grief in recognizing their familiar places, so much the region was scattered with sign posts with arrows and diverse constructions that the Germans had laid out for the needs of their troops and their supply lines. Long ago inaccessible, the forests were excavated with trenches and roads, so much that one could even glimpse through the trees a large sheet of water, the Duna flowing lazily its waves towards the Baltic Sea.

Around the castle, almost all the houses were burned and destroyed; that house, majestically dominating the great lake of Weyssensee, seemed moreover to have conserved its haughty aspect.

As a precaution, the Bartzels headed first for the rectory. The joy from the reunion with Mrs. Drozdowska and the Abbot Latlajtys was sincere and reciprocal. They all fell into each other's arms and question and responses mixed into a general brouhaha.

"Is Karp alive?"

"No, he died."

"From what?"

"From disease, from old age."

"And Anton?"

"Left for an unknown destination. We fear that he is preparing a nasty trick."

"And Ewcia?"

"Dead from chagrin after the departure of Anton."

"And Wercia, the daughter of Karp?"

"Married, she already has two children…"

The Abbot Latlajtys advised to the barons to go and see immediately the "Befehlshaber"[1] of the XXth Army Corps, whose High Command occupied the castle.

"They are all occupied!" explained the curate, but they will find for you maybe a place at the Regency."

Effectively, the Baron found a place at the Regency and it is there that the lords of Weyssensee settled in.

Ryffka wanted to rejoin her family and left for Dunabourg.

Mrs. Drozdowska took up again her former occupation close to the Bartzel family.

"Our domicile is very modest," declared the Baron the same evening of their arrival, "but we are truly at home and nothing is more appreciable!"

"And still… until when…" murmured the Baroness.

But, for the moment, it was the peace and they lacked nothing because inhabitants and neighbors, former workers and

---

[1] Befehlshaber: Commander.

friends, brought more provisions than they needed and were ready to render every service.

The Baroness welcomed as if they were family; after the ordeals and humiliations recently suffered, she had become much more familiar with the people.

The craftiest of the "muiziniks" reflected, "After all, we never know whom we will need... for the moment, let's put ourselves beside the barons..." They remembered the Russian dictum, "nie pliuj w kolodetz, woda prigoditsia."[2]

---

[2] "Nie pliuj w kolodetz, woda prigoditsia" : "Do not spit in the well, you will still need water."

CHAPTER XVII

A NEW TURNING POINT

If the Bartzels had theoretically recuperated their Weyssensee properties, they were, from the fact at hand, put by the Germans into the impossibility of exercising their rights; they needed each time the authorization of the German "Wirtschaftsoffizier."[1]

This young officer, the Baron von Straftsmannsberg, was, in fact, a man perfectly well bred and easily accorded all that they asked from him.

One day, he even went to the see Baron Bartzel in order to announce to him the good news; the High Command of the XXth Army Corps having received orders to leave, no longer saw any drawback for the proprietors to regain their former domicile.

The Bartzel couple went to examine the state of the castle; it still had some of the furniture but the beautiful library, object of the just pride of the Baron, had remained intact, excluding some vanished French novels.

However taking heed of the hindrances and the difficulties of a new change of homes, the Bartzels preferred to continue to live at the Regency.

Moreover, the general situation remained forever very precarious. The Russians were vanquished, the Emperor and his family had been assassinated, the Bolshevik bands no longer seemed to represent any danger, but the future for them remained no less than very uncertain. The Germans always boasted of winning victories on the "Western front;" nevertheless, the great fatigue of the war, which seemed to have no way out, was clearly read on all their faces; and then... there were these Americans and their inexhaustible potential which flowed in without interruption to come in aid of the Allied Forces.

The Baron von Straftsmannsberg was worried.

For the Bartzels, there was still the concern for their children. The parents could once again support the idyllic existence of Weyssensee; it is true that it was no longer a question of living the lavish existence as before the war, but the Baron,

---

[1] Wirtschaftsoffizier: administration officer.

always buried in his books, the Baroness, occupied with the housekeeping problems, were not bored and endured well enough the new conditions of their modest life. For the children, it was another thing! They had already lost a year in their studies and it was absolutely necessary to give them the possibility of finishing them.

The Baroness went to see the German officer, "Herr Leutnant," said she, "we need to think of the future of our children, we would like them to go pursue their studies."

"Nothing could be easier, Baroness," responded the officer, "send them to Germany; you will find there all sorts of schools and some of the best!"

"I don't doubt it, but our family is not German, we are Polish and would like that our children receive their education in Poland."

The Lieutenant became somber, "In that case, write to the Ober Ost-Kommando, but I doubt that he would grant your request."

The Bartzel wrote once, then a second time. Each time, the response was "abgeschlagen."[2]

The German lieutenant was nonetheless not a bad chap. He advised them to ask for the authorization to go to Wilno, city situated in the region of the Ober-Ost. That time, the response was positive. It was then agreed that with autumn approaching, the Bartzel family would go to settle in at Wilno.

That was their second exodus. Neither Mrs. Drozdowska nor the Abbot Latlajtys had foreseen then their dreadful tragedies that waited for both of them.

"In Wilno, the Bartzel were well at home; there were the family traditions for a long time implanted by the relatives, friendships and numerous acquaintances.

Philibert found there immediately what he was looking for: a group of Polish insurrectionists to which he enlisted clandestinely and which waited only for the moment of proclaiming the Polish independence of Wilno.

For the Germans, the situation visibly degraded. After the victory of the French on the Chemin des Dames, they yielded everywhere and retreated on all fronts. Came the abdication of the

---

[2] Abgeschlagen: refused.

Kaiser Wilhelm II and the installation, in their army of even Soviets that they had encountered in Russia. Those soldiers seemed nevertheless less scrawny and seemed more disciplined.

Day and night, an inexhaustible wave of German soldiers unfurled along the snow-packed streets of Wilno; they abandoned the conquered territories to the east and came back in mass towards the "Heimat"[3]. Their disorder was, it seems, only apparent because they perceived among themselves a tenacious will to keep a certain cohesion while crossing the country, sum total, hostile. In any case, all that was not natural to blocking their return home seemed absolutely indifferent to the Germans. However, one heard already the deafening boom of the canon near Dunabourg and of Kowno.

It was the moment where the two antagonists, Poles and Lithuanians, began to hoist their national flags; Philibert said his goodbyes hastily to his family and ran to rejoin the unit to which he had been assigned. Fully proud, he wore publicly his amaranth cap with a white eagle and attached a long cavalry saber to his civilian coat.

His comrades, still children, who had never handled either a gun or a saber, flooded in from all quarters.

"It is with these snotty kids that we will never be able to occupy, to hold and to defend a city against an army no matter how barely regular," the overseers of the Polish insurrection said among themselves.

They made then the separation into groups; a group of former war-weary soldiers with their horses and their arms would ride to Poland "manu militari," the rest, the most numerous among which Philibert found himself, would embark in some trains ready for the German occupier and transported directly to Poland.

Although always brutal, insolent and arrogant towards those that were not of their race, the Germans lent themselves, for one time, to facilitate this evacuation and deposed their cargo in front of the bridge that straddle a small river.

It was the front; from the other side of the river, they already saw the legionnaires of Pilsudski, who wearing a small cap carrying the Polish eagle without a crown, the "maciejowka," surrounded a heavy machine gun.

---

[3] Heimat: Homeland.

The arriving troops, all to the joy of seeing them, for the first time, true Polish soldiers, began to push up cries of enthusiasm; they are ready to throw themselves into each other's arms.

But the welcome was cold, disdainful even. "If you did not want to fight for Wilno, you could all as well have remained in the skirts of your mamas!" to them cried the legionnaires. The group of Wilno passed without glory in the middle of the laughter and the mockeries of the army of Pilsudski.

Philibert took leave of his group and went to pass some time with his Polish family in Warsaw and in the countryside. It seemed to him to revive in these places an existence that it had for a long time forgotten as if the people here had known nothing of the horrors, of the dangers of the war and of the revolution, prisons, executions, deprivation, famine and cold.

But his permission having come to its end, he left for the school of cavalry officers where he had enrolled. His abbreviated courses lasted only four months and he came out from it as an ensign.

The school was situated in a provincial city around Warsaw. The former Russian barracks, who served long ago in a regiment of dragoons, were large sheds in red brick, arranged uniformly along the dusty and monotonous route, opening up on a wide plain flanked here and there with tall poplars. When he arrived, they led some horses in the vast courses and the bugles sounded out in order to execute the transmission of commands.

Philibert led there a very hard life. The reveille sounded at four o'clock. It was necessary to dress quickly often in the cold and in darkness, then one ran to the call and to the prayer and one went to dress his horse. It is only afterwards that one had the right to rush out, the mess kit in hand, in the queue of comrades in front of the smoking kitchen.

Afterwards, there were the exercises, the handling of sabers, of guns and of lances, then the theoretical courses, and finally the time for lunch.

After a siesta of two hours that one made ordinarily in the piling up of hay in the stable, the officer cadets left for some maneuvers in pelotons under the command of their leaders.

That will last for four months.

CHAPTER XVIII

THE LIBERATION OF WILNO

After the treaty of Versailles, Europe began to mend itself from a long deadly war, uncertain for a long time. The names of victorious generals – Joffre, Foch, Pétain and French – entered into legend.

Only the Poland, resuscitated on paper, continued to fight on.

In the streets of Warsaw – Krakowskie Przedmiescie, Nowy Swiat, Aleje Ujazdowskie – the blue horizon or the kaki of uniforms of French or British missions became familiar. In the hospitable salon of the Polish capital, no one did not know "La Madelon" or the "Tipperary," but for the Polish soldiers, it was always the battle.

Soldiers coming from all corners of the horizon; soldier dressed in horizon blue of the division of General Haller, "feldgrau" soldier of the German army or legionnaire of Austria, and finally, the one of the eastern marches – the soldier with a Russian accent or with a Lithuanian intonation – who served in the Corps of General Dowbor-Musnicki and carried the long, grey hoods, the "shynel" with the "shashka," the short and curved saber which gave him a Tartar allure, by his side.

Soldier fighting also on all fronts as well against the Germans in Silesia as against the Ukrainians in the southeast or the Russians and the Lithuanians to the east and to the northeast.

That morning, in the grand barracks, where Philibert served, they celebrated the promotion of the new ensigns.

Several hundreds of them, impeccably aligned, waiting in the courtyard for the arrival of the War Minister. His car arrived finally at the street corner and the orchestra attacked the welcome march. A general, corpulent man who waddled on short, bowed legs, descended from the car and surrounded by several officers, passed rapidly by in review the promoted young who stood at attention with their saber and stared at him with their fixed eyes.

"Honor, officers!" proclaimed the general.

"Honor, General, sir!" resounded the powerful and unanimous response of the officers.

The minister seemed content, "They had a proud look,"

said he to his entourage.

"Gentlemen," he addressed the newly promoted, "I hope that you will always serve the Homeland with the same sense of duty and sacrifice that I believe to have read at this moment in your eyes! Viva Poland!"

"Viva Poland!!!" resounded the response as one single voice.

The ceremony was finished and the general immediately climbed back into his car.

Soon after, each one received his assignment. Philibert was sent to the 4th Regiment of Cavalry Chasseurs, composed principally of men of his country, the eastern marches.

This regiment entered into the army of General Zeligowski and one murmured that that he had for a mission to liberate Wilno from the Bolsheviks. Every army would make it seem as if they were revolting because the siege of Wilno by the Poles was quite contrary to the concluded treaties. "Provided that our government is taken by surprise," said Pilsudski. "Understood, Chief," responded that soldier in clicking his heels.

Since morning, the stockyards of Warsaw were encumbered with a great number of wagons; the army of General Zeligowski embarked for its destination. The platforms were swarming with soldiers from every branch: infantry, cavalry and artillery. The horses whinnied, the soldiers swore and some order burst forth from everywhere.

For a long time, the 4th Regiment of Cavalry Chasseurs had taken its place in the train, but it waited for night in order to leave. A thick pea soup in which floated fat morsels of lard was distributed; the soldiers were lying down at the side of their mount – the hay felt so good and they heard only the trampling of the attached horses – when finally, the train shoved off.

It was night; across the half-opened door, infiltrated the lights of the city; then, the train began slowly on one bridge under which one saw the great big sheets of water illuminated by the moon and the lamp-posts, it was the Vistula; one saw still the lights, the train accelerated and it was everywhere the black and impenetrable night.

The men snored, the wheels of the train always accentuated the same measure; the sleep and the night enveloped everything. Alone, a wind of a fine April blowing across the half-opened door brought a little freshness into the suffocating and smelly atmosphere of the wagon car. In a great silence, the military transport approached from the frontline.

Philibert woke up. The wagon was stopped. To the east, the sky whitened and a penetrating cold entered through the crack in the door. A trumpet blared. "Everyone out of the wagons! Bring your horses!" commanded the service sergeant. The people, the heavy eyes and the limbs numbed by the sun, made the horses exit by cursing. The pelotons, squadrons, the regiments arranged themselves already on the border of a forest. The sun invaded the earth, and in the fresh springtime morning, that madly smelled of jasmine while a nightingale sang its head off.

The cooks distributed the soup, then the pelotons, squadrons and every regiment penetrated into the great forest. "The enemy is not faraway," murmured the commander of the squadron at whose side rode Philibert on his sorrel.

The detachment left the forest; a great plain lifted up towards a hillside covered in several white houses. "Bartzel, take command of the first peloton," ordered the captain, leave the horses and advance in direction of that village. If one shoots at you from above, do not insist, we are going to go around them."

Philibert left his horses in the forest and deployed his peloton of skirmisher in a great meadow which extended up to the village. A fire fed by bursts of machine-gun fire welcomed them from the opposite side, the bullets whistled on all sides. "Lie down!" commanded Philibert, "and wait!" The machine guns stopped. "Up! Forward!" cried out the ensign. The machine guns crackled once again. "Lie down!" The silence. "Stand up! Attack!" No one fired any more. While Philibert had reached the village, the enemy had taken off; an enveloping maneuver executed by the regiment of Philibert, had forced it to evacuate its position. By chance, there had been only one soldier lightly wounded in Philibert's peloton.

After this first skirmish, the 4th Regiment of Cavalry Chasseurs no longer encountered any obstacle. It advanced across the forests and the fields, through villages and burgs. The inhabitants, if they were Polish of the same race and same religion, welcomed the military with bread and salt. The small cities where the population was composed, in majority, of Jewish proprietors, were fundamentally hostile to the Polish "pany."[1] In order to obtain what it was from this hateful and crafty population, it was necessary to employ the manner that the Jews understood so well.

At a given moment, Philibert, at the head of a small group of cavaliers, fell nose-to-nose upon a dozen Cossacks, commanded by a commissar, a giant wearing a "papakha"[2] The surprise was mutual and total. The Russian regarded the small Polish officer with great contempt. "Surrender, bieloruchka"[3] he screamed, in wanting to grab by the bridle of Philibert's horse.

That one had just enough time to draw his saber from its sheath and to strike at an angle the Russian in the neck.

The saber missed its mark and the commissar drew an immense "Kolt" and targeted his adversary. He would have killed him on the spot, but Philibert's orderly, having caught sight of the maneuver, shot down the Russian with one shot from a revolver without the Russian having had the time himself to squeeze the trigger.

The giant Cossack rolled from his horse and the detachment, deprived of its leader, fled into the forest. The commissar sprawled out on the grass, rigid and dead, while his horse followed the runaways.

They removed the arms from the dead and they took his papers from him in order to present them to IInd Bureau of the High Command of the regiment.

It is several kilometers from Wilno that ignited the first grand battle. While they headed towards a large village, the Poles were welcomed by rifle shots, bursts of machine-gun fire and a bombardment of canons.

The cavalry squadrons stopped in the clearing of the forest and the infantry battalions advanced into the fields while the canon batteries began to drench the village. The fire intoxicating from the shells lasted an entire hour, while the Polish infantry advanced slowly, encircling the suburban houses. Regarding the Russian canons, they were no longer shooting and their resistance seemed to weaken.

A trumpet sounding the attack rang out in front of the cavalry brigade, which bided its time in front of the border of the

---

[1] Pany: lords.
[2] Papakha: a furry hat.
[3] Bieloruchka: small white hand, man who has not worked with his hands.

forest.

"Sabers out! Forward!" cried the commanders of the squadrons.

An immense wave of cavalry bolted into a full gallop in the direction of the house straight ahead. Philibert, at the head of his peloton, fell into a sand trap bordering some small wooden houses. High sunflowers hid the windows. A sustained firing opened up on his sides and he saw some soldiers of his detachment fall from their horses.

Into an open window, from which it seemed to him that they fired, Philibert sent a burst from his automatic pistol. He felt that he had hit his mark. Then, there was calm, the cavaliers regrouped at the street corners.

Philibert went to examine the house in which he had fired; a fat Jewish woman, of a certain age, sprawled out dead, the others had fled. "All the same! One soldier killing a woman!" He was not proud of his exploit.

Fortunately, no one had seen him and he did not breathe a word of it to anyone.

Through a grand maneuver of encircling, the Zeligowski army approached the capital of Lithuania. Through the morning haze, the roofs of the most elevated houses were distinguishable.

No one expected any more resistance on part of the adversary. The entire 4th Regiment of Cavalry Chasseurs was occupied to polishing up uniforms and harnesses their mounts. They wanted to have a good-looking appearance. "And above all," barked the officers, "No obscene songs! The 'panienki'[4] of Wilno do not like the vulgar type."

It is in a perfect order that the Poles made their entry into the village of Gediminas and the Jagiellons. The General was at the head of his troop and the military orchestra struck up a suite of Viennese waltzes, which made the chasseurs' horses prance and dance. The inhabitants of Wilno came out en masse, offering immense bundles of flowers. Many cried for joy. "Finally! Finally! We have waited so long for you!!!" was heard everywhere in the streets.

As soon as Philibert's chasseurs had taken their quarters in a former barracks, the young man was presented in front of his

---

[4] Panienki: damsels.

squadron chief and asked him for the authorization to go and see his family. "Of course," responded the superior, "you are free until this evening."

Philibert saddled his horse, and in the company of his orderly, rushed towards Basztowa Street, where lived his parents. Still he had not needed to ring the doorbell because his sisters recognized him already from the window and alerted the parents. "Papa, Mama, Philibert has arrived!"

They threw themselves into each other's arms, and after a slew of embraces, burst forth the first questions and answers.

"How have you spent the Bolshevik occupation?"

"You have arrived just in time. The entire family had been lying on the list of people to deport. We were waiting for our arrest from each moment to the next."

"But, my small Philibert," interrupted the mother, "what favor could I do for you?"

"The greatest favor that you could do for us, me and my friend, who had literally saved my life during this campaign," responded the officer, "it is to prepare for us a good hot bath and let us change our clothes. Since Warsaw, we have not yet taken off our shirts and we have never truly washed up. We are devoured from the lice!"

The sisters prepared in a kitchen two bowls of boiling water, they brought for the two some of Philibert's clothes, which waited for him in the armoire, they brushed the uniforms and burned the old underwear and its lice in the courtyard of the house, which sizzled and emitted a fetid odor.

Amaldyne discovered a star on the epaulettes of her brother. "What is your rank?," asked she.

"During the campaign, I was named second lieutenant."

Several days after, the trains began to again run between Wilno and Warsaw. One of the first to leave was the Bartzel family.

The sister of the Baroness, the Princess Marjolyne Otwocka, impatiently waited for them in Warsaw.

CHAPTER XIX

PERSPECTIVES OF SOBIERZYCE

The Princess Marjolyne Otwocka, sister of the Bartzel Baroness, was very rich, but widowed and without children. She possessed an ancient and very beautiful castle at Otwocko in the south of Poland, and a ravishing and very stylish villa in the most distinguished quarter in Warsaw. It is there that with impatience, she waited for the arrival of the family of her sister.

The two sisters, who had not seen each other since the beginning of the war, stayed for a long while crying silently in the arms of each other.

"Poor Ermelyne," said softly Marjolyne, all that you could suffer... but it is finished now... we are going to live together... you are going to live at my home, I have enough space."

They were all reunited in the ravishing little boudoir of the princess while the hostess served them in some porcelain cups from Sèvres, a tea from China, accompanied with small dry cakes from the Wedel company.

They spoke of everything and the two twins cried a lot to their aunt: pretty, simple, gay, spiritual. While with one hand, Cathalyne held her teacup, on the other, she wrapped the collar of a large fox-terrier, which had accompanied the Bartzel family the whole war.

A miniscule Pekinese, sitting on the knees of the princess, observed the fox-terrier with its mean eyes, hidden by hairs and growled non stop.

The fox-terrier fixated on it in silence, then abruptly, it tore away from Cathalyne's hand and pounced with a single bound on the Chinese dog.

The small trolley with its cups and cakes was overturned, the fox-terrier trapped the little Chinese by the nape of the neck and rolled with its prey on the rug. It was the strongest, but the Pekinese defended itself with determination.

It would have surely succumbed if the two sisters had not intervened, coming finally to liberate the small dog, fully breathing hard from the battle and all covered with bite marks.

Because of it, the princess had tears in her eyes, and deep down she was irate but said nothing. That evening, she came to pay a visit to her sister and her brother-in-law in the rooms that she had prepared for them.

"We apologize so much, Marjolyne, for our dog," said the Baron, "but we could not abandon it. It was our best companion during the whole war. We are so much attached to it, my children and myself!"

"That was nothing," repeated the princess.

"Marjolyne," said after a pause the Baroness, "Sygmund and I do not know how to show you our complete gratitude, above all for your proposition to go live with you at Otwocko. But don't you think that it would be much more reasonable that we went to move into our little property of Sobierzyce that my father had left me as dowry. It would be a shame to not benefit from it, and in any case, we would not be far from you."

"You probably are right, Ermelyne," responded the princess, "but it will be necessary still to fill up the house that has remained empty and uninhabited during the war. I am going to help you however.

And deep down, she was not so displeased by this new project.

It is like that that the Bartzel family moved to Sobierzyce. The house had only one floor but sufficient amount of space to easily accommodate the family.

On one side, there was a small, very sunny garden, from the other, a small pond where waded ducks, very near to the village and its church, and farther away, undulations of yellow sand that extended until a forest of firs puny enough.

But the region was very much stocked with game, such as jackrabbits, rabbits, partridge and even pheasants, whose metallic calls were heard coming from the neighboring woods.

The Princess Otwocka brought constantly from her neighboring castle all sorts of tools and furniture for which the Bartzels could have a need.

Many times, she proposed to her sister loans of money that the Baroness refused consistently; she had however succeeded in selling at a very good price the pearls and the diamonds inherited from the Archduchess Olgeria-Ostwalda.

This money permitted her to reconstruct her housekeeping at Sobierzyce and soon to pay for the studies that her two daughters were going to do at Jagiellonian University in Krakow.

It was the life, modest yet safe.

Like everyone, the Bartzels followed closely the political events throughout the newspapers. For Poland, it was always the war.

They would also receive from the front the news of their son, Philibert; he was now in the First Lancers of Krechowce, the best of all the cavalry; he had received the Cross of War with the white-amaranth ribbon, had been named lieutenant and commanded the squadron. For his age, he was not even twenty years old, he made a blistering career. His regiment participated in the great offensive of Pilsudski on Kiev.

Then, suddenly, the news from the front ceased, the newspapers were bringing no more than vague indications and they heard no more from Philibert.

Little by little, the truth was up to date; the Poles had suffered a crushing defeat under the walls of Kiev. Under the push of the Cossacks of the Ataman Budyonny, they left the Ukraine and retreated into complete disorder towards their country. At the Bartzels' home, as everywhere, they were very worried.

Then, the trains of voyagers ceased running in the direction of Warsaw and of Lwow because the lines had to serve strictly for military transport. A great battle, which would be decisive, was engaged at the gates of Warsaw and Lwow.

With heavy hearts, they waited for… the miracle.

And here it was that the miracle arrived: the famous miracle of Warsaw. According to the combined plans of Pilsudski and the French general Weygand, a powerful artillery force was concentrated in the bend of the Vistula at the gates of Warsaw; bombarding day and night with all available canons, it stopped the assault of the Russians and broke open their front. Into the breech opened up in that manner, bolted numerous Polish regiments, who cut the Russian front, forcing the enemy to yield in a hasty escape. All the churches of all the cities and villages of Poland pealed the Te Deum for the deliverance.

Long afterwards, one recounted that the soldiers of Holy Russia," recruited into the Bolshevik offensive on Warsaw, would have seen on the sky the "Swiataja Bogomater,"[1] that prevented them from entering into the city.

---

[1] Swiataja Bogomater: the Holy Mother of God.

But one had not yet news of Philibert. One day, the Baroness received a notice from the Military Hospital of Krakow, inviting her to come see her son gravely wounded at the Battle of Korosten.

She left immediately. All pale, Philibert was lying on his bed; he had undergone a delicate operation, in the region of the lungs from where it had been necessary to extract a bullet. The operation had succeeded and the days of the wounded were no longer in danger.

The mother remained a whole week close to her son; that one received numerous visits from his relatives and friends; even his crippled father could come to see him.

His youth triumphed quickly over the injury, and Philibert could recount to his audience the last campaign of Kiev: the hikes of the cavalry across the steppes of Volhynia, of Podolia and of Ukraine, the spectacular cavalry charges against Budyonny's Cossacks, the sneaky maneuvers of the "tachanki"[2] mowing down entire squadrons, the terrible retreat, the desertion and escape from the regiments, and finally the gigantic battle of Komorowo where was engaged every flower of the Russian and Polish cavalry.

Then, there was the cavalry raid of General Rommel on Korosten. It is there that in a cavalry charge, Philibert received his wound, which could have be fatal.

At the end of two months of leave at the hospital, he received the joyous news; he had just been named captain and decorated with the "Virtuti Militari," the highest and the most envied of all military distinctions.

---

[2] Tachanki: small cart pulled by a horse and on which was placed a machine gun.

CHAPTER XX

THE FATE OF WEYSSENSEE

The Poland victorious over Russia, could finally breathe. The Treaty of Riga had just consolidated the eastern fronts. It kept Wilno and Lwow, but some large territories, like Livonia, where long ago, flourished Polish culture, would be placed outside its boundaries.

And it is there that the newly formed republics: Lithuania, Latvia and Estonia. These republics voted, without hesitation, for radical land reform. They leased to the former owners only a small tract of land and they deprived him of his former home; the rest was resold by the State to small proprietors. The former proprietors had the right, be it to keep, be it to alienate the terrain, which had been attributed to them.

The Baron Sygmund Bartzel discussed with his son about the attitude that they had to come face to face with a new situation. After a long convalescence, Philibert, save a light claudication, had indeed recovered from his wounds. He seemed even to have become more virile and more mature after his long warlike ordeals. He no longer displayed the little blue-black bar of the "Virtuti Militari," which he carried on the inside of his civil vest.

"Philibert," said the Baron, "you are my only son and the inheritor of the Bartzel von Weyssensee fortune. It belongs to you then to decide what we are going to do with that small portion of our fortune that the Latvian government wanted to leave us. All our traditions, since the XIIIth century, are attached to that region, but I do not want most of all that that must weigh on your will. You have the right to decide your own future… then you are going to see what it is necessary to do with Weyssensee… They reported to me that terrible things have happened down there since our departure."

"It would be necessary maybe to send someone to examine things at the site?"

"Yes, but who?"

"It is I who shall go."

It was then decided that Philibert would leave to see the former property of the Bartzel.

From Warsaw, he sent a telegram to a friend living in

Dunabourg in order to announce the day of his arrival and he left. The trains ran now as before the war.

After a voyage without incidence, rather comfortable, Philibert descended at the Weyssensee station.

It seemed to him that nothing had changed since he had gone there the last time: the same, silent, little station surrounded by sand, the same yellow flowers in front of the window of the station chief, who at that moment, waved a small, red flag for signaling the departure of the train.

Rare faces appeared in the windows, throughout his movement; they regarded with curiosity this young man in whom they seemed to recognize the son of the former proprietor of Weyssensee.

Philibert left the station. Spot of sorrels stamping the ground impatiently, maintained by the firm hand of the coachman, not a Tilbury impeccably spruced up, but a modest chariot, padded with hay and pulled by one horse in front of the entrance steps. A young woman covered in a grey shawl, sitting on the high bale of hay, held the reins in her hands.

She recognized and called him, "It's through here, Mr. Philibert!" It was Wercia, the former "beauty" of Weyssensee, daughter of deceased Karp, married and mother of two children. They had sent her to bring back the former lord from the station.

The car went through the forests and the fields that he recognized well, with small detours, some getaways and aspects that were to him familiar since his most tender childhood; here is this tree at the corner, here is the crest of the forest from faraway… nothing had changed. Even this small breeze of fresh air, which blew from the harvested fields, was to him familiar.

Wercia was loquacious; she recounted how the Bolsheviks had assassinated Mrs. Drozdowska and the Abbot Latlajtys and burned the castle.

"After your departure," said she, "masses of disheveled Bolsheviks unfurled throughout the district. They did not harm anybody, but stole all that fell into their hands. Mrs. Drozdowska and Father Curate had very well closed the castle and took the keys and the Bolsheviks did not have the time to break into it.

"Afterwards arrived the authorities. There was a commissar who searched for the counter-revolutionaries and collaborators with the Germans. 'Where are they hiding?' they asked to the village. 'There aren't any among us,' we responded to them.

"Everything changed when Anton arrived in the village, you know, the former huntsman of the Baron. He had become a very important person and did not want to speak to anybody. It is on his indications that they arrested Mrs. Drozdowska and Father Curate and that with a small group of barons, they incarcerated them all in the village school, the one that your mother had built. They must be tried.

"Their trial took place there the next day. The judges sat on a podium around the grand table, which served long ago for billiards for the barons; the accused, surrounded by numerous militia members, had their benches not far from there and the entire hall was full of people from the village.

"Mrs. Drozdowska was the first to be interrogated:

"'Drozdowska, you are Polish originally?' questioned the president of the tribunal.

"'Yes, from Warsaw.'

"'You were accused of having collaborated with the aristocrats and the Germans. Is that true?'

"'I did not collaborate. I was in the service of the Bartzel barons and I did my duty. That's all.'

"'But you have already spoken in German with the German occupiers in order to defend the interests of the capitalists against the people.'

"'It was not against the people. I spoke German, of course. But how could I have done otherwise? Moreover, is it not the Germans, who brought Lenin into Russia? These Jews, sitting high above among our judges, do they not themselves also speak German even better than myself? Is it to say that they are traitors to the people?'

"They started to laugh in the room.

"'Silence!' screamed the Tribunal President.

"It was next the turn of Father Curate.

"'Latlajtys, you are Latvian?' asked the President.

"'Yes, I am Latvian.'

"'Too bad for you. Because you also, you are accused of collaboration with the aristocrats, the counter-revolutionaries and the Germans.'

"'I did only what was my duty as priest and pastor.'

"'There does not exist any priests or pastors in our constitution,' howled the President.

"It was next the turn of the barons. Those had, according to any probability, effectively collaborated with the Germans.

"At the end, the President announced that the examination of witnesses was not necessary, since all the accused had avowed being counter-revolutionaries and the collaborators with aristocrats and Germans.

"The judges withdrew. We waited for the verdict. In the end of several minutes of consultation, the judged came back into the hall; all the accused were condemned to the penalty of death.

"We started to protest in the hall; everyone here loved Mrs. Drozdowska and Father Curate. But they imposed silence upon us.

"'If you do not want to undergo their fate, shut up!'

"The next day at dawn, the condemned were led to the place of their punishment. They must have been shot in the border of the forest of the place of our summer swims.

"Mrs. Drozdowska and the priest marched side by side, in silence, reciting each on his turn the rosary. The barons, there were two, followed them with dignified.

"They stopped in front of the woods and they ordered the condemned to dig their graves; it was a grave two meters deep, two wide and two lengthwise.

"It was noon when they aligned them along the grave. They began just then to sound the Angelus in the church, habit that had been conserved.

"Mrs. Drozdowska and the priest had still the time to say they forgave their enemies. The barons declared seriously:

"'Today, it is our turn, tomorrow it will be yours.'

"A salvo rang out, it was repeated in the echoes throughout the forest and they heard it distinctly from the village. Mrs. Drozdowska and the two barons were killed on the spot, but the Abbot Latlajtys whimpered still and one had to give him a finishing shot.

"That evening a swarm of unknowns came to set fire to the castle. It seemed that they were acting on the expressed order of Anton who had said:

"'They destroyed even the last vestige of feudalism!'

"Since they all had left, we disinterred the body of the priest and of Mrs. Drozdowska and interred them in the cemetery.

The entire village was there. And if you saw all the flowers that they brought each day to their graves!"

Wercia had terminated her tale when they entered under the arch of the gate of honor, which faced the alley of chestnut tree leading to the castle. The door remained still intact with its blazons, its crowns and its figures which decorated the superstructure.

But the castle was no more than a skeleton; its black walls burned off by the blaze, looked over the emptiness from its wide-open windows.

Philibert remained still some days in Weyssensee. He lived in the rectory with the new curate. The next day, he went to see his former friends in the village. Everyone was overjoyed to see again the young baron.

"You know, we loved your parents very much! All that they did here: schools, co-ops, factories… Everyone benefited from it!"

Philibert heard only that. But he realized very quickly that in the very rare exceptions, the people were satisfied with the changes; each hoped to have his own parcel of land, they were all among themselves, all peasants, all Latvians, they had their own government and there were no longer any need to wear out their tongue in order to speak a bad Polish or a worse German.

"I am despite everything only a stranger here," wondered Philibert, "my culture, my interests, my families are in Poland! I have nothing more to do in this country!"

He took again the advice close to sure friends and through a notarized act in Daugavpils – like that on now calls the former Dunabourg – he sold the rest of the Weyssensee property.

And it is in that manner that for the Bartzels von Hohenwaitzen zu Weyssensee, disappeared the last vestige of the epoch called feudal.

SECOND PART

TOWARDS NEW RUINS

CHAPTER I

BALL AT OTWOCKO

The Princess Marjolyne Otwocka, sister of the Baroness Bartzel, belonged, through her deceased husband, to one of the first aristocratic families of Poland.

It is true that the Otwocki from Otwocko were only one lateral branch of this family, less rich, less powerful than the one of their relatives from Lwow, which led a lifestyle quasi-royal, or even from Krakow to which belonged the most ancient and the most beautiful manors of this historic city.

But with his castle in the Stanisław Poniatowski style, its parade of luxurious salons on the ground floor, its numerous and ravishing rococo apartments on the second and third floor, its twenty thousand hectares of fields and woods, of prairies and ponds, she was a very great lady; she was considered as such by all.

Marjolyne had a good heart and would have done everything for coming to the aid of her sister's family. They were almost the same age – Marjolyne being a little older –, they had been raised together in the Court of Vienna and very young, married almost the same year.

Widowed and without children, Marjolyne would have well wanted to will her fortune to the Bartzel family; alas! Otwocko, as majorat, could only be transmitted to a descendant of the family of the Otwocki princes.

Furthermore, her sister, Ermelyne, was extremely susceptible and even vexed since she sensed what they wanted to give her as charity.

But what Marjolyne could do in all peace was to contribute to the establishment of her two nieces, Amaldyne and Cathalyne. This was not easy either because as well as young, pretty, friendly and cultivated, these young girls had become after the war the "poor family."

It was necessary however, to not despair; the princess organized a grand ball at Otwocko, at which she invited some young people of the Polish aristocracy, among whom her nieces used the occasion to make the useful acquaintances for their future.

Marjolyne inspected her wardrobe; there were two elegant and very pretty dresses, one was pink, it would fit very well the brunette Amaldyne, the other was dark blue, that one underlined better the charms of the blond Cathalyne. It only had to have them readjusted and adapted at Herse's shop in Warsaw,

The aunt spoke of it to her nieces and invite them to spend several days together in Warsaw. "But above all, say nothing of the goal of our voyage to your mother," recommended the aunt, who feared to arouse the petulance of her sister.

The three women made a very agreeable trip in the new "Cadillac" of the princess and stayed several days in Warsaw, in the beautiful Otwocki villa of the elegant quarter of the Aleja Roz. They came back very satisfied with the two dresses finely folded in the grand boxes of the Maison Herse.

It is, without a doubt, the first time that we saw at Otwocko so many automobiles aligned under the umbrage of the century-old oaks, which in the middle of this October, were covered in a flamboyant gold.

And it happened again… Always in fashion, the guests abandoned more and more the ancient horse and buggy to replace them with elegant Alfa-Romeos or solid Buicks.

Gentlemen in English cloaks, donning the brilliant top hats, having in their arms ladies in long dresses, entered non stop through the door largely opened, while the accents of an orchestra came from the grand hall where the ball had begun.

Lacing up their tall riding boots , some gentlemen in long tailcoats sketched out the figures of a rapid "fox-trot" or a languorous "tango," which since the end of the war, replaced more and more the old waltzes and the polkas of their grandmothers.

In the crowds of guests, the two Bartzel sisters, clothed in their dresses from Maison Herse, considered as the young girls of the house, did the honors and helped their aunt receive the numerous guests arriving.

They were accompanied by only their mother because the baron had preferred to stay at home in Sobierzyce; his first cousin, Msgr. Edward von Hoffish-Buxwolden, archbishop of Leningrad, had just been, following an exchange of prisoners, liberated from the Butyrka Prison and expelled from Russia to Poland; his first visit was to the Bartzels and Sigmund could not leave him alone.

A little later, arrived Philibert Bartzel. He was in uniform of a cavalry captain and all decoration out, thin and young, moved forward limping slightly, supported by a cane.

"Ah! finally our national hero!" screamed his aunt catching a glimpse of him from faraway. Philibert approached, kissed his aunt's hand and disappeared into the crowd.

In the beautiful milieu of the ball, a great upheaval was made at the entrance door; he announced the coming of the head of the family, the Prince-Duke Géopard Otwocki, man richissimo, who led a royal life in the most sumptuous castle of Poland.

The Court of Austria gave him the title, none other than Highness Serenissimo, but Highness Serenissimo and the Gotha[1] ranked him between the first and second party, that is to say between the famous princes and the royal princes. Moreover, he received only in his castle and consorted with only the princes by blood and the most famous stars.

The Count Barszcz-Lipszyc accompanied him in his capacity as Premier-Secretary; "The most intelligent man that I have ever met," says the Prince-Duke, in presenting his secretary to Marjolyne, who rushed towards the door in order to receive the Head of the Family.

The Prince-Duke, a little, fat man middle-aged, a disdainful grimace on the mouth, passed through the crowd and came to sit in an armchair at the side of the lady of the house.

"Say then, Marjolyne, who are these two young girls, in blue and in pink… quite pretty?"

"But those are the daughters of my sister."

"Of your sister?"

"But yes, my sister Ermelyne, married to a Bartzel."

"Ah, yes, I remember, they own a very beautiful property somewhere on the shores of the Baltic Sea."

"They no longer have it since the war."

It seemed then that the interest of the Prince-Duke for the Bartzel girls subsided just a little. He directed the conversation towards other subjects.

Amaldyne and Cathalyne had however a very grand success during this soirée. They danced less with the numerous Otwocki because those – that they were of the baronial, count or princely branch – evolved rather in their own family and preferred to marry among themselves.

But there were numerous Bartzels von Pikiliszki, of the

---

[1] The Almanach de Gotha was a directory of European nobility and royalty and was published between 1763 and 1944.

Krakowian branch of the family, and there was also that Prince Czerski and a Count Pozecki who seemed to take a very special interest in the Bartzel girls; Amaldyne whirled frequently in the arms of the Prince Czerski and the harmony seemed perfect between Cathalyne and the Count Pozecki.

The two young people were not extremely rich but possessed pretty properties in eastern Poland and carried excellent Polish names.

Ermelyne seemed satisfied, readjusting in her graying hair, a magnificent diamond tiara that her sister had loaned her for the circumstance, confiding in her, "You can well accept it, it belonged to our common ancestors."

The ball ended after midnight, with a magnificent mazurka led by the Prince-Duke himself, who showed, in this circumstance, how much he had kept in his blood this former verve and this bravery, which were the very own of the Polish race.

The Prince Czerski and the Count Pozecki held absolutely to walking their boots back to the car while the baroness said to them with her most engaging smile, "See you soon, I hope, sirs!"

CHAPTER II

THE BARTZELS IN SOBIERZYCE

The months, the seasons, the years drifted away while the Bartzel family became accustomed and began even to love this new modest yet calm life that it had to from now on lead in its new residence.

Regularly, each morning, in winter as in summer, Ermelyne, at the ringing of the bell of the neighboring church, went to mass. In the small somber country church, she sat on the lordly pew, while several old women of the village, invisible under the gloomy shawls, whispered the rosary in the obscurity of the nave.

Came the old curate of the village, accompanied by an altar boy and the mass took place in this mysterious language, having become universal in the Latin Church; if the priest did not always latch on to the terms of it, the little boy rendered it totally incomprehensible, but the baroness was growing older and aided him always from her pew.

Ermelyne loved to stay a long time in the church after the end of the Holy Sacrifice. In the presence of her Creator and Master, signaled by the little glowing lamp in front of the tabernacle, she felt happy, calm and soothed. During the winters, the wind raged into the lime blossoms behind the stained glass, but here it was the silence; during the summers, the concerts of birds burst out into the branches of these same trees, singing a joie de vivre, indestructible, eternal.

She went afterwards to rejoin her husband for breakfast. While Sigmund drank his coffee, Ermelyne poured herself some tea drawn from the grand samovar that she had near her. The drink was boiling and the baroness loved to drink several cups of it in succession; she laid down several of them in front of her, refilled them and emptied them constantly, arriving so at drinking seven cups of tea in a row.

It is afterwards the time for the mail. It is necessary to write and respond to numerous letters and above all, wrap large packages with solid gray paper and tie them with string skillfully.

Because the Baroness Bartzel was a great provider for the churches of the eastern frontier of Poland. Almost all the afternoons, she hitched up her small cabriolet and accompanied by her "groom" Wladzio, aged 13 years old, she strode through all the parishes of the surroundings in search of old chasubles, chalices and candelabrums. She put everything into a sack and sent the contents, be it to the bishop of Pinsk, be it to the curates with whom she had a rapport beforehand. The bishop of Pinsk had even written to her one day, a letter of thanks, in which he called her "the benefactress of our churches."

The occupations of her husband were of another order. His first cousin in Paris, the Marquis Tamerlan des Etoiles, had made him open a correspondent's column in a grand French economics newspaper. His articles were not very well remunerated but they gave him a very interesting occupation. He studied the Polish newspapers on a given topic and each month, he composed a summary of the economic situation in Poland, which the editors of the "Journal économique" appreciated very much.

Amaldyne and Cathalyne stayed little at the house. They spent almost all their time at their aunt's home in Otwocko, helping her to administer her immense manor. At each time, the two twins prepared their hope chest because the aunt had stuck to having their weddings celebrated at Otwocko, whose setting was more prestigious than the one of the modest residence of their parents in Sobierzyce.

Amaldyne and Cathalyne were engaged both on the same day, at the same hunt, in the vast woods of Otwocko. It was on the crackling snow, while waiting for the beat to come, that the Prince Wladimir Czerski and Amaldyne Bartzel, like so that the count Hippolyte Pozecki and Cathalyne Bartzel, exchanged their promises of marriage.

The aunt was rather disappointed. She would have preferred that the fiancés were of the Otwocki family, which would have permitted her to will her fortune. Because Marjolyne was very attached to her two nieces so gay, helpful and spiritual.

"And to say that this animal of Géopard," – remarked she – "this Prince-Duke Otwocki... comes to announce to me his engagement with an American multimillionaire, divorced, Golda Meirdorf, older than him... What a degradation!"

"The Prince-Duke knows well what he is doing," remarked judiciously Amaldyne "he is reserving maybe a surer future than in Europe..."

"You are maybe right, my child," – said very softly the aunt having become pensive.

The one that they saw the least at Sobierzyce was Philibert. He came there sometimes in rainstorms in his convertible "Fiat," gift of Aunt Marjolyne to the "national hero," in order to leave again the next morning. He followed, so-called courses of philosophy at the Jagiellon University in Krakow, but worked little, too occupied to do the "bomb" with his former comrades of the regiment. He was not truly engrossed by his theoretical studies and on the other hand, abhorred the stays in the country and the field work.

But it was satisfying neither for him nor for life, and that was seen on his face shut, taciturn and sullen.

"What has he become, my little Philibert!" lamented the mother.

"He is going to marry and all will be well," concluded the father.

CHAPTER III

LORD AND LADY BEECHFOREST IN SOBIERZYCE

This morning, Sigmund Bartzel found in his newspaper, the "Kurier Warszawski," the whole page with photographs, dedicated to the arrival in Poland, of a certain Lord Charles Beechforest, accompanied by his wife and daughter.

He came, one would learn, as a guest of the Polish government for the important financial negotiations between the United States and Poland.

Regular visitor with the President of the United States, one of the principal magnates of Wall Street, he would have arrived in his own yacht from New York to Gdynia and would have rented the entire Bristol Hotel for his stay in Warsaw.

There had also been in the same newspaper, his photograph, in front of his boat, in company of his family.

"Could that be our former Kurt Buchenwald?" pondered the Baron. The very fuzzy clichés does not leave much room for guesswork.

Several days after, a letter decorated of a baronial crown, arrived by the mail at Sobierzyce. Sigmund opened it; Lord and Lady Beechforest – he read on – asked to be received in the afternoon of the following Sunday. Bartzel responded that his wife and himself expected Lady and Lord Beechforest at the indicated hour.

Punctually, at the scheduled day and time, a powerful dazzling Lincoln stopped in front of the entrance steps of the modest house of Sobierzyce. A chauffeur and a domestic wearing a black and rigid cap, were sitting in the front seats. Since the arrival of the limousine, the domestic jumped out of the seat and rushed towards the back door in order to open it.

Yes, it was indeed the former steward of Weyssensee, accompanied by his wife. But today, he was in the latest English style: monocle in the eye, grey top hat whose style had been launched recently at the racetracks of Epsom. His coat and his suit clearly came from the best trendsetter in London.

His wife, Zinaida, had not changed very much: always as agitated and prattling as through the past. She wore a small scarlet red suit, displayed charms, small rings or other pendants and emitted a very strong yet very pleasant perfume, with the eau de Cologne from Dior.

"How much time, how much time since we last saw each other!!!," exclaimed she at the door to Mrs. Bartzel, who stepped towards her,"How is your spouse doing?"

"But he waits for you," responded the baroness affectionately embracing her former acquaintance, "he is always suffering and could not come to greet you."

The baron, sitting in his armchair, tendered his arms towards the newly arrived guests, "What joy, dear Lord, to have come among us accompanied by Madam your spouse."

"You will stay to dine and sleep over at our home?" asked the lady of the house, somewhat anxious.

"Probably not," – responded the Lord – "we have still so much to do, only a cup of tea, if possible, and we will leave again."

The ice had been broken; the Lord approached his armchair of the baron and the two ladies retired into the adjacent room to chat in their own way.

"Baron, sir…" began the Lord Beechforest.

"But I beg you… without the 'sir'… we are equals, you have become a person infinitely more important than me," interrupted the baron.

"Certainly, the importance of the financial power is not to be denied, but there exists also the superiority of the seniority and the tradition that you will always keep… But let's cut to the chase; you have certainly guessed that I have come to Poland for an important mission of which our President and Wall Street has charged to me. If I bought this title of English baron, it is that it is indispensable to me in my relations with a Europe plunged always up to the neck in the snobbism from before the war.

"But I have another reason to come to see you, a family matter that is held deeply in my heart. You recall my daughter Barbara…?"

"The kindest little girl that I have ever known," intercalated Bartzel.

"Thank you," – continued the Lord – "eh well! I brought Barbarka on this trip. She is at this moment in Warsaw at the home of her grandmother Ryffka."

"Hold on," exclaimed his interlocutor, "I did not know that Madam your mother was in Warsaw?"

"Yes, long time ago arrived from Courland. But let's come back to my daughter. Imagine, my dear friend, which Barbara has put it in her head to become a Catholic nun and to go on a mission to Africa. When we arrived in the United States towards the end of the war, I sent her to do her university studies in the Catholic University of Villanova where she had taken accommodations with the Reverend Sisters of the Holy Hill in Pennsylvania. It is there that they put this idea into her head. I have well tried to deter her from this project, to divert her, and I have sent her to all the balls on Fifth Avenue. She was an incredible hit! She could marry Ryff Goldberg, the oil millionaire, or even with Abbie Cyngman who had five hundred thousand in steel mills! But nothing doing; it was 'No' and always 'No!' It is not that I hold that she must have a rich marriage because we ourselves have enough money. But I would like that she had a normal life of a married woman, mother of a family, happy. I have then thought this; she maybe has still some attachments with Europe, it is without a doubt that this impedes her from marrying normally. You know, she spoke often and with much tenderness of your son Philibert. I wondered whether she will make this long trip, in our yacht, across the Atlantic, this is going to change once she has again encountered Philibert; that will give to her maybe other ideas...? What do I know?" And the father choked back his sobbing.

"I have the intention," – he continued – "to organize during the carnival a grand ball in the salons of the 'Bristol' in Warsaw. Barbara will see there some young Polish folk, maybe her former comrades your two daughters and above all, if possible, Philibert. Would you be in agreement in order to invite them to come there? And if you can, come yourself with your spouse. You will do all that we could to make your stay pleasant."

"But yes, but yes, dear friend, we will do everything to help you."

In an adjacent room, Zinaida recounted the same worries to Ermelyne. While summing up, she broke down into tears, "A girl so pretty, so intelligent, so rich, who could have the entire world at her feet... to bury herself like that in the anonymity, in a total obscurity, in an uncertain future, unknown... no, it is truly too strong..."

Afterwards, the Bartzels and Beechforests together drank tea. They recalled again many things from the past. Towards the end, on the initiative of Sigmund, the baroness brought a bottle of Castellane Champagne and they clinked glasses to the "Bruderschaft" of the two families; it was decided that each one would call everyone from now on by his first name.

CHAPTER IV

A GRAND RECEPTION AT THE BRISTOL HOTEL

That day, a long crimson rug descended from the glass door of the Bristol Hotel until the street; they waited at the reception organized by Lord and Lady Beechforest, the imminent arrival of the President of the Polish Republic, Ignacy Moscicki.

A dense crowd of journalists with their cameras, police officers in uniform and in plain clothes, Swiss in dazzling frock coats, three-cornered hats and halberds in hand, blocked the main entrance.

Some long, black limousines, marked with the white eagle or a departmental plate, led without ceasing the government representatives or some from the diplomatic corps. They stopped a short moment, then left again, made a turn and went to park on a neighboring plaza, the largest of Warsaw, that they called long ago Saxony Plaza; now, it was the Plaza of Marshal Pilsudski, soon it would Plaza Adolf Hitler, later, another still...

Lord Beechforest waited for the signal of the arrival of the president of the Republic. A group of persons surrounded him: the Prince-Duke Otwocki having at his side his fiancée, Mrs. Golda Meirdorf, very well dressed and very charming indeed, as well as the Duke of Kent, accompanied by his aide-de-camp, the Lieutenant Lord Glencross-Warwick, dressed as a Horse-Guard, who at this moment, amused his entourage, in recounting some extra-ordinary jokes.

In a small boudoir to the side, as her husband, but seated, Lady Beechforest waited for the President Moscicki. She was surrounded by the entire family Bartzel to which the Princess Marjolyne Otwocka was tied.

Barbara chatted joyously with the two former comrades, Amaldyne and Cathalyne, having become respectively Princess Czerska and Countess Pozecka. The marriage had taken place the last autumn, at Otwocko and had been blessed by Uncle Edward, Baron Hoffisch-Buxwolden, formerly archbishop of Petersburg.

Philibert stood to the side, always taciturn and dreaming. He was however very moved by the encounter with his former comrade and friend during wartime.

Uncle the bishop also had already arrived. He carried his

long, red "feriola" and had greeted at the entry Lord Beechforest, "Oh! How is everything, Mr. Kurt?" When they had made their point to him that he had to make it to Lord Charles Beechforest, he had made like he didn't understand.

Suddenly, a young officer exclaimed from the entrance, "The President of the Republic!" Lord and Lady Beechforest already went to the front, and everyone stood up. The President and Mrs. Moscicka stepped forward accompanied by the ambassador of the United States.

The military orchestra, set up in the ballroom, blasted the Polish national anthem and following the one of the United States. Everyone stood at attention. Afterwards, the President and his group entered into the ballroom.

The President, holding the hand of Lady Beechforest, opened the ball with a polonaise. As second pair, came Lord Beechforest and Mrs. Moscicka. Followed a long procession in which Babarka led Philibert by force because that one did not want to dance. In effect, he always limped.

Once the polonaise finished and once the President left, the true ball began. The delegate of Marshal Pilsudski, his aide-de-camp, the General Sobielewski, invited Barbara into the first pair to dance the mazurka.

It was a special mazurka, where with the rhythmic gallop of the dance, added the acrobatic pirouettes of the oberek. The general, who was no longer a spring chicken, executed it magnificently while Barbarka, svelte and zestful, whirled around her dancer like a butterfly.

The room applauded. Seeing the general in his fifties sweat and huff, the old Baron Bartzel, seated in his armchair in the corner of the room, was taken with such a crazy laughter that in each instant, he was obliged to catch his breath.

From the other side of the room, the Duke of Kent and Lord Glencross observed the dance, and imitating without flinching the gestures of the General, royally amused himself. Evening, remaining alone in pajamas in their room, they referred together to the mazurka, of a more expressive manner. Nobody could doubt while in several years, that same general, charging on horseback in the lead of a cavalry division against the German armor-plated vehicles, perished with his entire unit.

Barbarka was a crazy hit, she was truly the queen of the

ball: her beautiful eyes glaring under the rich black head of hair, her harmonious body of a young girl, expressing a nature and an ease that fascinated every eye.

Philibert watched her with his somber and sad eyes. And however, after each new dance, Barbarka rushed to rejoin her friend and to wait, near him, the succession of the figures.

During an intermission, the ball left room for a famous quartet of violinists, accompanied by a pianist of great renown and by the famous black singer from New York, Dilly Fann. It is at this moment that Barbarka, seated at Philibert's side, in the half darkness of a small library asked to that one:

"Philibert, why are you so sad and so shady?"

"Because I am jealous of you," responded Philibert.

"I do not know what you want; you do not want that I dance with the others, you do not want to dance yourself. What must I do?"

"Do not prevent me from being jealous… I am in love with you."

"And you would maybe like to marry me?" But love and marriage, it is not always the same thing. Love is often only passing while marriage is forever."

"But it is that you would like to be married to me forever!"

"And you know what that means: forever, not only when one is young, but also when one becomes old, not only when one no longer has the desire of the other, but also when one begins to truly get on one's nerves… Could I support you? Me, I am not so sure of it."

"Maybe have you someone in your sights?"

"Nobody. If I wanted to marry, it would be with you. But I do not want to marry."

"Why?"

"Because I am thinking of falling in love… with God…"

"Ah! Is it possible?"

"Listen, Philibert, it is not that I do not love the earth and all the pleasures that it presents to us. You have well seen that I had fun during this ball. I love the society, I am attracted by the boys, as you yourself are by the girls. I am completely normal.

"But, you see, when I hear, for example, a tango, that dance which expresses the best all that implies human love, I feel a great sadness, an immense nostalgia; I see that as the expression of a functional love, but what is not truly feasible in this ephemeral and imperfect world.

"Deep down, all that luxurious display, all those balls, dinner, gatherings that my father organizes, I have had enough until I am nauseous. For me, it is but only empty, vain and ephemeral. There I take part, most of all, in order to be pleasant to my father, but deeply, that bores me profoundly.

"Although that could seem to you bizarre, I feel truly happy only close to God, in his intimacy, when I admire the beauty of nature and when I reflected on kindness, the beauty and the power of The One who created all these things. It is to God that I would like to consecrate myself and voila why I have no desire to marry."

"Yes," remarked Philibert, "but you also, you do not realize the frailty of this 'marriage' with God which comprises the worst risks that the marriage between humans... All that you say is but only emotions, and the emotions are unstable. If you would lose your inclination towards God, what would become of you?"

"Do not speak so fast, Philibert," responded Barbarka, "there is, albeit maybe unconscious, a profound philosophical base to my religious feelings; the nature 'speaks' always and always eloquently, of the authentic existence of a God True, Beautiful, Powerful and Intelligent, completely independently of our feelings. It is to this God that I want to consecrate myself."

"Yes, but this 'intellectual' voice that you believe to perceive by meditating on nature it is only one very weak glimmer, which is so often swept away and extinguished by the push of feelings of passion and through everything tragic that happens to us in our lives. Because the life is not the immaculate mirror of the Goodness, Beauty, Intelligence and Power of the Creator. Much to the contrary!"

"We could discuss it still for a long time," responded Barbara, "but I admit that the 'marriage' with God is not possible without a particular vocation from Above, a special grace from God. At each moment, we need this grace, as it is needed also for the human marriage. Without grace, no family life, without grace, no religious life. The vocation is needed for everything! And me, I believe to have the religious vocation."

In another small adjacent salon, Ryffka Buchenwald had sat down on a sofa at the side of the Baron Bartzel. She had just arrived from the quarter of the Nalewskis where she lived with some relatives; in her grey robe with glittering spangles, she resembled strangely to an old armchair that they had just descended from the attic.

"Tell then, dear friend," remarked softly the baroness, "that seems to work out between Barbarka and Philibert. We see them always together. There they are, again, immersed in the endless discussions in the library."

"Tssst, tssst, not so sure, not so sure," responded the old Jewish woman. "These days I have discussed a lot with Barbarka; she is completely fallen for her God, a Christian God of course, but is God not the same everywhere!? I fear that we must make the sacrifice of Abraham ready to immolate Isaac..."

The orchestra played again the airs of dance. But Barbarka refused all invitations and remained close to Philibert until the end of the ball, two o'clock in the morning.

Lord Beechforest stuck to remaining until the end close to the exit door in order to say goodbye to all her guests and thanked them all. By passing by her, her friends of Wall Street, the multimillionaires Abby Grinspan and Fox Zitrin, gave him great, friendly taps on the back; "Well done, Kurt! Well done!" they told him.

At the end of this January, it was strongly freezing the snow-covered streets in Warsaw, but until the end, there was a crowd of bystanders in front of the "Bristol," which stayed to catch sight through the large windows half frozen and the lower blinds, the winding down of this ball about which the newspapers had spoken so much and attending afterwards of the exit of the members of the government, of the diplomatic corps and celebrities of the world of the arts.

When the Bristol Hotel plunged again into night and sleep, the hosts were only half content because the fate of their daughter remained always uncertain.

CHAPTER V

WOLODIA AND PHILIBERT

The young Czerski and Pozecki couples, as well as Philibert, decided to still remain in Warsaw until the end of the carnival.

They had all received some invitations to the grand balls at the "Blue Palace" from the Zamoyskis, at the home of Radziwills, the Potockis, the Raczynskis and others still, which inevitably prolonged their stay.

Philibert did not want to abandon his assiduities close to Barbara because he was madly passionate about her and each day went to see her. Unfortunately, Barbara could not decide, every night, she bitterly cried. Ah! If all that would end! If she could finally go home to the Holy Hill Sisters where the peace of heart and the happiness of soul waited for her! But the father did not want that because he always hoped.

Aunt Marjolyne offered to her Bartzel nephews and nieces the hospitality of her villa in the Aleja Roz and it is there that one morning, Philibert received a secret message from the embassy of the United States, asking him to present himself there as soon as possible.

He was received there "stante pede" by the ambassador in person who called him into his office, locked it with a key and said to him in an undertone, "I asked you to come for the identification of a certain young man who claims to have fled the Soviet embassy and has asked us for the right to asylum; he told us that you knew each other well."

The ambassador pushed a buzzer and at the end of several seconds, a young man passed through the door at the end of the room and stopped.

"Wolodia!" exclaimed Philibert, "what good wind brings you?!"

The young people threw themselves into each other's arms. The ambassador could certify that the affirmations of the young Soviet were true.

In order to facilitate a free exchange of opinions, he brought them into an adjacent room and withdrew.

Philibert and Wolodia had a great secret in common that

they had never ever divulge to anyone; at the end of the Soviet-Polish war, Wolodia had saved the life of Philibert.

It was during the retreat of the Ataman Budyonny, at Korzec in Volhynia. The Russian troops withdrew hastily, the Poles attacked. In the melee which ensued, the Lieutenant Philibert Bartzel was made a prisoner and led in front of the High Command of the Soviet Division. Every white officer – as well as every red commissar – risked at that time being shot by an adversary.

The Divisional Tribunal would have decided like that, if it had not been the intervention of the divisional commissar of the G.P.U.,[1] Wladimir Kurtowitch Buchenwald.

The latter made as if he had not recognized the prisoner and Bartzel, having understood the game, did the same. "Listen, Towarishchi,"[2] – said the all-powerful commissar of the G.P.U., "before he is shot, I need to interrogate this Polish officer, he can furnish some secret information of which I have a need."

The tribunal consented without saying a word. The prisoner was incarcerated in a barn and his guard was entrusted to the military police, commanded by Buchenwald in person. The commissar came to see Philibert the same evening, chatted for a long time with him and it was agreed between the two of them that Philibert would escape this same night at precisely two o'clock, through an exit that they had located in the building. The commissar tried to imperceptibly lure the guard away; next, while the disappearance of the prisoner would have been certified, they would shoot and, if possible, pursue him. But in the night without a moon and in the middle of the deep forest, in addition with the Poles being extremely close, Philibert would have every opportunity to escape.

"But you will never speak of this to anyone," concluded Wolodia, "If not, it is my certain death."

"Word of an officer and a friend," responded simply Philibert.

Thing concluded, thing done. No one was ever astonished by that escape, such that the Poles were closer than they had believed, and the fired salvos behind the runaway triggered a general battle and the frantic retreat of the Soviet detachment.

---

[1] G.P.U.: Soviet Police.
[2] Towarishtchi: comrades.

Wolodia recounted his life to Philibert, "At the beginning, I made a dazzling career in the Soviet Russia. I climbed sky-high in rank and they gave me full confidence. I was considered as one of the hardest and the most fanatical in the Party. I was a militant, unapologetic Trotskyite. But everything changed with the arrival of Stalin in power. Stalin detested the Jews – and I was considered as a Jew; Stalin was a sectarian and rigorist doctrinarian – me, I was for the tolerance and the liberty – Stalin, he was a static communist – me, I was for the dynamism and the evolution.

"The worst was that we had not the right to express freely our opinions. They incarcerated us in the madhouses, they imprisoned us, they sent us into the concentration camps. Several of our own were even just simply eliminated, be it clandestinely, be it after a monkey trial.

"At that time, they could reproach me for nothing because I had remained always loyal towards the Party and the government. But my ranking had fallen. They sent me then to the embassy in Warsaw to hold a post rather inferior to that of technical advisor. They knew that I spoke Polish well as well as other foreign languages; they believed that I could render still some services to them.

"For a time long enough, I had realized what waited for me under the regime of Stalin, I had then decided to benefit from the first opportunity and to part company. At the desirable moment, I asked for asylum from the embassy of the United States and here I am!

"And the last straw is that the Soviet embassy had not yet discovered my escape, which happened this morning…"

Afterwards the two young people spent in the office of the ambassador, who in front of Philibert listened to the abridged version of the "curriculum vitae" of Wolodia, and concluded, "I voluntarily accord you the right of asylum but for your own safety and for reasons of general order, I would like that no one, I mean no one, apart from your father, Lord Beechforest, be informed until your debarkation to the United States."

"Captain Bartzel," said the ambassador to Philibert, "would you like very much to take your car and go communicate to Lord Beechforest – but only to him – the news of the arrival of his son, and bring him here afterwards, always in your car, not to the embassy of the United States but into the annex that we have on the side. I would be very grateful to you if you render this service for us. Your friend will remain with us."

Philibert with his "Torpedo" was in a wink of an eye at the Bristol Hotel. Lord Beechforest was dressed for visits and encouraged them wholeheartedly, although he had, with sadness, certified their uselessness; Barbara cried, but always said "no."

His face metamorphosed, became radiant, young and joyous when he learned through Philibert that he went to see his son in an instant. "If Barbara leaves me," wondered he, "at least that one will stay with me and I will have not worked and slaved in vain during my whole life!"

"But above all, say nothing to anyone, not even to your wife!" recommended severely Philibert.

"Yes, of course, Zinaida is so gabby!" But he could not hide his joy bubbling over. To the stupefaction of the personnel of the hotel, this dignified and calm gentleman, rather sad and worried, started to run down the stairs in order to pounce as a joyous kid, into Philibert's car stationed in front of the entrance.

From that moment and most of all after having received the news of the arrival of his son in New York, Lord Beechforest was less reticent to return to the United States.

Zinaida, to whom her husband had communicated the news without further commentary, was overjoyed also and prepared in succession to come back as soon as possible to the United States and kissed Wolodia.

Barbara had red eyes because to have to abandon Philibert cost her dearly, but this novel, which had no way out, began to weary her, and with a broken heart, she decided to accompany her parents on their return voyage.

Philibert was heartbroken, but feeling that he would obtain nothing from Barbara, he had to submit to his inevitable fate.

The Beechforests were so hurried to return to their home that they sent their empty yacht and took the first military plane for the destination of the United States.

CHAPTER VI

AT THE BEECHFORESTS' HOME IN AMERICA

Wolodia settled in New York at the home of his father, who was satisfied with having his son to help him. They married him soon after to a young American, whose pregnancy was confirmed at the end of five months of marriage.

The grandparents burst with joy; the so recent dynasty of the Lords Beechforest was going to continue.

Wolodia busied himself with his father's affairs with skill and care; he was intelligent and energetic. Of course, there was his Marxist past, communist even, but he carried also new ideas and the conceptions that could be proven.

Vlady – it was the American nickname of Wolodia – frequented the same club as his father: "The Sons of Solomon." It was a club, very closed off, of which his father was one of the vice-presidents.

There they turned on to Broadway, an avenue, wide yet, which seemed narrow, because so high on each side were the buildings, which let anyone see only barely a fringe of a blue sky in which floated the white clouds.

A rapid and silent elevator opened up into the hallway richly carpeted on the 60th floor, a melodious buzzer rang and they discovered the salons of the Club. On a soft Persian rug were placed some armchairs covered in lion skins; on the side of each armchair were located small tables in a Chinese lacquer furnished in heavy ash trays in Baccarat crystal.

Big French windows opened up on a long loggia in a row from where the intense traffic of the street down below seemed an incessant movement of busy insects.

The temperature of the salons was always pleasant: perfectly well heated during the winter cold, deliciously air-conditioned during the summer heat.

Son of powerful Lord Beechforest and sole inheritor of his immense fortune, Vlady were very well received at the moment of his first introduction to the Club of the "Sons of Solomon."

They knew well his advanced ideas on the economy and the politics, but they did not take them too seriously. "That will pass with age," said the millionaires of the Club.

The young Lord Beechforest advocated the fundamental reform of the capitalist system. "They can no longer base the economy," said he, "only on the pursuit of the greatest profit: to sell at the highest prices, to buy at the lowest price, enriched the ones at the expense of the others; the rich countries grow richer, the poor countries grow poorer. I admit that a rich country brings indirectly the affluence to all and that in this manner in the industrialized countries – most of all in Western Europe – the proletarian class has practically disappeared. But it is not the case of underdeveloped countries that constituted the two tiers of humanity; to buy at a low price their raw materials and to sell it at a heavy price the articles that we produce from those can only impoverish these countries instead of enriching them.

"The charity thanks to which we tried to remedy this impoverishment is ridiculously insufficient and even if it was not sufficient, she could constitute only a palliative, whose result is finally harmful because it encourages the underdeveloped populations to laziness. No, what is necessary, is to raise their intellectual and moral level, to teach them to be self-sufficient through their own means."

"Yes! In order to nourish serpents with their own milk... to produce and to reinforce future enemies... No!" groaned sarcastically Kipper Goldfisch from the other side of the room.

"In any manner, Mister Goldfisch, they are already our enemies and they will be it even more if we leave them in misery and ignorance. In a world where intercontinental information will grow enormously, the thousands and thousands of backward and uncultivated men will be much more dangerous than an adversary enlightened by civilization and culture. Because these non-civilized beings will let themselves be trained more easily by a nefarious propaganda than people to whom they will have taught to think, to judge, to reflect.

"The economy based only on the principle "make money" must be, once and for all, abandoned. The economy must not have for the primary goal money, but man. It is for man that it is done, for any man, no matter his race and no matter the continent from where he comes. It is the only manner of avoiding the injustices, and flagrant inequalities which are the cause of all the revolutions and the wars; humanize your economy, rip it from the blind power of money!"

"But how do you want to get there? It would be necessary for that an organization, a planetary power which only could impose its will on all the peoples of the world! Yet, we are far from that! It is only a utopia that you advocate," remarked the wise Bill Cukerman.

"Today utopia, tomorrow probably necessity before which everyone will have to accept," concluded the young reformer.

Leaving the club, the members exchanged their opinions on the latest discourse of the young Beechforest, "It is really beautiful, all that he says, very idealist and charitable, but he knows nothing of life. The practice will soon teach the young lord that the maxim that prevails is this one: 'if I do not eat you, it is you who will eat me.'" Because these distinguished men were raised on the principles of Hobbes's philosophy: "Homo homini lupus."

They were still far from the philosophy of Teilhard de Chardin, who began only to teach that all in the world is based on the synthesis, the unification, the creation of love.

*
* *

Barbara was in her second year as postulate with the Holy Hill Sisters in Pennsylvania. She had found peace and calm in the conviction to serve her God and her Lord in all that she did.

One day, at the moment of a prayer vigil, she caught cold and had to be confined to bed. The doctor was not overly worried and assured that her pain would pass soon.

But the fever did not diminish, on the contrary it increased. The doctor declared an acute pneumonia and was vehemently worried because it seemed to be the symptoms of a rampant phthisis.

The heart of the young nun weakened every day and her strength diminished rapidly; also the Mother Superior of the convent believed in her duty to warn Barbara that she was in danger of dying and to ask her if she desired to see her family.

"In any case, " said the Mother Superior, "we will not let your parents stay too long because you are too tired."

Her father, her mother and her brother were warned by the nuns and received into the hospital at the bedside of the sick. All seemed terribly frightened.

Barbara smiled weakly in seeing their grief-stricken faces and spoke to them with difficulty but with a great calm, "I feel that I will soon go into the other world... I am overjoyed by it because all my life was only a preparation for this moment where I could finally unite with God... this God to whom I have consecrated my heart and my life... I wanted to say goodbye to you, mama, to you papa, and to you Wladimir... and how much I love you... Please write, mama, to Philibert how much pain it caused me to break up with him... but I want to remain loyal to God and to his son Jesus Christ... to whom I gave my heart."

The visitors had burst out in tears, but a nun in a white habit and veil was watching and made them leave immediately, "It is time to leave, it is not necessary to wear out the patient," said she.

Three days later, the Beechforest family learned that Sister Barbara had piously left this world. They were all shattered, but all at once, filled with the inspiring feeling of having had in their family, an authentic saint.

From the modest convent of the Sisters of the Holy Hill the death of Barbara was reflected widely across everything that counts in America and in Europe; some telegrams piled up on the desk of Lord Beechforest, they arrived from the White House, from the Vatican, the Queen of England, from the President of the Polish Republic, from the Duke of Kent, from the Prince-Duke Otwocki and from some many other personalities.

But the funeral was the simplest of the world in the modest cemetery of the Holy Hill Sisters. The crowd of the attendants was great and they saw, among others, all the members of the Club of the Sons of Solomon. They were lined up all side by side, strapped in their long black coats: Ryff Goldberg, Abby Grinszpan, Fox Zitrin, Koper Goldfisch, Bill Cukerman and others still. During the last benediction of the casket at the cemetery, they had all removed their top hats, except Rabbi Heizholzer, who – for respect for the God of Israel – had kept his wide felt hat on his long haired and bearded head of a former Biblical prophet.

After the burial, "The Sons of Solomon" reunited at their club, Broadway Avenue. The Beechforests, father and son, excused themselves their absence and no one was astonished.

They evoked the incomprehensible death of this young girl who had not yet reached twenty-five years. Nothing from them comprised neither sense nor reason.

"If she had lived normally," said judiciously Bill Cukerman, doctor reputable within the hospitals of New York, "that would never happened to her. But this incomprehensible gesture of refusal of human love in order to live a religious and abstract love, there is what is natural to kill a healthy and normal organism."

"It would be necessary to vote for a law through the Legislatures, which prohibits the vow of chastity that the Church imposes on young men and girls, who consecrate their lives to its service," exclaimed Ryff Gildberg, former suitor of Barbara.

"Barbara, she is a lost life, nonsense, a defiance to reason, she was in fact a suicide that serves nothing and no one," added Fox Zitrin, who could not forget the soirée at the "Bristol" where each one was on their knees before this "goddess" of charm, beauty and intelligence, "no, I will never admit it."

These gentlemen were all grouped in a long loggia from where the street, seen from the 60th floor, seemed an immense and deep corridor, boxed in between the walls of the buildings which soared sky high, letting burgeon only a thin fringe of an azure sky. Rabbi Heizholer was there also himself and meditated deeply.

"Listen, dear friends," said he finally, "you see here only the grey stones, the worried movement of the human masses down below in the street, of the elevated houses, where happened many sad and little enlightening events, disputes, maliciousness, jealousy, treason, dishonesty, where they think only to enjoy this world, locked away in the narrowness of its surroundings, without escape, without horizons. But, high above, between this pile of stones sad and desperately monotonous, opens up a fringe of the sky, into the infinite hereafter. Eh well, for me, Barbara, it is that; she recalls for us in a sad world without escape, that this gleam exists in the pure sky and that there is a God above.

CHAPTER VII

THE DECISION OF PHILIBERT

In the Bartzel family, everyone was profoundly moved by Barbara's death. Even though she tried, yet she disappeared from the mundane life, to retire and to consecrate her life uniquely to God, Barbara had remained the child that they loved and admired since her infancy; in fact, Barbara was a part of their family.

The most touched by this deceased woman was Philibert. Externally, no one perceived his chagrin, but at the bottom of his soul, Philibert was deeply disturbed.

The contact with Barbara had shown him the serious side of life of a real-life religion and had made him reflect on all those that consecrated their existence to the grand causes. He had encountered some of them on the front, even among his enemies, the Communist commissars, who before being shot as per regulation by the IInd Polish Bureau, had affirmed to die without regret for the future of the humanity. And this brother of Barbara, his friend, was it not also from the same caliber as those who live and sacrifice for a cause?

Philibert was terribly ashamed. The idle and light life that he led these last years seemed to him, in this light, an immense and guilty loss of time, and he started again from then on to work seriously. He took his exams at Jagiellon University and obtained good diplomas in philosophy.

His religious life steadily felt the effects of it; from now on, he would no longer ever miss Sunday mass and they saw him even sometimes kneeling in front of the tabernacle of the churches. His mother said nothing of it, but she was very satisfied.

Consecrating his life to a grand cause... the one of the Christ... to become his soldier, his cavalier... his priest... became an idea that preoccupied him more and more.

Once, in the silence of the little church of Sobierzyce, he kneeling contemplated Christ on the Cross, dispossessed of all, he seemed to hear the tender and suffering mouth from the Crucified, as a response to the offering of his heart, "You want to offer yourself to me and become my priest? But do you know what is a priest? You are still full of lusts and of terrestrial ambitions, but the true priest, it is the crucified, it is I.

111

"Look at me, who was dispossessed of all, abandoned by all, who suffers without consolation, without recompense, abandoned even by my Father in Heaven, who served Him however during all my life – that is the priest, it is I.

"You will be, same as me, misunderstood by your superiors, by your comrades, the world, the Church, unless it was always through your mistake, but often because of clumsiness of your too fiery love for Me.

"Your works, which merited the most flattering praise in the beginning, will soon one after another be vilified, forgotten.

"You will march from defeat to defeat and you will ask, tired in your spirit and in your body, to be liberated from worries and suffering of the terrestrial existence and you will have to again lift yourself and continue.

"They will strip away from you even the possibility to continue and you will remain in the total shadows, not knowing how and through where to continue and you will need to wait for a long while for a new ray of sunshine to retake a new path.

"Your life as a priest will always be a failure, it must be a failure because the ideal is not of this world. Do not forget that there is no greater failure than My death on the Cross and however, it was not through my glory but through the cross that I overcame the world.

"Priest – yes, but priest dispossessed of everything and cast aside always. To be a priest, you must become the Christ on the Cross. Then you and your work will overcome… after your death, as for me…"

Philibert understood, but he did not back away tooo much; a too powerful attraction held him close to Christ.

He confided his intentions to his mother. She was transported to seventh heaven, "You could not give me any greater joy than to announce this news to me."

She was already seen with her son, a priest in front of the altar, while the graces from heaven descended upon them, filling their hearts with a joy and peace, which are no longer of this world.

"He found the true sense of life," she wondered, "he is going to feel what I have lived myself so many times during my prayers after Mass."

The father was much more reticent, "Philibert does not realize," confided he to his wife, "what is the life of a priest, how hard and difficult it is! And he has nothing to make him a priest! Light, superficial, unstable that he is, he will never be able to support this life of continual sacrifice! He was unhappy all his life! It is through scorn, through caprice, that this idea has come to him."

The cousin the bishop, Baron von Hoffisch Buxwolden, who found himself on a visit at Sobierzyce, likewise gave his opinion.

"Listen, my friends, rarely a vocation is truly quite pure and limpid. I admit it, Philibert is a whimsical sort, a romantic, he is too complicated a character, one does not always understand him and I wonder often if he knows himself.

"But the vocation is not much of an affair of a temperament or of a character than before all a call from God. Yet, what do you know if he has not received this call?

"And furthermore, do not forget," added the bishop in laughing, "Philibert is like me, a 'feudal.' If he truly found his Lord, he will try to serve Him faithfully as a knight of Christ. I wish him at least…"

The Baron von Hoffisch-Buxwolden, formerly archbishop of Saint Petersburg, was well placed for preaching the "feudalistic" spirit because this Courlandese lord, by having some of his shortcomings, had also his good points. Man of an "incredible courage," Philibert's Jesuit professors said of him.

Having lost his diocese, suffered a long time in the prisons of Butyrki, expulsed from Russia, living as an exile in a religious house in Warsaw, this old man approaching ninety years of age, half blind and pretty much deaf, had lost nothing of his vigor and his fiery allure. Walking always on foot, he ran, straight as a candle, the streets of Warsaw and without any aid, leaped even on to the moving tramways.

Nothing could demoralize him. He had always the pleasantry in his words. When once, he slipped on some stairs and rolled with all his weight from the second floor to the first and when the frightened clergy, seeing him lying on the ground, rushed to help him get up, the angry old man stood up quickly on his own means and said, "They had taught me that an intelligent man always falls without doing himself any harm."

At the end of his life, when his superiors confiscated from him everything even his Institute that he founded in Poland for preparing the missionary relief for Russia, this courageous prelate supported this latest ordeal and humiliation, not without the most vehement protests, but without being discouraged.

The youth loved him and surrounded him until his end because he had always a funny and pleasant word and behaved with them as if he was their age. It was he, moreover, who led Philibert into his first steps towards the priesthood.

CHAPTER VIII

THE DEATH OF THE OLD BARON

Sygmund Bartzel visibly declined. Ermelyne tried hard to augment the attention and care, save money in order to make him pursue cures at Busko or at Ciechocinek, the paralysis of her husband progressed rapidly and Sygmund felt his end coming.

He was very much indeed surrounded by his wife and family. The Czerskis and the Pozeckis accompanied by their children, came often to Sobierzyce of their faraway properties on the western Polish border. The sister-in-law, the Princess Otwocka, remained constantly very attached to him; she came to see him almost every day, because she valued very much the intelligent and pleasant conversation of her brother-in-law. Occupied by his theological studies, next to the bishop of Warsaw, Philibert had, on the other hand, become almost invisible.

But he seemed to succeed well enough and under this support the father became used to having a priest for a son. "Only," contemplated the old baron, "my only son having become a priest, there will no longer be any Bartzels after my death. There will be, of course, some Bartzels of the Krakowian and Warsawian line, but those of Weyssensee are going to disappear. For Ermelyne obviously, this viewpoint doesn't exist. She is Bartzel only through marriage and besides begins to replace her former passion for her high Austrian ancestry, through a devotion more and more pronounced. With the end of the fortune, here is the end of our family.".

Despite worrying, these considerations became blurred in front of the threats of a new war. Germany became more and more aggressive. A certain Austrian corporal had taken power there and exercised a stronger and stronger pressure on its neighbors, which sooner or later, would trigger a general conflagration. "What will become then of Poland, the biggest target of all the countries, and our properties, the great fortune of Marjolyne, the properties of the Czerskis and Pozeckis and even our small property of Sobierzyce with its five hundred hectares?"

It is the fate of his family that preoccupied him because he clearly realized that he no longer had much time to live.

And however, he still lovedlife, he loved it more than

before in its most humble and its most imperceptible events.

A simple sunrise, the sky in the east fringed in gold, a small fresh breeze entering through half-open window, the chirping orchestrated by birds in the tall lime trees, which cover the house with their shadow all that procured for him an inexpressible respite in his suffering and filled him with a youth that seemed to him eternal.

"As she is yet beautiful, this earth of God!" murmured he in ecstasy. But soon the suffering took hold of him again and his strength abandoned him.

The doctor arrived from the small city of Otwocko, warned the baroness that the state of her husband had become very worrisome and that it was necessary to expect the worst.

It was night when she called the old curate of Sobierzyce, who administered the last rites and attended to him in his last moments. The baron was going with dignity into the other world, but he breathed with more and more difficulty, a last hiccup made him quiver and rendered his soul to his Creator. The horizons of the sky and of the earth became lost in the infinite, an unspeakable light lit everything up, and he saw...

In the coffin, where he had been disposed, his face had the inexpressible majesty of those who died in God's peace.

The funeral was the simplest, but the Princess Otwocka insisted on her brother-in-law being buried in her family's vault. Surrounded by relatives and friends, Philibert celebrated the burial because the uncle-bishop was at the end of his life and would soon have to succumb.

"You will now be all alone at Sobierzyce, we are going to live from now on together," said Marjolyne to her sister, who transported her affairs to the castle of Otwocko.

CHAPTER IX

A REUNION OF YOUNG BARTZELS

Having terminated his works in the diocese, the Abbot Philibert Bartzel climbed into the Miodowa Street tram and descended on the Unja Lubelska Square.

He went around the statue of the aviator, whose modernism and ugliness fought over the first place, then he headed with a rapid gait towards a lateral street, situated above a rigid escarpment from where the view plunge on to the wide-open green spaces of the Lazienki Park; in the middle of the latter, the Belweder palace, historic residence of the departed marshal, Józef Pilsudski, made a white spot.

He rang the doorbell of a small very modern hotel, work and the property of his first cousin Boryslaw Bartzel, who inhabited it in company of his brother. These first cousins belonged to the Bartzel branch of Pikiliszki and carried the title of count.

Boryslaw had done his excellent studies at the Polytechnic of Warsaw and was considered as one of the most talented architects in the capital. His brother, student in the same establishment, was preparing to follow the same path.

There was a family reunion among the Bartzel brothers; they waited for the Czerskis and Pozecki, who came back from a voyage abroad. Everyone was curious to know their impressions.

A pale tea was poured into miniscule cups of China and some dry cakes with almonds waited on a small saucer when the Czerskis and Pozeckis entered into the "living room."

"Me, I do not want any of your cold and tasteless tea of a student, I want some real hot tea!" exclaimed Cathalyne while taking the cups back to the kitchen while Wladimir Czerski and Hippolyte Pozecki began their narrative.

They had traveled in Austria, Italy, France and Germany.

The anxiety in Austria had been great; the government of the Chancellor Schuschnigg expected an imminent push from Hitler.

Italy lives always in the euphoria of the great Duce; they showed, to all and sundry, the magnificent Roman Autostrade, which went around the Coliseum and the Campidoglio.

117

France was in prostration. They had visited to their very charming uncle Ermentien, Marquis of Tamerlan des Etoiles, whose family descended from the Merovingians and who was the first cousin of the deceased Sygmund Bartzel. The uncle invited them to a very fine lunch accompanied by excellent wines, but he was very worried; "Among us," he said, "nobody has any desire to make war and however, I believe it inevitable... we are legitimately proud of our victory of 1914, but battered and tired... we believe in the inexpugnability of the Maginot Line... Provided that we are not mistaken." Paris pleased them enormously: what unequal harmony of elegance and magnificence!

They passed again through Germany. That one was in full preparation for war. In the cinemas, they saw only war films, ultra-modern tanks knocking down the walls, demolishing houses, crossing rivers, everything accompanied by the frenetic applause of the whole room. Few people in the streets, Germany, claws drawn, was readying silently to leap with a single bound on its prey and crush it by surprise. On the border, the German employees were of the latest insolence and arrogance.

All of them, who were there listened, in a dream-like state; men were, for the most part, reserve officers of the Polish army and perfectly realized that their army, although valiant, would have troubles holding back an assault by the Germans.

CHAPTER X

BEGINNINGS OF THE WAR OF 1939

From the annexation of Austria and Czechoslovakia by Germany, the Poles were convinced that their nation would be the next prey of Hitler.

No one in Poland wanted this war, all feared it; they perfectly realized the disposition of the forces between the two countries. The accusations without end repeated by the Germans on the Polish provocations on the borders of the Reich were then absolutely false and even ridiculous.

But without exception either, the Poles were angered by the impudent aggressiveness of Nazi Germany; they had well seen that no concession was capable of stopping his insatiable imperialism, someone must say to him finally no. And this no was delivered the first time by Poland.

It was then only a partial surprise when on the morning of the September first 1939, the Warsawians realized that this time the alarm sirens and the passing of planes were no longer simple exercises but marked the beginning of a war.

The loudspeakers of the capital quickly sounded patriotic discourses, optimistic news on the entry of the English and French allies into the fight, on the first success obtained by the Polish troops.

And the dread of spies was installed throughout the entire nation; everyone became suspect, all that touched from close by or from faraway the Germans was condemned, even the cassock of the priest, however so respected, was not protected.

Under penalty of the most severe sanctions, prohibition was enacted against listening to enemy radio; the radio of the nation had to suffice and it was always optimistic or taught nothing. It was equally forbidden to listen to the idle gossip of the runaway from the West, which was less reassuring.

The night was silent and tranquil, Philibert turned lightly the knob on his radio to the German stations. What he heard made his hair stand on end; the Germans announced that they entered into Poland like a knife through butter, they were already approaching the big cities like Krakow, Kielce, Poznan, Bydgoszcz.

The next day, after Mass and during breakfast, he

communicated this news to his colleagues with whom he formed a parish team. "But the Germans lie always," was their response to him, "it is astonishing that you would pay so much attention to their affirmations.!"

Fearing being accused of antipatriotism, maybe even of a certain complicity with the Szkopy,[1] the Abbot Philibert did not persist. Alas, very soon, everyone had to realize from the evidence; the situation was far from being excellent, the innumerable wagons of refugees, coming from afar and blocking the streets of the city in order to cross the bridges and reach the right bank of the Vistula, were sufficient proof for it.

There was no longer any doubt when the booms from the canons, first faraway and deafening, becomig more and more distinct, began to envelope the horizon, and when they learned that the government and the diplomatic corps abandoned the capital and fled away from the enemy.

Remained however the President of Warsaw Starzynski, who more and more hoarsely, harangued the good people, announced to them that he had taken control of the government and that the capital was going to oppose the Germans until the last human life.

Each day, the battle moved closer. The continuous rumbling of canons coming from the west, from the north and from the south, could only forewarn the beginning of a formal siege. The first shells had already rained down into the streets.

More and more audacious the enemy descended with the sinister whistling until the rooftops of the houses in order to drop there, in a deafening swarm, their cargo of bombs. The city burned. The furious riposte of the Polish anti-aircraft defense was more and more timid and finished by stopping completely.

With the water pipes and the electrical installations of the city having been destroyed since the first days of the siege, there was no longer any water, and only, the candles distributed a little bit of light. The women were going to look for water in the Vistula.

After the first weeks of the siege, the provisions started to go missing, also the inhabitants had to go off to carve up slices of meat off the cadavers of the horses, which were sprawled out in the

---

[1] Szkopy: the Krauts.

streets and on the squares of the city.

Since the start of the war, Philibert's parish distributed a free soup to the refugees. They were close to 140 and came from all the parts of Poland. This soup was often their only nourishment and they lied down, pell-mell, in the garden and in the cellars of the former cloister that had been, long ago, the rectory.

In order to supply everyone, they needed to constantly renew their stocks: cans of fish, vegetables, potatoes. It was an entire expedition to reach the supply center.

Philibert was charged as well as a very likable Poznanian, both former soldiers, accustomed to bombardments.

They would chose the moonless nights, Philibert sat on the seat of the tricycle, which was had a large trunk in the back, the Poznanian ran on the side.

They had to follow Marchalkowska Street, important axis of the city, which was located under the incessant shooting of the enemy; the street was strewn with debris of glass, pavement ripped out by trees uprooted and inverted. Here and there, they encountered a cadaver and an odor of the burned reigned everywhere.

The tricycle advanced into the middle of the shells which pulled up trees, exploded against the walls of houses and the pavement of the streets.

After having done the loading up, they returned. But, after several tries of this type, the Poznanian refused to continue. Deep down, Philibert was satisfied because he himself also started being scared.

They approached from the end of the third week. Under an incessant bombardment which lasted day and night and impeded everyone from sleeping and from going out, even the hardest patriots wished for the end of this siege, which seemed foolish to them.

After three weeks of resistance, Warsaw capitulated. In a room with cracked walls where the cold air of a fine September penetrated through the windows without panes, Philibert had his first night of tranquility.

CHAPTER XI

THE GESTAPO

With the arms keeping quiet, all of Warsaw went out into the streets: the ones looking in the stores, which started to open, for some provisions or some material to repair the damage caused by the bombardments, the other to do a damage assessment in the houses, the hotels, the public buildings, the churches of the capital.

The German army had entered into the city and very numerous cars carrying the plaque POL[1] patrolled the streets in all directions. Philibert found himself at the corner of a sidewalk while one of the these cars stopped in front of him, an extremely elegant officer got out of it and invited him to follow him, "Bitte, folgen Sie mich." Philibert realized that he was arrested and protested with vehemence, "Sie haben kein Recht, it is against international laws," cried out he in an excellent German.

The German drew his revolver from its holster and Philibert had to obey. "Against international law!!!" giggled the officer who sat next to the chauffeur. The car continued its march. As soon as the officer saw a priest in a cassock, he invited him to take a seat in the car. There were already five priests in the back seat.

"What do they want? What are they going to do with us?" was asked among the companions of Philibert.

The car stopped in front of a huge gate covered with barbwire; it was the Pawiak Prison. The officer made his passengers get out in a corridor, but stopped Philibert, "You, stay there! Put yourself against the wall!" Philibert obeyed.

The police officer stepped forward and with all his strength, delivered a punch on the chin of the prisoner. Philibert had a lot of pain but did not say a word. "There, that will teach you," said the officer.

The prison filled up with cassocks. There was even the grand chancellor of the Parish and a Jesuit known in the entire world. With any evidence, the Germans began their operations with a raid on priests; it was necessary since the beginning to intimidate the small insolent people who had dared to oppose the

---

[1] POL: Polizei.

full power of the race of lords; and since the priests were considered as leaders of this nation, it was necessary to begin by scaring them.

The "Pawiak" was in a deplorable state; the windows were broken by the bombardments, there was no water in the faucets, in the toilets excrement not emptied was accumulating, the little cells were overpopulated and the bedbugs crawled along the walls in endless battalions.

But, this time still, the imprisonment was only a warning; after two weeks of detention, all the priests were reunited in the corridor of the prison, harangued by the Gestapo chiefs and for the most part, released. Philibert found himself among those who were liberated.

But the Poles were not so easy to put on their knees. Heroes of a resistance of 150 years under the occupation of Russian, Prussian and Austrian empires, they continued still. As always, they were all alone because after the fourth partitioning of Poland between Stalin and Hitler, the Polish cause seemed definitely lost.

It was the opinion solidly established by the Germans, who from now on transformed the Polish national anthem from the epoch of Napoleon and who, instead of "Poland is not yet lost!" sang "Poland is once and for all lost."

The remark of a little Polish nun who, to a proud German of the victory of a pagan and unholy Germany on a pious and religious Poland, responded just simply that it was necessary to still wait for the end of the war, could not weigh heavy in the eyes of the victor.

Since the start of the occupation, the Polish resistance was being organized, the clandestine newspapers appeared, some acts of sabotage were signaled and the Germans concluded, "Jeder Pole ist unserer Feind. Every Pole is our enemy."

For his part, Philibert had only a little faith in this resistance, he believed it useless for the moment and even harmful to the interests of his country. This resistance was premature and these small pin pricks stirred up vengeance and suffering disproportionate with the consented sacrifices. However, they had, in any case, no effect against an enemy, who was then on the apogee of its power and of its successes.

And however, Philibert – because of the resistance, which

he had opposed since his arrest in the streets of Warsaw – was poorly noted in the offices of the Gestapo; two fat Germans in uniform came to collect him at the rectory and bring him again to the prison.

This time, Philibert offered no resistance and went even in front of the police. Polish soldier, he had remained, but not involving himself in politics and exclusively consecrating himself to his priestly occupations, he thought to have the clean conscience and to be able to explain himself with the Germans.

Since his last detention, the conditions of life at the "Pawiak" were slightly improved. They had replace the panes in the windows and the warm temperature in the radiators rendered the atmosphere almost bearable in the beginning of this November; they could also freshen up because the faucets had been fixed and worked, the same as the toilets; on the other hand, the bedbugs had lost nothing of their pugnacity.

Philibert found himself in a company of Polish priests, very interesting and cultivated, but all were always cramped: dozens in a cell that was meant for two persons at the maximum. On the side, in one isolated cell, the hero and chief of the Polish resistance, President Starynski, was letting his beard grow in waiting for his condemnation to death.

They rarely saw the Germans in uniform and the surveillance of the prisoners were assured by former Polish bureaucrats who showed so much comprehension and kindness in the eyes of the detainees. One of them brought to the priest even hosts from the neighboring church so that those could continue to say Mass.

The prison, already overpopulated, was always filling up; at the end of three months, there had been several enlargements and Philibert found himself among the lucky ones. He later knew that it had essentially been due to the intervention of his mother; this one had addressed some influential relatives in Germany.

The latter had kept some importance in a Germany always respectful of its ancient traditions; the German aristocrats, in addition, served faithfully their homeland by fighting in the first class on all fronts; they found even a certain number of them in the Nazi party. It is only later after the assassination attempt against Hitler that they will be suspects and enemies of the regime.

CHAPTER XII

THE GERMANS AT OTWOCKO

The do-or-die resistance with which the Polish machine guns, tanks and canons clashed with Germans in front of Krakow and Czestochowa, was swept away in little time, and Otwocko was occupied by the enemy since the first days of the war.

A little after, the Princess Otwocka received the visit of an enemy colonel, to whom his chiefs had confided the administration of the region. He was called the Count von Bleufontaine and had descended from an ancient Huguenot family established for centuries in Berlin.

Plump, smiling and charming, the colonel seemed to have little taste for the career of arms. "Excuse me," he said to the lady of the manor, "for entering like this into your prerogatives as proprietor, but in war as in war, I am obliged to obey my superiors."

He could speak German and was overjoyed to hear the two sisters express themselves in his maternal tongue with so much ease and without the least accent.

"But are you not German?" asked he, "you speak German as if it was your 'Muttersprache!?'"

"We are, in effect, originally Austrian, but you are not mistaken about it; both of us are married to Poles, and we consider ourselves, my sister as well as myself, as Poles," retorted the princess.

"I am not asking you to have pro-German sentiments..." responded the colonel, satisfied to have at least to do with well bred individuals who did not seem to breathe that deep-rooted hatred, which was the natural rule between "Krauts" and "Polakken."

The colonel settled in the castle and was treated by the two widows with every respect due to his duty and to his functions; they facilitated the task for him and they did everything in order to render his life pleasant.

Graf von Bleufontaine took it as friendship for these two ladies, so gentle, so polite, who even reminded him of his family. He was however not so naïve, different things seemed to him somewhat suspect: like the presence in the castle, with their children, of the two nieces of the lady, the Princess Czerska and the countess Pozecka.

They had arrived, allegedly from their properties situated in eastern Poland which was now in the hands of the Bolsheviks. It seemed that they had had all the troubles in the world to cross the front line and to flee the barbarian hordes of the Soviets.

But no one spoke ever of their husbands. However, the two ladies were young and everything led to thinking that those were in life and in age to serve in the army. Where were they? What did they do? The colonel Bleufontaine never posed these indiscreet questions. It was however not his role but the one of the "Geheime Staats Polizei." And the colonel feared this one more than the two Polish ladies. The visits of the police officers put him strongly ill-at-ease.

During this time, the Prince Czerski fulfilled the role as cook of the castle and the Count Pozecki the role as gardener. Former officers of the Polish army – the Count Pozecki had even been seriously wounded at the beginning of the war – they refused to give themselves up as prisoners of war and lived now under the assumed names at the home of their aunt in Otwocko.

The two young men quickly contacted the Polish Resistance, which began to form in the great forest of Otwocko. It is there that they had their radios, their arms depot, their general quarters.

The resistance was politically very divided; there were on one side, the Whites, who formed the Home Army and on the other, the communisants or communists, who fought under the name of the Peoples' Army. They hated each other but formed a common front against the Germans.

Lacking supplies and clothes, looking always to stock up, the resistance fighters, white or red, came often to the castle and reclaimed sometimes under the threat their patriotic tribute. The Princess Otwocka had to please everyone and at the same time to not arouse too much suspicion from the Colonel Bleufontaine and still less suspicion from the Gestapo! The situation was often delicate and dangerous.

But, for the moment, it is instead the calm because the resistance, in its beginnings, was still timid and the German all-powerful.

CHAPTER XIII

THE WARSAW GHETTO

After his liberation from prison, Philibert went to pay a visit to the old friend of his mother, Ryffka Buchenwald. She had refused to follow her son to New York, affirming, "I have nothing in common with a Lord Beechforest and his Wall Street," and preferred to remain in Warsaw, among relatives who conserved their ancient Jewish traditions.

Ryffka lived not far from the rectory of Philibert in the Jewish quarter, grubby and smelly which teemed with a crowd, always agitated, gesturing and speaking a "Yiddish," half-German, half-Polish. To the non-initiated, it would have seemed that everyone were only arguing or maybe performing a rather ridiculous comedy.

A good number always wore the "tallit," which resembled the cassock of the Abbot Philibert and the "yarmulke" which barely covered a bearded, long-haired head while their "pejsy" fell on the temples in curls.

Ryffka's house was miserable; the wooden stairs, fully shiny and slippery from wear and tear, led to the floors. Philibert rang on the first floor. Ryffka herself opened the door for him and Philibert entered into his apartment.

This one had nothing in common with the external aspect of Nalewski Street; the cleanliness and affluence jumped right out immediately. The furniture was modern, the floor covered in a great, thick rug. On a pretty bookcase of the Empire style, Philibert noticed a very beautiful portrait of Barbara before her entrance into the order; among the photographs of the Buchenwald family, he saw also those of his father and his mother, the Bartzels.

"My mother was very worried about you," said Philibert sinking into a large club armchair, "how did you survive the siege? Did you suffer? Was your house bombarded?"

"Of course," responded the old Jewish woman, "we had suffered much, we were very scared, but what do you want? We are in the hand of God and the one who knows can also overcome his panic. They are above all the planes that impressed us; in entering through Nalewski Street, you have maybe noticed the three immense holes in the pavement, barely filled in now? That is the work of the bombers. We believed to live our last hours…"

"Fortunately all that is now in the past," replied Philibert, "but what are you counting on doing at present? It is not a secret for anybody that the Jews are particularly persecuted by the Nazis who, one says, are preparing for some acts still more terrible. Nothing will stop this demonic mob. They speak now of constructing in our quarter a wall that would permit to enclose and to imprison all the Jews. Is it reasonable that you stay here? My mother proposes for you to rejoin her at Sobierzyce or at Otwocko. You would be safer over there."

"Listen, my dear friend, I am old and I do not have long to live. How I die in one manner or another, makes no difference. But my dearest desire is to die among my people, with them, in its faith, who I have always seen in them the people of God. If this people must suffer, I will suffer with them. Thank your dear mother so much but tell her that I will remain here."

In effect, soon began around the Jewish quarter the construction works of a gigantic and powerful stone wall, covered in barbwire, pierced only by some large gates, guarded by some German and Polish police. All who wore the Star of David was assembled again in the interior.

Like that, Philibert's church and two others were enclosed in the compound of the ghetto; the priests were commanded by the Germans to leave the quarter, but the diocese was opposed to it and gave the order to Philibert, who spoke German fluently, to discuss it with the relevant enemy authorities.

This opposition by the Catholic clergy to the orders given by the "Deutsche Behörde" offended the Germans and before being received by the responsible "Hochleiter," Philibert had to wait some long hours.

"We have very well told you, didn't we, to leave these places?" said that German while receiving Philibert. "Why didn't you obey?"

Philibert having had a spontaneous gesture of a former soldier, "Herr Leiter," he said nicely in standing at attention, "our religious authorities gave us the order to remain and we cannot leave without their authorization."

The argument carried and Philibert obtained the necessary permissions for the three churches with the obligation to have the passes renewed at the completion of their term. But finally, the travel permits were there.

And life in the ghetto continued. More and more, it became a nightmare, not only for the persecuted Jews, but also for the priests forced to live and to work among these poor, unfortunate wretches.

A half million Jews piled in as into a prison in this tight quarter of Warsaw, population very poor for the most part, began to die from diseases, from starvation and from cold.

Some skeletons in rags, half nude, ran through the streets in the middle of the day, grabbing the bread transported in the basket of the housewife and fled while they bite into it with beautiful teeth like famished wolves. In the morning, barely covered by a snow fallen during the night or by newspapers, some nude cadavers were strewn over the sidewalks and in front of the houses.

The excursions of small "yuppins" through the holes pierced under the restraining wall, did not suffice in stocking up supplies for the families, if they were not too often a tragic failure: a little cadaver sprawled out at the side of the hole, skewered by a bullet well adjusted fired by a German gendarme.

There was always a crowd in Leszno and Chłodna and other streets, an agitated, chattering, trafficking crowd. They sold whatever – spools, old scissors, rusty knives – always with the same refrain: "To whom, to whom, because I return to Mamie's home."

But they inferred more and more the anxiety of this crowd which always sensed more clearly the atrocious end that waited for them. These people resembled the wildcats that would be moved always in the same direction, forwards, backwards, going around in circles, instinctively looking for the escape from a too tight cage.

The three Catholic parishes did everything possible to alleviate a little the fate of these poor people; they distributed soup – more and more insipid, whose boxes of canned food supplied the principal consistency – but which could take the place of nourishment to some people who had no other food.

The evening, they organized some conferences for the numerous intellectual Jews of the ghetto; the social encyclicals of the Popes Leo XIII and Pius XI were discussed there and the listeners deplored that the popes did not give enough concrete solutions to the worldwide political and economic problems.

It is in the churches at the time of religious services, that the souls found again the most of peace: the silence in mankind, who is finally alone in front of his Creator and Master. The person of the Christ Jesus, who had appeared to their race and had undergone the same ordeals, became to them more and more familiar and dear although had some trouble to recognize His Divinity.

But the long months drained away and the end of Israel approached inexorably. The gold collected by the Jewish community no longer sufficed to push back the deadline of their denouement. The Germans decided to liquidate the Warsaw ghetto. On large notices, glued to every corner of the walls, announced the deportation of the non-working population of the ghetto – women, children, old people – towards other destinations. All these persons were obliged – under penalty of death – to present themselves in the grand stock yard at the scheduled time and day.

Already, the first groups of children and women guided by the white batons of the Jewish militia, headed towards the switching yard; all were resigned, even the young mothers who did not have any milk for their babies. At the head of a great Jewish school – from which all the children held each other's hands – walked Doctor Korczak, who had refused to separate from his students. They went all towards martyrdom, into the gas chambers of Majdanek, of Treblinka or elsewhere and for the most part, realized.

It was in the ghetto like a fat baton embedded into an anthill, a stampede without precedent; the streets filled up then with a crowd of countless men and women, in the middle of which the "rickshaw" – this bike with a seat became the sole method of transport – was fighting its way with difficulty. Everyone was seized by a "patriotic" work fever and looked to make one's self useful in the Thousand-Year Reich.

Workshops, almost factories, filled with sewing machines, were installed everywhere, even in the halls of the Catholic rectories. There they began to sew sheets and clothes for the German army, decimated, stopped in the winter cold in front of the walls of Moscow and Leningrad.

The Abbot Philibert ran to Nalewski in order to get some news from Ryffka Buchenwald, his mother's friend, "She left, also you will find her maybe still in the switching yard," one said to him. But Ryffka was no longer there either.

"She followed a transport for Majdanek," Such was the last news that he obtained. Identified maybe despite her to her compatriot Jesus of Nazareth on the mount of Golgotha, did she in her last moment recognize her God in Him? Only God knows.

The Catholic priests remaining in the ghetto were more and more tormented; the passes were delivered to them with parsimony and for an inadequate period; to the ghetto gates, which looked out on the Aryan side, they underwent some quarrels more and more frequent, in the evening they received by telephone the threats predicting to them the worst sanctions if they did not leave immediately the ghetto; the nights became awful when the Germans began to execute their prisoners just in front of the church doors. It was up to the priests to bury the cadavers abandoned by the Germans.

Finally, all the priests were convened at the General Quarters of the Gestapo where they were ordered under the penalty of death to leave the ghetto in the next twenty-four hours. He had barely the time to gather the strict necessities, the registers of civil state and to rent a horse and wagon; the next day, they had to be at the foot at their new domicile situated on the other side of the wall. So much good as well as bad, they were all housed in the neighborhood of the ghetto. The windows of Philibert's room, on the third story of one building, looked out just on the wall that marked the border between the Jewish and Aryan sides; there he had looked over the entire ghetto.

It is then that began the last chapter of the Jewish drama; assassinated under whatever pretext, beaten like wicked animals, brought finally through, hundreds of thousands, like beast of burden into the gas chambers, they revolted and stirred up an armed resistance. And Warsaw heard again the rattling of rifles and machine guns, the detonations of grenades; the fire had taken possession of the quarter and the black plumes of smoke rose up above the city.

The Jewish resistance was tenacious and fierce and it lasted close to a month until the death of the last combatant. It was so much more meritorious that the Jews were alone in a very small number and could only oppose the Germans only with totally pathetic arms.

Later, Philibert read some novels about this resistance. One of them, titled "Mila 18" and whose author was named Uris, described with a lot of skill the extraordinary exploits of the Jewish resistance fighters crushing and annihilating some entire armored divisions of the Waffen SS. No one knew anything of it at the time. Moreover such successes had been impossible, due to the flagrant disproportion between the two forces in place.

But the suffering and the resistance of this heroic people, persecuted during so many centuries, brought another victory, a moral one. Because from that moment, the mistrust, the misunderstanding, the hatred of the Jew – whose motives were rather visceral than justified – ceased suddenly among the Poles. Those Poles felt from then on a great pity for this old people, so unjustly persecuted and who had given to the world Christ and the apostles.

On the other hand, the hatred of the Germans, authors of all these crimes, increased to the highest degree. And they did not need to wait long because they stirred up the insurrection of all the Poles against the Nazi occupier.

CHAPTER XIV

THE WARSAW UPRISING

Since the defeat of General Rommel in the sands of Arabia and the great disembarkation of the Allied armada in 1942 on to the north coasts of Africa, luck began to abandon Hitler's cause.

His army always trampled along forever until Moscow and Leningrad, then in 1943, it was the heavy defeat of the VIth before Stalingrad and the capitulation of Marshal Paulus. Despite the German counter-offensive attacks, the Russians retook the initiative and began to throw the enemy back outside of their borders.

If the Germans obviously weakened on the fronts, the activity of the "Geheime Staats Polizei" had not slowed down so much; to the contrary, it seemed that it clamped much more; the raids, the imprisonments, the deportations, the shootouts became a scourge to which everyone had to become accustomed.

It is true that the Polish resistance, behind the backs of the Germans, showed its teeth more and more; they spoke only of sabotage of German trains and factories destroyed; just lately, a group of Polish resistance fighters, disguised as German soldiers, succeeded in stealing the very own car of the Gestapo chief, the General Kutschera, who met his maker there.

But the German response intensified; for each German killed, ten hostages – men totally foreign to the resistance, even priests in cassocks – were hung in the streets or shot, heads covered with sacks, in every corner of the city. After that, the concierges of neighboring houses made, with their brooms, all this blood flow into the gutters. Some invisible hands placed there, during the night, armfuls of flowers and the clandestine war continued no less.

Every person who went out into the street was no longer certain of returning home in the evening; each one could think that the car, covered with a tarp, stopped in front of his door or at the street corner, was the one that transported him to the "Pawiak."

Whoever could, fled into the forest which swarmed with resistance fighters. While Philibert, the last time, came back by train from the home of his relatives at Otwocko, the border of the forest bordering the train tracks, was invaded by a crowd of men, who impassively watched the convoy pass. There was obviously several Germans among the passengers, but neither them nor the resistant fighters in the forest, seemed to want to trigger the least hostility; that would not have even been worth the trouble.

Moreover, the Germans began to doubt the armed Poles and except if they were in force, avoided provoking them. On the other hand, the Russian front always approached closer to the Vistula, the canon did not stop booming day and night, always more distinct, behind the Konstantynów Forests, on every horizon to the east.

The evenings at the end of summer of 1944 were splendid and Philibert watched with pleasure from his window high above on the fourth floor, through the silent ruins of the ghetto tragically pacified, the glorious sunset. It seemed to him to already announce to the world the liberation from the Hitlerian oppression. Because, despite all the German denials, it was certain that the landing in Normandy by the Americans, British and French had succeeded.

Philibert often went to see one of his parishioners, a lady of a certain age, who was very up-to-date on all the events.

There they met at her home some important people in charge of the Polish resistance and even some young Polish officers just arrived by plane from Great Britain and parachuted into Poland in order to lend aid to the Resistance. The lady offered them a clandestine shelter in her home.

The young people also flew over France; according to them the regime of Marshal Pétain would have encouraged the proliferation of numerous sympathizers to the German cause in France, which thereafter could hobble the activity of the Allies.

The people in charge of the clandestine Polish government very well realized that they did not have a firm grip on the Polish youth, which was already stomping the ground and kicking like a horse, refusing to be reined in, in order to resume the hostilities against the Germans. But they themselves did not yet believe that the launching of a veritable war was possible. "Our secret army is well trained and organized," they said, "but it can only assure the maintaining of order during the transfer of powers between the Germans and the Russians."

Nevertheless, during his last visit, the lady in question announced simply to Philibert that the clandestine Polish army was going to launch the hostilities that same day, at four o'clock in the afternoon; the siren of the power plant was going to announce it to all the population.

In effect, on the way home, Philibert encountered every five or ten meters some groups of young folk who carried suspicious objects in their swollen coats or under their gabardines.

The Germans were invisible; suspecting something, they were hiding behind the bunkers and other fortifications that they had beforehand laid out in different places around the city.

As the lady had announced, precisely at sixteen hundred hours, the prolonged yowl of the siren announced the start of the insurrection. They began immediately to shoot, here and there, then arose the rattling of machine guns and the explosion of grenades.

Up on the roofs, appeared, one after the other, large white and red flags fluttering triumphantly over the Polish capital. Towards the evening, it was a question only of victories, of German tanks captured, of strategic points ripped from the enemy. Besides, the Russians were already extremely close, on the right bank of the Vistula.

Philibert foresaw nothing good; he did not believe in the victory of the insurgents no more than in the help from the Russian communists; by contrast, he was convinced that the German riposte would be terrible, as well against the city as against the inhabitants. Plunged into sadness, he expected the events. Thereafter, he knew that he had been right, the Germans were quickly heartless towards the Polish of all ages, civil or military, who fell into their hands.

Since the start of the hostilities, the inhabitants of the house, inhabited by Philibert, had barricaded it from the interior and had dug holes as the openings in order to reserve them as emergency exits in case of fire; everyone lived like in a fortress.

Often, they heard the violent strikes against the barricaded door, but no one was in a hurry to open it.

However, one beautiful morning, the concierge brought into Philibert's room, on the fourth floor, a young man and two adolescents in paramilitary uniforms. They all wore American hats much too big for the two soldiers who were still only children. They were the first insurgents that Philibert had seen.

"Father Abbot," said the oldest, who had the rank of an officer, "We have chosen you, or rather your window, in order to shoot at the 'Szkopy'[1] from high above. Everyone declined, was scared, invoking that there were children, who are going to exact revenge... You, you are a curate, you are not scared, you risk nothing!"

"There it is, as always," wondered the priest, "the others do foolish things and it is to us to suffer as a result of it." But he had an idea. "Listen, Commander," it is in that manner that the subordinates called him, "obviously, I cannot refuse my window to you, but if the Germans, that you want to dislodge, abandoned the blockhouse on their own accord, you will no longer have any need for my window to bombard them."

"Of course, but how to do that?"

"I am going to take care of it, I am going to speak to them from this same window."

"But they are going to kill you."

"Not necessarily."

The window opened out on the former ghetto, whose wall had remained intact. Behind that, there was a hospital in good shape as well, that Philibert knew well since the time he exercised his ministry. It is in that hospital that the Germans were entrenched, they had made it into a fortified position.

The window of Philibert's apartment, on the fourth floor, towered over not only the wall, but also the hospital, which was a low-rise building, and if the Poles had had a thing other than the few grenades in hand that they possessed then, they would have been able to cause great damage to the enemy. But the Germans ignored that.

Philibert felt no hatred against the Germans; having done some long studies among them, he knew well their language that he spoke without an accent. He relied on them.

As he had done it, quite recently, in the refectory in the seminary, he put a stole over his cassock, covered his head with a biretta, opened wide the window, made a grand sign of the cross and began his harangue in German.

"Dear German soldiers, I am the curate of this parish, therefore your pastor as well as the one for the Poles. The Poles have charged me with asking you to abandon that hospital which they need; you will have your life spared and will go where you

---

[1] Szkopy: Krauts.

want, keeping your arms. Each to his own: the Poles are here among themselves and you, you come from Germany."

There was a grand silence on the entire front. The gazes spied from a place or another. Then, voices arose from the German side, "We trust you, Herr Pfarrer, come and see us, we desire to speak with you."

Philibert had a lot of fear, but since he started it, he needed to continue it. Through a subterranean passage, he went out into the street, clothed as he was at home, in sandals and without a hat because he counted on returning soon to his apartment. While approaching the reinforced wall of a blockhouse and seeing the cadavers of young Poles, who had probably tried to take it right there through an assault, he had a moment of hesitation. From their windows, the Poles acclaimed him however.

It is then that a Polish insurgent came to join him; "We will go together," he said, "I am going to accompany you." A Polish officer having joined them, all three penetrated into the blockhouse and entered into the hospital. Before each window, there was a heavy machine gun and groups of soldiers were lying on the side. They also acclaimed the curate.

They climbed to the upper floor where Philibert exposed the thesis for which he was the advocate; he wanted to demonstrate to the Germans the uselessness of prolonging a combat which, in any case, was for them a dead end. The Germans had to understand well that Warsaw had ceased to be defensible for them since the Russians camped already on the other side of the river. It was then in their interest that the Poles do not impede them from tranquilly reaching their homes.

The Germans sitting around a large table listened attentively to Philibert. They seemed very indecisive; visibly, they did not know the forces of the Polish insurgents and feared the Russians very close to the vicinity, also they had to feel alone and surrounded.

But the Polish officer did not hear it with this ear; he commenced simply to insult the Germans by demonstrating to them all their weakness in face of an adversary, who could crush them.

Finally, he was convinced that the officer, who was only a subordinate, will go and notify his superiors and that until his return, there would be truce between Poles and Germans.

But, before the Polish officer had come back, a violent shootout had started in the street by the Poles. Furious from what he believed was a lack of loyalty on the part of his compatriots, Philibert rushed into the street, and being placed between the two fronts, began to protest. He had not noticed that his other Polish companion, who had accompanied him everywhere, had disappeared in the scuffle.

A certain lull was established nevertheless and Philibert that his Polish compatriots acclaimed from the other side of the front by crying out, "Viva the curate! Viva Poland!" benefited from the occasion to do a harangue of circumstance addressed to all. He therefore exclaimed, "So everyone lives! Germans, Communists, Jews, Poles!" But he realized that his sermon, despite being appropriate to satisfy everyone, and perfectly ecumenical, did not carry. They were still very far from Vatican II!

When Philibert had finished his discourse, a German soldier, the same one, who had made the Polish parliamentarians, approached the priest and told him in full haste, "Listen to me, flee quickly, I will accompany you, in a moment, it will be too late."

"And my companion, where is he?" asked Philibert.

"He is arrested and will never leave anymore."

"Then, I will also stay." Obviously, in such circumstances, it was morally impossible for Philibert to abandon his comrade.

The arrested companion was in a smoke-filled room on the second floor, in the middle of a very heterogeneous group of soldiers, railroad workers, Ukrainians in uniform, who constituted, according to all likelihood, only a garrison of chance.

He was very much beaten, but since he saw the priest enter, his face lit up with joy, "As it is so good for him to have come back," he said softly to Philibert.

On that, the Germans brought fat morsels of lard and they ate and smoked together, everyone discussing politics. With his outspokenness, Philibert forgot and critiqued the politics of the Führer, who according to him, fully remaining very great, led his people into a disaster. The majority of the Germans shared without a doubt his opinion, but it was for them too soon and dangerous to avow it.

The night already fell. The two prisoners were led into a small, adjacent room. The priest was invited to sit down, but he had decided that his companion had to remain the whole night standing, the hands raised, and the two men lived under the threat of a gun. At the end of a certain time, no longer being able to take it, Philibert pounced furiously on the German guard and screamed at him, "So, at last, kill us rather than making us suffer."

The discussion became venomous and they had to call a bureaucratic superior. This one seemed to belong to the police, but he was very well raised. "Tell me then, sir," Philibert said to him, "for what reason, do you torment us? We both came here in the capacity of parliamentarians well disposed towards you..."

The bureaucrat seemed to apologize, "Listen, Abbot," he said, "to you, we have nothing to reproach, you have almost the entire garrison in your favor; but your companion will be judged and he has a very good chance of being shot."

The intervention of the bureaucrat was however efficient because the two prisoners were led into another room; this one was very narrow and barely lit with a skylight, but the floor had been covered with a thick layer of hay and they finally left them alone there. It is then that his comrade explained to Philibert the true reason for his misfortune. "While you were discoursing in the street, I spotted their munitions depot and it is then that they arrested me."

"Oh! Above all, stick strictly to your role as parliamentarian," Philibert implored him.

From that moment, the surveillance of the Germans on their prisoners became apparently less strict. The guards brought them things to eat and numerous were the enemies which came to talk with them. These thanked them for their friendly intervention, the others asserted that they had never been more amused in their lives. The bureaucrat so polite recounted to Philibert the Polish officer who had accompanied them and for whose return they waited, had showed for a full response, his fist through the window frame; he added that besides the Poles on the other side had asked for his news. To the contrary, the small soldier, who to honor his words towards the parliamentarians, wanted to make Philibert go out, was shot on order of their commander. The bureaucrat even led Philibert to see his cadaver, but this one did not understand fast enough.

To the contrary, the fate of his misfortunate comrade became more and more precarious. Some officers, with alarming countenances, entered more and more often into their cell and announced to his impending death. Philibert intervened energetically and asked that they shoot them both together, "Both, we are only parliamentarians, if you shoot one, you need to shoot the other." The German withdrew without saying a word.

At the end of several days that had seemed an eternity to the prisoners enclosed in their cell, they no longer heard the noise of the battle, which just recently, raged by shaking constantly the walls of the hospital, and a pleasant lull succeeded. At that moment, the behavior of the jailers became dry and imperative, and armed guards were posted in front of the cell. It is hardly as if the two prisoners now obtained the authorization to go to the restrooms. It seemed that the Germans in Warsaw had received from Italy some essential reinforcements and that the Poles on the opposite side, seeing that they risked being encircled, had abandoned their strategic positions.

Night had fallen when they made the two Poles leave their prison. Żelazna Street was deserted, strewn with broken glass; there they smelt the burning, some shells, in a sinister whistling, exploded and raised red flames. The houses on the other side burned. Philibert caught sight of a purple fire coming out of the windows of his apartment and he understood that all that he had was going to be consumed in the blaze.

An escort, which had as its leader an officer, waited for the prisoners in the street. The officer, a true soldier of the "Wehrmacht," was perfectly wrapped in his elegant uniform; he seemed cold and distant, but impartial.

They will encounter in the street, a group of the "Hitler Jugend." Philibert was known and the group exclaimed for his immediate execution, asserting that he was the worst of traitors among those who proclaimed themselves as friends of Germany. But the officer defended him energetically and transmitted afterwards the command of the convoy to a young soldier of the "Göring Panzer Division" which had been recently brought in from Italy to destroy the Warsaw uprising.

Seeing a priest's cassock, some men belonging to other German detachments encountered along the way, threw insults at Philibert. That one refrained from having soaked his priests' hands in blood and affirmed to the contrary that he had looked for a way to establish the peace.

The young soldier of the "Göring Panzer Division" seemed

suddenly overcome by the ideas of peace and fraternity and convinced of the futility of wars with no way out. The convoy passed through the deserted streets of Warsaw, with all its burned houses, encountering here and there on the ripped-up pavement covered in debris, cadavers of insurgents burned acutely by the flame-throwers, all black, huddled up from their final convulsions, with their white teeth, which seemed to draw an atrocious laughter.

Afterwards the group arrived in front of a very vast neo-gothic church that Philibert knew well from having done one of his first curacies; it served the Germans as a gathering place for all the Warsawians, women and men, old and young, insurgents and civilians, whom the Germans had captured in the city during the fighting.

Everyone here had undergone a first triage, after that a large number of persons were led to the train station in the suburbs in order to be deported to Germany where waited for them the forced labor, the camps, or even better the prison. Philibert was one of those and the officer-controller declared to him that it was in order to punish him for having intervened in military operations.

When the train started on its way, Warsaw was burning; the uprising must have still lasted several long weeks. A cloud of smoke already covered multiple cadavers, among whom were four young Bartzels of the Oswicie branch and the father of the brother-in-law Pozecki of Philibert, who met his death by serving, on order of the enemy, the covering fire for the German tanks launched against the insurgents.

CHAPTER XV

DECISION AT OTWOCKO

At the end of the Warsaw uprising, at the approach of winter of 1944-1945, the situation seemed, for the moment, stabilized on all fronts. To the West, the Rhine posed a considerable obstacle to the continuation of the offensive of the Allies while to the east, the Russian trampled before the Vistula.

However, apart of the unconditional fanatics of Hitler, everyone was convinced that it was only a partial setback and that soon, under the combined push of its western and eastern enemies, the all-powerful Germany was going to collapse.

At the castle of Otwocko, the whiteness of whose walls appeared nicely across the grand bare park they discussed fiercely..

Benefiting from the hospitality of the Princess Otwocka, the refugee relatives arrived from all parts. Just recently, they had welcomed the two Bartzel brothers from Warsaw, Boryslaw, the bachelor, and Widzislaw, recently married with his young spouse and their baby.

It is from extreme justice that they had escaped the claws of the "Geheime Staats Polizei;" as their residence had burned and as Warsaw had been systematically destroyed by the Germans after the insurrection, they looked first for a roof; yet, what simpler than going to the aunt's home!

Boryslaw Bartzel and Wladimir Czerski, who deep down detested each other, were for once, suddenly in agreement; they would not remain in Poland after having tasted the German occupation in order to again undergo the Russian occupation. Both young men had already met up with the Bolsheviks at the beginning of this war and had barely escaped deportation. How many of their friends and relatives died from the cold or from starvation in the Siberian "taiga[1]?" How many others had been at Katyn, or elsewhere, shot with two bullets in the back of the neck? If they had to die in Germany, the family would receive at the very least a death certificate…

"No, we will not remain in Poland!" said unanimously Czerski and Boryslaw Bartzel, "we will instead flee to Germany,

---

[1] Taiga: forest.

and from there, we will try to reach the west."

Widzislaw Bartzel and Hippolyte Pozecki professed with fierceness the same opinion; from what they had overheard, they had been able to come to an exact opinion of what was the N.K.V.D., which rated well, if not better then the Gestapo.

But the Baroness Bartzel was difficult to persuade; she began to age and had lost the taste of abrupt changes, of uncertain futures; she had suffered enough from the imposed exiles through the first world war.

However, in Germany, there was also Philibert, her son the priest; he was just released from a new prison and worked now as a requisitioned worker in a factory in Schweidnitz[2] in Silesia. Before dying, she had wanted to see him again… maybe help him?…

"I will accompany you," declared she with a decided tone, "on condition that you pass through Schweidnitz and that I can go and see Philibert there." That itinerary did not much suit the others, but willy-nilly, those had to make the best of it.

With the princess Otwocka, there was nothing to do; although older than her sister, she had still loved to explore the unknown horizons, but at Otwocko, she was on her own terrain, affluent with responsibilities, whose abandonment seemed to her cowardice.

But everything changed, when she saw her curate, the Abbot Nitwicki, her counselor and friend, "You know, Princess," said the old curate, "I would not have any objection if you accompanied your family to Germany. Of course, I will miss you very much because you have always been as good for the church as for myself, a truly ideal lady; I will then lose so much with your departure. But I do not see either what yourself and the others gain by ballasting there. In any case, the inevitable accession of the communists in power, be they Russian or Polish, your role of lady is done once and for all. You would know nothing of your holdings and despite your services and your qualities, you would be exposed to the greatest dangers. Leave, I give you my complete blessing."

And the Princess Otwocka, finally, decided to join the group of her relatives.

---

[2] Schweidnitz: now Świdnica in Poland.

There were more Germans at the Otwocko castle. For a long time, the Graf von Bleufontaine had been transferred. He had been too dangerous, given the current situation, to let him reside alone in the castle. At this time, the district swarmed with bands of Polish insurgents, rather red than white, and the isolated Germans risked being easily assassinated.

But the administration of the nation was still in the hands of the occupier and some strong German garrisons were stationed in the cities and the most important towns. In order to obtain the authorization to move around, above all if it was a matter of going into the Reich, it was always necessary to speak to the German authorities.

They decided then, in the castle, to send a delegation to the Oberkommandant, the Ritter von Nosek, an Austrian, who, everyone said, was genial and complacent. The group from Otwocko chose as delegates the Prince Czerski, grand lord, cultivated and artistic, who spoke fluent German with a slight accent singing with the Hungarian aristocrats, with whom, before the war, he had hunted a lot and in the second place, Boryslaw Bartzel who had the genius of the diplomatic "combinazzioni," he had tested it in this regard by "miraculously" escaping an imminent deportation to Siberia, during the entry of the Soviets into Poland at the beginning of this war. The entire family observed them from the windows of the castle while both of them left: Czerski rather slow, calm and thoughtful, Boryslaw gesturing and discussing abundantly, marching to a staccato pace.

Both of them were very well received by the Ritter von Nosek. The Germans were flattered by the preference given by these Poles to the Germans over the Russians. But at the heart of the matter, the procedure was as such not legal because the German authorities had the right to help in this manner only the German nationals.

"What if," suggested Boryslaw Bartzel, "we are going to leave with our horses, so-called requisitioned by the German military authorities, for an evacuation into Germany."

"Excellent idea," responded the Oberkommandant, "because we must also evacuate our horses."

"We will be then your 'Spitze,'"[3] resumed Boryslaw. The Ritter von Nosek smiled.

The same day, both young men received the passes for Germany, in the names of the Durchlaucht Prinzessin Otwocki, of the Reichsbaronin Bartzel, of the Prinz Czerski, of his wife and his three children, of the Graf Pozecki with his wife and his two children, of the Graf Bartzel with his wife and one child and of Graf Bartzel, the bachelor. Several persons who accompanied them were also mentioned on those documents.

"You will be followed by our detachments until the German border, it will be safer for you. Our convoy will probably leave after Christmas. Prepare yourselves then and good luck," concluded the Ritter von Noseck.

Meanwhile, Widzislaw Bartzel, who had ties with the national Polish army, reported to him the resolution of his group and received his "non obstat." Moreover, the Home Army no longer had much to say, overwhelmed as it was by the Peoples' Army.

The inhabitants of the castle believed to still have ahead of them several weeks before leaving and therefore they tranquilly prepared their departure. But the deafening rumbling of the canons, which were reinforced in successive waves, began to worry them; it is then that arrived a messenger from the Oberkommandant, dressed in plain clothes, "Prepare yourselves because the next night, we leave," he said simply.

---

[3] Spitze: vanguard.

CHAPTER XVI

THROUGH GERMANY

It was night, a soft night in a fine December with snow falling in fat flakes and melting on the ground when the wagons of the Otwocko castle came to line up in the German convoy.

Alone the faraway noise from the canon and the blaze burning on the horizon, behind the forests of the Vistula, announced the close front.

The commands were given in a low voice, and the wagons of the castle aligned in the following order; Hippolyte Pozecki and his family took the lead. He was, from the military viewpoint, the most senior in rank; he had even been wounded during this war and he had a strident voice of command. Nobody knew horses as well as this former cavalier, one of the best known in Poland. They understood it and obeyed him on a single crack of the whip, with the least pressure on the reins. His group confided to him then the command of the convoy. But as he knew only the rudiments of German, they appointed to him the two grand specialists of this language, the Baroness Bartzel and the Princess Otwocka who helped him in turns.

The second car had for passengers the Prince Czerski, his family, and two domestics. The third was led by Boryslaw Bartzel, accompanied by other service personnel. The fourth car served for the baggage and some accompanying people. Bringing up the rear, in a fifth wagon, were Widzislaw Bartzel, his family and one of the old ladies in the family, expert in German.

The wait was long before everything was ready, then on the blast of a whistle from the German Kommandant, the long convoy set out. It crosses some sleepy villages, some forests buried under a thick blanket of white snow, from the fields, which disappeared into the invisible infinity of the night. Everything was silent and the children fell asleep in the arms of their mothers.

From time to time, some German officers stepped up to the group of Poles and asked by murmuring if anyone needed whatever, if the children were enduring the voyage well. They were armed to the teeth, carrying a combat helmet and were abundantly armed with machine guns and revolvers.

Former officer, Pozecki observed them with curiosity and

almost with envy. "You are looking at my weapons," to him said the German officer, "eh well! We need to be fully ready to fight because these forests are infested by insurgents and if they do not attack us, it is that they knew we are ready to return fire."

The dawn already began to poke through on the horizon when the convoy moved nearer to the former border of the Reich. The morning was very fresh because during the night, it had started to freeze. The sky brightens up more and more with the radiant light of the sun. From near the Vistula the loud booms reached them.

"The Russians must have crossed the Vistula," rumored softly the Germans, Pozecki became pale; if he did not speak German well, he would have understood them sufficiently. By entering into the Reich, the German military must have abandoned them because they were going farther south, towards Austria. From then on, Pozecki had to assume the entire responsibility.

Noticing a beautiful farm and seeing his tired wife and children, Czerski shouted to Pozecki to stop but that one refused, "And if a band of Cossacks having broken through the front came to surprise us? No! Forward!" shouted he while cracking his whip. The convoy continued on its route.

Abandoned by the Germans, the Poles advanced alone into the snow-covered plains of Silesia.

They had always towards their back the thunder of the canon fire, the paths of communication were more and more blocked by the wagons of Germans – Reischdeutsche or Volksdeutsche[1] – followed by small fully joyous French prisoners, who accompanied the German families in the flight ahead of the Bolsheviks.

The Germans were clearly very afraid of the Russians; those burned the farms and houses, raped women, from the youngest to those 80 years old, respected nothing or nobody. "Eh," joked Mr. Bartzel in front of his sister, "shame that we have left; we would have been able to even have some success among the Russians!" The two ladies smiled.

Pozecki had all the troubles of the world to fight his way through this entire crowd and to maintain his group compact. That group would stop in the night in the farms; he was generally well

---

[1] Reischdeusche, Volksdeutsche: Germans of the Reich, originally German.

received but encountered also some fanatics, who recognizing strangers, slammed the door in their face, released their dogs in pursuit of them or even called the gendarmes, "You only have to stay home!" shouted they to the Poles. But they could do nothing against the voyageurs because the latter had their papers in order and provision tickets, which gave them the right to buy some white bread and some sausage in the stores where they found many things.

Other times, the Polish travelers encountered on their way only kindness and hospitality. Numerous were the rich peasants, who inhabited magnificent farms and two-storied houses. They had a very long tradition behind them and were perfectly informed about the current situation. It seemed that they were even enchanted to run into people belonging to the camp which would soon triumph.

They often pitied Poland, which had suffered so much through their fault and all the more, they had enormously suffered themselves; on a shelf of the chimney of the dwelling, how many times did they see a row of portraits of German soldiers covered with a black veil, and the proprietor explaining, "There he is, my son fallen under Stalingrad... here another son dead at Moscow.. and that one there was killed during the campaign in France..."

After a thick soup with "Knodeln,"[2] it often happened that, on the tacit sign of the proprietor, they were going to listen to the radio during the evening; the proprietor tuned in directly to the BBC from London, who had neatly its preferences on the impassioned discourses about Goebbels, which aroused only smiles of commiseration.

Next, they were going to go to bed in a guest room on the third floor, perfectly clean, but glacial because even in this country of coal, they did not heat all the rooms during the winter. On the other hand, gigantic comforters which went up to the ceiling, kept the heat under the sheets throughout the whole night.

*
* *

Arrived finally at Schweidnitz, in a crowd of countless

---

[2] Knodeln: meatballs.

runaways, the Polish travelers easily found the domicile of Philibert.

He inhabited a miniscule room, in a private house consecrated to the Catholic works, across from a magnificent parish church, in front of which stood the statue of a Piast[3], which had formerly reigned over this region.

Philibert came back from the factory where he worked and the reunion with his family was for the priest-worker a very happy surprise.

"Eh, how are you, Philibert?" asked his brother-in-law Czerski who saw him first, "have you suffered much?"

"Yes, most of all at the beginning; they made us work hard; afterwards, for a trifle, I was punished with two months of prison; then I truly suffered from hunger. Then, that was better, the work became easier, they assigned me a personal room and I could even say Mass in the evening in secret. In the end, they proposed to me to become German."

"And you consented to it?"

"Of course not."

"The least that they could say is that you would have poorly chosen the moment," cynically remarked the brother-in-law and both of them started to laugh.

His mother was absolutely adamant that Philibert accompanied them in their voyage towards the west. But he needed to obtain the authorization of the Arbeitsamt, which employed Philibert. Luckily, the Director of the Work Bureau, Herr von Brinken, was complacent and Philibert obtained the necessary papers. "Don't' be discouraged," said Ben von Brinken to Mrs. Bartzel and to her son who was leaving his office, "we will win, the secret weapon is going to change the situation!"

"He can even run now with his secret weapon," said Philibert to his mother when they had closed again the door behind them, "the principal is to be able to say goodbye to them."

The abbot took his seat in the third carriage, next to his single first cousin, Boryslaw Bartzel, and the voyage continued.

They crossed the Neisse, then the Elbe, wide and powerful river and they found themselves in the heart of the ancient kingdom of Saxony. The canon fire to the east faded. On the other

---

[3] Piast: First royal dynasty of Poland.

hand, the activity of American and British planes intensified. Day and night they flew over this industrial region.

The nights became terrible. The air raid sirens operated non stop, followed closely by the explosions similar to earthquakes, after which the entire horizon fully glowed with the purple of the fires.

At that time, Leipzig, Dresden, had become a heap of ruins and hundreds of thousands of inhabitants were entombed under the rubble.

But the Poles prudently avoided the great cities, chose rather the back roads which linked the villages and the towns of lesser importance.

Then it was Thuringia, with its mountains covered in firs of a deep green. Always well informed, Boryslaw pointed out to Philibert a place obviously under heavily watched, hidden in the underground passages, behind powerful rocks. "I believe that it is here that they prepared their secret weapon." They would have been able to learn many interesting things from the mouths of the Polish workers who worked in this region.

From Thuringia, they descended into Bavaria and it is here that, through the general agreement, the voyagers decided to make a stopover. The two aged ladies found pretty much a normal way of life, one at the mayor's home, the other at the curate's home, in a region very attached to the traditions and to the Catholic religion.

Anticipated by their German friends that the Bolsheviks probably invaded the neighboring Thuringia, the Poles decided to push more towards the south of Bavaria.

They followed the magnificent highway, one of the rare glories of the Hitlerian regime, which led to Nuremberg and to Munich.

They crossed a vast fir forest which pushed high and heavy on the mountains of the Frankengebirge.

At a place called Kronenburg, they saw a picturesque and a grand castle which arose majestically in the middle of the mountains covered with woods.

"Ah!," shouted Ermelyne, "but it is the castle of Aunt Mitzi, and if we would go to pay her a visit?" The group of Polish carriages got off the highway and took a sinuous and rigid route, stopped before the castle walls.

Accompanied by her son-in-law, the Baroness Bartzel rang

at the door of the great castle. They waited long enough, finally an old domestic opened it.

"We would like to see Madam the Duchess von Kronenburg," said Ermelyne, " we are her relatives."

"Die Frau Herzogin left for her villa in Tyrol," responded the domestic, then noticing the distinguished genre of the visitors, he added, "but if you want to speak with the steward?" And he made Ermelyne and her son-in-law enter.

The steward immediately arrived; he was very polite, "We are some relatives of the Herzogin," explained Ermelyne, "I am here with my sister, a princess Caramanlys, like me. We come from Poland accompanied by our family in six cars…"

"Quickly, quickly, I am going to telephone to the Frau Herzogin. The public telephones no longer work, but we possess a special cable," said the steward, eager and complacent.

He came back ten minutes later, "I just telephoned the Frau Herzogin. She greets you from her villa in Tyrol and bids you welcome. If you want to benefit from the hospitality of Kronenburg, she very willingly lends you her castle." Then, he added softly to the address of Czerski, "The castle is requisitioned by the Reichsführer Himmler. The Herzogin prefers that it was you who occupied it. In any case, the Reichsführer will not come to live here."

The Polish voyagers were enchanted by this unexpected tale in the magnificent surroundings of this castle. They unhitched the horses, gave them to eat some hay and oats that they transported with them and to drink this water so pure and so fresh which bursts out of the mountains, then they tentatively put their children to bed in the well heated rooms of the steward and went themselves to visit the sumptuous rooms of the historic residence of the Dukes von Kronenburg.

Everything there was in white marble and with a chandelier of a hundred candles hung from the rococo ceiling of the ballroom, which had two hundred meters of length by one hundred meters of width.

In order to warm up his fingers a little, Czerski, a talented pianist, sat in front of the piano and began to tickle the ivories. The "Bechstein" seemed a little like it had a cold, but the keys responded well. Then little by little, Czerski moved to the modern dances, to the Charlestons, to the boogie-woogie, so they started to dance in the entire world.

"Come, Cathalyne, we are going to warm up," said Pozecki discarded his "bekiesza" [4] and taking his wife by the hand. Cathalyne did the same and both began a step of a "samba" on the parquet well waxed.

The others followed: Widzislaw Bartzel with his wife and Boryslaw with the one of Czerski, Amaldyne. Czerski played a tango that Boryslaw Bartzel executed with the perfect motions of a veritable mathematician of dance.

Marjolyne and Ermelyne, whose hair already became tinged with a pretty silvery white, were sitting side by side and took pleasure in seeing these couples dance, still young, distinguished, vigorous.

Only the Abbot Philibert, who was the youngest of the group, but also the tiniest and apparently the most morbid, observed the scene with a melancholic eye. Even if he had not been a priest, he would not have been able to dance because following his wound contracted in the war of 1919-1920, he always limped slightly. Moreover he had caught a soreness in the back which he attributed to the chores imposed in the German camps and he was worried about it.

Czerski stopped playing. "Brrr, it is too cold in this castle!" exclaimed Pozecki putting his fur coat back on, "I could never live here." "Neither could we!" cried out together Widzislaw and Boryslaw Bartzel.

Only Wladimir Czerski, accustomed to the lordly castles of Hungary, seemed pleased by it. They decided then that he would take up residence in the castle whereas on the advice of the steward, the rest of the group would go settle in a nearby village.

---

[4] Bekiesza: small Polish fur.

CHAPTER XVII

THE ARRIVAL OF THE AMERICANS

Czerski persuaded Madam Otwocka to stay with her family in Kronenburg; they succeeded in organizing their life pretty much comfortable, under benevolent eye of the steward of the castle while the rest of the group scattered into the houses and the farms of the vast village of Wartendorf.

Pozecki and Widzislaw Bartzel were hired by some Bavarian peasants, whose coarseness and toughness did not always make their lives easy. But they preferred to go unnoticed and loved the field work. Pozecki, who knew horses well, was a counselor appreciated in this subject, whereas Widzislaw Bartzel, young engineer-architect, was many times called by the neighbors to design the plans for buildings that they planned to construct.

Boryslaw Bartzel lived at the home of the mayor of the village, he talked with him about politics and general questions whereas the Abbot Philibert, accompanied by his mother, resided at the home of a rich Catholic peasant, with the daughter, Greta, for whom Ermelyne gave lessons in English and French.

In Reglitz, Philibert got along with the eldest; he obtained the authorization for him to say his Mass and to preach in the small filial church of Wartendorf. The faithful compensated him by bringing him a great quantity of eggs, from which he made the family benefit, and who had shortly served as bartering money against American cigarettes.

From his window looking out on the courtyard in back, Philibert heard, each morning, the cackling of numerous chickens, which laid their eggs; from time to time, a cock stood tall on its legs and launched a strident call; the pigs growled in the mud, the cows mooed in the barn, the horses stamped their hooves in the stable, which smelled of manure, hay, milk; nobody would have believed that the war was raging on.

And however, the American planes were each day more numerous, more audacious. Filling the sky with a powerful vroom, they flew over the district in great formations with encountering the least resistance on the part of the German anti-aircraft batteries; as for the helicopters, they descended sometimes until the height of the rooftops of the houses.

To the north, at the east and to the south, it thundered day and night and the nocturnal horizons lit up all around into a great, big, sinister inferno. Near the Rhine, the increased canon fire announced that the fighting for the river had commenced.

Some detachments passed by without stopping: convoys of evacuated prisoners, British always dignified and calm, Hindus picturesquely wearing turbans, Soviets incredibly dirty and dishonest. The French prisoners, employed in great number on the farms, received also their evacuation order. Greta cried because she had a great French friend, with whom she spent long hours in the barn. But, before the order had been able to be executed, all the French had disappeared like by an enchantment into the nearby mountains full of woods, with the obvious complicity of the German population.

Then all of a sudden, the news spread like wildfire; the American tanks had crossed the Rhine and pushed along to the east!

A German garrison ran up to defend the village of Wartendorf; an officer, some soldiers armed with grenades and machine guns, a canon and a cavalry regiment of the Hungarian honved.

But since before the arrival of the Americans, the German garrison disappeared, like into a mirage, and the regiment of the honved hid in a neighboring forest waiting for the favorable moment in order to surrender to the enemy.

Finally some rascals from the village, climbed on the ridge overlooking the burg, announced in great, big cries the arrival of the Americans, "They are coming! They are coming!" they shouted sliding down the side.

Everywhere, the white flags were hoisted while at the back of the village, they saw cautiously advance three small reconnaissance tanks covered in dust and carrying long antennas similar to fishing lines.

The Americans questioned the populations about the presence , the number, the armaments of the Germans while the children of the village kneeled down while brandishing the white handkerchiefs.

The night fell on Wartendorf liberated by the Americans. The next day, since morning, it was without interruption an invasion of assault tanks en route across fields towards the cantonal city of Reglitz.

Some American soldiers, handsome tall boys very strong ; they did harm to no one; but they were very poorly raised and disrespectful. They broke into the barns, stole the eggs from underneath the chickens and sought out the company of young girls, to whom they offered cigarettes and chocolate.

Around evening, appeared numerous amorous couples; G.I.'s walked arm in arm with the blond "Madels," trying to make themselves understood, smoking cigarettes and eating chocolate. With slight astonishment, Philibert caught sight of Greta – who had however cried for her little Frenchman – in the arms of an American: "She had quickly changed, if not the camp, at least the individual," thought he.

After the unstoppable passage of the third army of General Patton, the events moved faster: suicide of Hitler, capitulation of Germany. During this time, spring made the trees flower anew and still a little shy, the sun reheated the hearts which know once again the hope of recovered peace.

The Americans set up in the conquered nation. Philibert and his mother received a summons to the General Headquarters of the UNRRA[1] in Reglitz, in order to undergo the "screening"[2] and their registration. There they found the rest of the family.

The General Headquarters of UNRRA was situated in the vast building of a former high school. Some American officers followed by elegant secretaries entered and exited from former classrooms arranged in the offices. Here and there, appeared the haughty silhouette of a British officer. Wrapped in the magnificent uniforms of the former Russian Empire, the Soviet officers behaved, to be blunt, as lords and masters. Solitary and sulky, the French officers occupied the offices that UNRRA had so much wanted to lend them. Among the millions of deported foreigners which populated at that moment the Third Reich, each nation was searching for its nationals.

"Are you Polish?" asked the intelligence officer of the UNRRA while looking at the dossier when Philibert and his mother had entered into the office, "how does it happen that you are left to your own devices and not released from a prison or a concentration camp.

[1] UNRRA: United Nations Relief and Rehabilitation Administration, International Bureau for expatriots.
[2] Screening: police interrogation.

"It is not, sir, that I have not tasted those prisons and the Nazi camps, more so than many others," responded Philibert, "but foreseeing their end, the Germans gave us the choice between them and the Bolsheviks, and my family and I chose the lesser evil, that is to say the Germans."

"But you have acted as traitors. The Germans are our enemies and the Soviets our allies; you therefore have preferred our enemies to our allies…"

"The Soviets, your allies!" shouted Philibert sarcastically, "you are soon going to realize for yourself and you will change your opinion quite quickly!"

Then came the turn of Ermelyne Bartzel. It was already an elderly lady who did not present any special problem for the intelligence service.

"Your name, madam?" asked the officer in English.

"Madam Ermelyne Bartzel de Hohenwaitzen," responded the lady.

The officer having some trouble writing that name, Ermelyne presented her visiting card. He read on it in French, "Ermelyne, née princess de Caramanlys, widow of Sigmund baron of the Empire, Bartzel von Hohenwaitzen zu Weyssensee."

"It is good, but in all that, how can I know where are your first and last names?" asked the American. Ermelyne showed him. The officer wrote on his register, "Erma Bartzel, profession: teacher."

The other family members all pulled through it in the same manner. The officers asked them still if they wanted to return to Poland, to which they responded unanimously and without hesitation, "No, not to a communist Poland."

Czerski had some difficulties because he inhabited the Kronenburg Castle which had been requisitioned by the Gestapo chief, the Reischführer Heinrich Himmler, but in the end everything was sorted out, and like the others, he obtained his "Displaced Persons Card."

While returning home, Philibert noticed that the former camps where the Germans previously kept their prisoners, was currently swarming with Polish workers or Russian soldiers.

All that barbwire and those observation posts served at present to keep in captivity the people who, willingly or by force, would be returned to their country of origin. If the Poles did not seem particularly unfortunate, they felt for the Russians a profound sadness and a great misery because Stalin's law, every Russian prisoner was considered as a deserter.

And however, even among the latter, one heard the sounds of the "balalaika," the songs of the nostalgic "dumki" and one saw them dancing the "trepak" with its acrobatic "prisiudy." Deep down, everyone was overjoyed with the end of this war.

The Polish family reunited for the last time at the home of the Pozeckis. The half-brother of the two elderly ladies, the Marquis Bardzopolski, invited them by letter to come to live with him in the United States. He had been married since the war, had become an American citizen and lived in Philadelphia in a vast a comfortable house. Edelfred proposed to pay for the voyage and the stay in the U.S.A. for his sisters.

The Pozeckis received another letter. It came from Lord Vlady Beechforest, who remembered the one, who could have been his wife, the blond Cathalyne of Saint Petersburg. Very cordially, he invited the Pozecki family to take over the management of a farm that the Beechforests possessed in Pennsylvania. He himself would also pay for the voyage. The Widzislaw Bartzel family which was on the best terms with the Pozecki, decided to follow them.

Czerski chose France, notion of old and high culture that he preferred to America that he judged as a nation still too young. Boryslaw was of the same opinion.

Philibert Bartzel who had fallen seriously sick and could no longer continue his ministry in Germany, also thought of going to Paris where he could be operated on by a surgeon of world renown.

It was then that the dispersion of the group, no one knowing for how much time, maybe for always…

They left behind them a Europe profoundly murdered, ruined and depopulated, so divided and shared between the influences of two superpowers, Moscow and Washington, that from now on it had ceased playing the primary roles on the world stage.

Always like David facing Goliath and despite its courageous efforts to liberate itself from the subjugation of its neighbors, Poland simply changed occupiers.

Germany, terribly tried for reason of its own crimes, now laid down, humiliated and impoverished while the members of its government, climbed together on to the scaffold. But behind this miserable, façade, tireless and disciplined, the German people already prepared the resurrection of its economic power.

France and Great Britain, winners of the first world war, were going to bear more and more difficultly the influence of the great winner of this war, the United States, which pushed back into the shadow their bygone prestige.

And to the East of this Europe, which looked to balance Stalin's Russia, the other victor of the war, climbed to the apogee of a glory that it had never yet reached through all its history in order to become the most dreaded power in the world.

The map of Europe had changed. An uncertain and fragile equilibrium seemed to be designed.

But already from some farther away limits of the terrestrial globe, other rumors, other voices, other claims started to make themselves heard, which risked to upset this barely established equilibrium.

They came from faraway Asia: from Japan which loosened its too tight bonds and completed a spectacular leap in its economy; from China, in the territories and in the infinite populations, which putting its multimillenium wisdom in service of its indispensable reforms, reached the rank of superpower, equal and as dreadful as the greatest in this world.

They were making heard more closely these voices, the terrible famines of India and of Black Africa which made some entire populations perish, were carried by the waves of radio and television, in the most diverse districts of the globe.

They began to cause serious difficulties for the richest and the most powerful country in the world, the United States; Cuba, the republic of South America already claimed rightly or wrongly, but in a manner more and more urgent, the part of the proletarian nations in the international capitals.

And soon, the situation was going to begin to capsize. They will no longer be the Rich Countries which continue to impose their law on the Third World, but the latter, which, a repository for the sources of essential energy to the industrial development, will influence through adroitly applied blackmail, the workings of world politics…

Philibert recalled from a dream that he had had while still a child, while they brought him towards his first exam in the school of Saint Petersburg; the locomotive projected into the black night a multicolored smoke little by little along the march of the train, it developed into swirls, constantly spiraled, changed color, became agglomerated in order to dissolve and to be reunited again, scrambled non-stop, in order to draw in the nocturnal sky figures more and more fantastic and extravagant. He already saw, maybe unconsciously, that that had to be the image of the world, always unstable, cruel and terrifying image despite its beauty, reflection of a perpetual change of an incessant evolution towards an unknown future.

But above all that, there was still his God, to whom he was consecrated as a priest and that it seemed to him to have constantly served – despite his indignity, his infidelities, his mistakes and his falls – during all his life. This God, who had never abandoned him and whose presence in his life, he had always felt. In everything that he had lost, in everything he was going to still lose, it remained always this God and alone, his God. "Lord, stay with me!" prayed he softly. And his soul squeezed still closer to The One that appeared to him as the sole Stability.

THIRD PART

IN A WORLD THAT CHANGES

CHAPTER I

ABBOT PHILIBERT'S PROBLEMS

A little after the end of the war, Philibert arrived in Paris. Without delay, he had to have an operation. Without a penny in his name, it is only thanks to the compensation from social assistance and after a long stay in the hospital that he was finally set free from his pain without having to reimburse anything.

For his convalescence, he reached the hospitable domicile of his relatives, the Marquis Tamerlan des Etoiles, who inhabited a former particular hotel, in the 7th arrondissement. At the graceful entrance stairs of this building, waited since XVIIIth century, a sedan chair padded with scarlet cushions decorated with gildings. It still served for the movements of the great-grandmother of the family, duchess de La Vielongue, who died very old at the beginning of the XIXth century. One recalls the duchess as a person having so much spirit and writing even some novels that some considered a little obscene.

In the rooms a little somber but with a cozy aspect, whose large windows opened up on a silent and chic street of the Saint-Germain quarter, were hanging some portraits of the Tamerlan family. They recalled the celebrities of this old, aristocratic family which was said to have descended from the Merovingian Dynasty. The marquis was married to an American from an excellent family; he was a good and intelligent person. Himself, of a very distinguished style, spoke perfect English, his French had even acquired, it seemed, a light British intonation, the one maybe of the Jockey Club. The marquis had just justifiably took off his uniform as a liaison colonel close to the British army, a post that he had occupied until the end of the war.

Paris barely came out of the hostilities; there were still bread tickets. Philibert was nevertheless immensely surprised and comforted to see counter to what he had contemplated of the devastation at the time of his long exodus across the plains of Poland and Germany, this magnificent city so much spared from the ravages of the war. He believed to be living a dream!

As good as weakened by the operation that he had just undergone, Philibert tirelessly ran through the streets of the city, his eyes being able to be satiated with the panorama of the Seine and some majestically historic silhouettes of the Louvre and of Notre-Dame which were liberally thrown into the radiant sky of spring. The horizons of Paris was not yet blocked by the modern skyscrapers, and the noise of the incessant and stinking flood of traffic did not yet impede him from tranquilly enjoying of the picturesque charm characteristic of the old city; at the street corners, in front of numerous dance halls, one heard the accordion playing. And one could always sashay peacefully on the banks of the Seine, in search of rare books among the famous secondhand booksellers.

With his health being reestablished and as he could live indefinitely in the care of others, the Abbot Philibert looked to take up his work again. One opportunity being presented in a Franco-Polish parish in the Center of France, Philibert jumped at the chance with joy.

His new parish was situated on the banks of the Loire which spread its wide lazy waters throughout the immense sandy beaches. The interior of the country was very rugged and covered in rich pastures of bright green, on which, almost all year round, grazed some white cows called Charolais whose meat had a world-wide reputation. From multiple somber forests bordered the pleasant landscapes. In the hollows of the valleys, shimmered throughout the foliage of the trees, the water of the pure lakes with which the region was scattered. In the distance, appeared the bluish line of the first foothills of the Central Massif.

The country conserved some vestiges, difficult to discover, from the faraway gallo-roman wars; in addition, the towers and the massive walls of numerous castle-fortresses gave to the old burgs, which overlooked the valleys, an authentically Medieval style. They were on a ground long ago hard-fought between the Armagnacs and Burgundians.

This rich and beautiful country, so full of history where the simple countryside expresses the softness of the grand parks and of the castles, was inhabited by a gay and social population, which loved red wine, steak and fries, as well as a good joke and a little Gaulish. Fine gourmets, eaters of frogs and escargot, the inhabitants resided in the opulent farms or in some villages, which stretched for many kilometers At the time when Philibert arrived in the district, even the richest residences did not seem to hold to the appearances and to the modern comfort; the people preferred simpler conditions of life. The outhouses were in the back of the garden and their door was swept by tempests.

The breeders of Charolais livestock worked with much knowledge and love, but the farms emptied each year of their inhabitants because instead of the grooming of the beasts, the young preferred the office or the factory. Fortunately, the work hand was more and more replaced by mechanical equipment; the combine harvesters and bale-tying combines, more and more numerous, began to furrow the fields.

Some sizeable factories opened the doors, offering to the young, in the closest city, a work perfectly remunerated and in pleasant conditions. The swarms of bicycles of the factory workers rapidly gave way to lines of particular cars. Like the others, Philibert's parish benefited from it, and the entire population grew richer in the blink of an eye; the houses were equipped with electronic material and even the exterior aspect of the old hovels were rejuvenated and embellished. There were no longer any roofs, which did not have a television antenna. The proletariat had disappeared.

*
* *

It is in these surroundings and this milieu that from then on the Abbot Philibert was going to practice his ministry. Among his parishioners, the most practicing belonged to the old, traditional families. Exemplary was the practice of the lords; despite lacking domestics, they continue no less with it to "reign" in their residences from a bygone past by maintaining around them the good manners of the former France. Then, came the rich farmers who still did like their parents and grandparents. The least practicing were the workers, and however, the funerals and the grand festivals no longer saw any free space in the church In his ensemble, the people were believers and hardly anymore let themselves be impressed by the sectarian cries of the enemies of the Church, who became scarce. However, as the standard of living augmented everywhere, there was no longer any reason to assimilate the Church to the capitalists and to the enemies of the people. The sign of progress and rallying was frequently the subscription to the "Pèlerin" edited by the "Bonne Presse."

Besides his small French parish, center of his pastoral radiance situated around a marvelous Roman church with a modest rectory, the Abbot Philibert served several Polish colonies of the department.

For the most part, it was a matter of the family workers working in the coalmines which extended under the woodsy hills of the entire nearby region.

The Poles were still very numerous on the arrival of Philibert, and they were powerfully supervised in the associations, such as the Sainte-Barbe and the Saint-Rosaire.

Behind there banners and their flags, they flocked en masse to celebrate the grand occasion in the parish church, which filled up with their powerful voices singing Polish hymns.

Excellent workers, they quickly arrived at making themselves small fortunes and constructed, on the picturesque slopes with woods, some ravishing modern villas.

But, by gentrifying and taking the habits of their skeptical French neighbors, they lost, not only their national traditions, but also the faithful practice of their religion. Towards the end of his ministry, the Abbot Philibert saw at his Mass no more than a few dozen native-born Poles.

*
* *

Before becoming, much later, the oldest according to age in the canton, Philibert, at the arrival in his parish, counted still among the young. He had replaced his bicycle with a moped, then he exchanged shortly that for an automobile, which permitted him from then on to more easily go to the different points of his ministry. Philibert was well heard with his neighboring colleagues, for the most part still traditionalists; they sang the Mass in Latin, the back turned to the people, the priests discussed, read, wrote in the newspapers. The discussions and the polemics were often bitter, but did not impede the best friendship from surviving.

Little by little, the old priests passed away, one after another and the relief was more and more difficult. Because of the lack of more new candidates each day, the grand seminary emigrated progressively into the other diocesan city farther away. The rare young priests, who arrived, formed teams and professed the opinions contrary to those of their predecessors. The old canons treated them as originally dangerous, verily even as "heterodoxies." But after the Vatican II Council and the accession of young bishops, it was the turn of the old priests to not be on the same page.

Philibert loved to speak with one of his young neighbors, very thin and very dark; the latter never jokes, and his eyes shone with an internal fire. He had replaced his cassock with a simple sweater and read only "l'Humanité." His attacks were direct, often vulgar, he asserted that such was the method of Saint John the Baptist.

"It is through your fault," he declared to Philibert, "that the Church stopped attracting the souls! Your conservative and stagnant religion, which only proclaims that an abstract faith without going to the man and which does not truly practice the charity, has broken the contact with the people of God; you have ruined the religion! Your faith, all in abstractions, is exempt from the realizations and that is why the world turns away from the Church!"

"You are particularly right," responded tranquilly Philibert, "in effect, it could be only a theocentrism, all in a vertical dimension, made us too often forget the other dimension, horizontal and anthropocentric. What is, however, contrary to the words of Christ even, according to which we will be judged by Him according to our approach towards men, to which Christ has revealed himself. But you exaggerate by confining yourself uniquely in the horizontal dimension and by abandoning like that the departure point of all religions, which will remain always theocentric. You say, 'It is, through mankind, the other, that we arrive at God.' Oh! Unfortunately not, Sir! It is often the contrary; through his fellow man and throughout his fellow man, which is often mean and always imperfect, we risk instead to lose God, what has happened to so many of those who follow you! We will say then; it is through God alone that we can obtain and exercise the true charity, the one of Christ on the cross dying for his enemies. Man, always a sinner, can be loved in a perfect and selfless way that for God, because of God and through God! If the Man-God teaches us a perfect charity, it is because he is God and not because he is man. Only God can inspire the true Christian charity in us."

"It remains," continued the young priest, "that your ancient representation of God, all in Thomist abstractions, could reach only a "philosophical god," at the most a "Yahwist," who no longer convinces anyone. Moreover, we no longer have a need of philosophy because we reached directly the living and historic Christ. The Bible suffices amply for us. It is through the concrete, the human that we search for God.   Your philosophy, your apologetic is instead a cumbersome weight and not a contribution towards God."

"Do not go so fast, dear colleague!," exclaimed Philibert, "do not reject the philosophy outright! Because reason will always keep its rights. A plausible God for reason, a reasonable idea of God, we will always be necessary. I would again willingly admit that the abstract theodicy which one has taught us in our old seminaries has become insufficient for a great number of people. But this apologetic is not the only one. We have today a Christian philosophy, which all by keeping the value of a plausible reasoning, presents to us a less abstract approach, then less detached from man and brought closer to the Man-God – it is the one of Teilhard de Chardin, all of whose philosophical reasoning emerges directly in the same mysteries of the Christianity.   Here the theodicy becomes christodicy. Does this philosophy, which you knew like everyone else, disagree with you?"

"Teilhard agrees with me only as revolutionary which has upset a rotten world. But, positively he is worth nothing. Negated by the scientists for his unpardonable synthetic extrapolations, negated by the philosophies whose consecrated method he abandoned once and for all, negated, by the theologians as an antitheological gnosis, it is not worth more than a suspended poem in the air without any serious base."

"Dear colleague," smiled Philibert, "it seems to me that by reasoning like that, you are infinitely more conservative than me. For you live always in the firewalls of the ancient School. To limit one's self to the strict analyses without admitting the possibility of synthesis, is not truly scientific. To consider that only the abstract categories of philosophies embrace fully the entire truth, is not philosophical either. To see an antitheological gnosis there where a philosophical approach gives a justifying plausibility to the gratuitousness of the Revelation is no more dignified than a truly theological thought. If Teilhard proposes to use a universal synthesis in the world, if he operates, not only with the strictly abstract concepts, but also by employing some arguments taken to the sensibility of all of mankind, if he renders finally the Christianity reasonably plausible and comprehensible to every thinking being, – I do not see that one can refuse him the value of being an eminent man of science, a grand philosopher and a perfectly orthodox theologian. And this is more serious than even the most beautiful of poems! It prevents such that the poetry is attractive and it is in that manner that Teilhard becomes a thinker all the more engaging.

"You other Christian progressives," continued Philibert, "you are all, more or less, marred with Marxism.. Oh! I am not reproaching you because of it, I would even say that, in a certain manner, I am grateful to you. For, at least, you made the Church come out of the doldrums of a feudal stratification in which it risked being frozen. You have like that opened to it some humbly human horizons, wider, more democratic, less haughty, less insular and less narrowly nationalistic. Here I recognize it, you did an excellent work and rendered an immense service to the Church. I love very much Latin and I believe that nothing is capable of replacing the magnificent Gregorian choirs, but it is not I who will reproach you for having introduced into the Mass the dialogue of the priest and of the people in their vernacular tongue, no more than having inaugurated the communion into the hand, that I find even more hygienic and more convenient. Why I am reproaching you is for having borrowed from the Marxist dialectic only the 'antithesis' and for having in this way abandoned the 'thesis,' without which no 'synthesis' is any longer logically possible. I understand Stalin and above all Mao-Ze-Dong; the brutal rupture with the past and the refusal to be left to the soft pleasures of synthesis, were maybe the only means of effectively imposing a necessary new order. But in principle, as well as the 'yang' and the 'yin' of the Chinese philosophy that the 'thesis' and 'antithesis' of Hegelianism and of Marxism have, when all is said and done, only a sole goal: to establish the unity of a 'synthesis' or of 'Tao,' which supposes the substitution, but not the abolition of the 'thesis.' Contrary does not mean contradiction. Do not abolish the past, as have done the Marxists, Chinese or Russians. It is not through the total disavowal of capitalism and the principle of liberty of the person that you will arrive at constructing a better world. If Lin Piao had raised these ideas against Mao, he would, without a doubt, only be ahead of his time. I would say, more squarely, that our 'antithetic' attitude which rips the baby from his mother, risks making from it not a normal man, but an artificial being, against nature. That is moreover the type of your Marxist ideal!!!"

While his interlocutor was listening to him with a somewhat amused interest, Philibert continued, "I know how much you are a believer and I do not ignore that your sole aim is to convert our sole valuable adversaries, who at this time are the Marxists; I admit also that in order to reach that goal, it is necessary to employ not only the language of the adversary, but even the background of its thought and to discover in its philosophy all that is found in it to be positive. This approach is justly offered to us through the Teilhardian philosophy. Its evolutionist base, borrowed from the paleontology, is dialectic but the inverse of the Marxist dialectic, it all is entirely striving for the synthesis. Not that the antithesis plays no role in the Teilhardism: as well as the painful trials and errors of nature and its tragic collisions, but even its straying and its sins are proven, ultimately, necessary for the progressive workings of the world. But in this scrambling of spontaneities who are the base elements for all things – the essential orientation – the one that explains the evolution certified throughout the centuries towards some forms of existences more and more perfect – is unquestionably their best unification, an always more perfect synthetization, otherwise said, in order to employ a Teilhardian term, the 'amorization' of all things. And how too could it be otherwise for every believer who according to the expression of Vatican II, understands that God is most of all love and that his work can be only the work of his love?!"

"All that is only a beautiful utopia, without any possibility of practical application. The world in reality is the contrary to this utopia," sighed the young priest.

"Not at all!" retorted Philibert, "it is just the contrary! What impedes the world from advancing is very often the pessimistic attitude of man. The ancients said, 'nothing changes, it is always the same thing.' You say, 'The world evolves, but we do not know its orientation.' Teilhard said, 'The world advances and its orientation is the development of the charity in the universe.'

Who else but Saint Paul in his letter to the Corinthians described for us the charity as the sole thing that will never die. For, from now on, it constructs an eternal world since here-now, the lone revivable world, the one that announces the New Heavens and the New Earth. It outlines what can be the Kingdom of God. The exterior forms of the world can pass, crumble, die without the charity in God being prevented from establishing from the present – patiently and invisibly – the Kingdom of God. Each time that the particulars or the nations understand one another, listen among themselves, unite with one another, not in order to hate but in order to love, they construct a world eternally durable. It is here that resides the essential contribution and merit of Teilhard; to the paralyzing pessimism, he opposes a spiritualizing and optimistic orientation. Maybe…, one day…, the fundamentalists as well as the others, who have not yet admitted it, will they finally understand all the good that Teilhard brought to humanity; the fundamentalists will be reassured of what progress will not break from tradition, and the others will be better oriented in all that they will undertake."

"I would admit it maybe, but how do you want to translate it into your life?"

"It is our entire mentality that would need to return and to change," responded Philibert.

"Then let's wait," resumed the younger.

"Maybe you, not me," concluded the elder while melancholically smiling.

*
* *

The seasons, the years passed.

The cycles of the glorious springs, the hot and sleepy summers, the golden and melancholic autumns, the winter tempests howling into the old chimney of the rectory, constantly took turns. The Abbot Philibert uncontrollably grew old.

He became more sedentary, voyaged less. But it seemed to him that his life, while losing his extensivity, always gained in intensity. Nothing, no event bothered him anymore; the least thing clothed a beauty, an interest that he had not known before. What imported to him the anonymous crowds of the Parisian boulevards, compared to his parishioners, of his children in the catechism, of his old friends, whose life he knew in its least details and who had become his family. Before the lives of others, before this grand world of God, so beautiful everywhere, his own affairs lost their importance and faded more and more. His own person disappeared for himself, before disappearing for the world. "Deo sit gratias," said he softly, by finding more and more softness in the arms of his God, of his Master and Lord.

CHAPTER II

IN THE UNITED STATES

It is from le Havre that one of the first boats had to depart bringing the emigrants from the last war to the United States. It was called "Le Fiacre de Paris;" it was very huge, but also very dilapidated; this crossing of the Atlantic must have been one of its last.

And however, what a beautiful ship ! Immense, it raised its three powerful chimneys, slightly leaning towards the rear, above the swarm of countless small boats – trawlers, flagships, tugboats – which swarm around this colossus. By its majestic allure, this king of the oceans stands over all.

Marjolyne and Ermelyne, followed by the Pozecki family and Widzislaw Bartzel, were already on the deck and waved goodbye to the Czerskis who came to accompany them on their departure. The eldest had the melancholic looks, only the children seemed enchanted by the extraordinary adventure that awaited them.

Finally, the "Fiacre de Paris" released a terrible mooing, which reverberated into the entire bay, chased away the seagulls which flew away in flocks over the waters, and scared the small children. The colossus of the seas slowly started on its way in order to move away towards the infinity of the ocean.

A cold wind started to blow on to the deck and the passengers all went back to their cabins. Marjolyne and Ermelyne occupied together a luxurious first-class cabin with a bedroom and a salon; it was their brother from America, the Marquis Bardzopolski, who paid all the fees for them. The Pozecki and the Bartzels, young still – to whom the Lords Beechforests had offered to pay their passage – not wanting to be tactless, had chosen some cabins situated on the second-class deck.

"As they must be fortunate, our grandmothers, in their pretty cabins above!" said the eldest of the small Bartzels to the oldest Pozecki.

"When we will be their age, we will do the same!" exclaimed his cousin in the guise of consolation.

The night already enveloped the waters of the English Channel and on the British side, which ran alongside the boat, appeared the lights of dwellings while the gong rang out to call everyone to the evening dinner.

Everyone went down the large staircase; across a suite of salons carpeted in red, glittering with mirrors, and furnished with deep armchairs and small armoires filled with jewels, one reached the grand dining hall; it was magnificently illuminated by immense chandeliers.

Among the small tables covered in immaculate tablecloths, crept out a horde of young domestics, dressed in all white, an orchestra played softly.

"Ladies, through here! Gentlemen, through there! And you, the children, follow your parents!" commanded with a serious and polite voice, a maître d' dressed in black.

The children found the meal excellent : a little chicken consommé, a delicious sole à la Colbert with some purée and some meringue to lick one's chops. They had even permitted them to drink some drops of an excellent Beaujolais served at room temperature.

After the meal while the men had gone to the bar to drink their cognac, the rest of the family conversed in the immense armchairs of the salon. "We have it good on this beautiful boat," whispered the little Bartzel to his cousin Pozecka. "Yes, so much better than in the cursed Europe," acquiesced with a voice barely perceptible his little cousin, while shyly watching the expressions less cheerful of the elders.

While the others returned to their cabins for the night, Pozecki and Bartzel leaned with their elbows against the parapet of the deck; they remained for a long time silent and meditative, while smoking their cigars and contemplating the sea.

They had now left the English Channel and the boat had joined the desert of the ocean. The night was beautiful and the water tranquil. The full moon threw a long luminous trench on the waters. Faraway and inaccessible, the countless stars vacillated on a sky without a cloud. They barely heard the sloshing of waves which beat against the flanks of the grand ship. The odor of the cigar floated around the two men.

"I am not worried for our future, but we will need to elbow our way through," said Bartzel after a pause.

"The children and we others, we will quickly adapt, as for the grandmothers, I fear that at their age, the change will be too brutal," remarked Pozecki.

Began the regular and monotonous life of a week of travel. Each morning, the Catholic chaplain said the Mass in a corner of the grand salon, which they had arranged for this circumstance. Most often it had only Ermelyne as an attendee. For the latter, it was a consolation that she always appreciated to the highest degree.

The meals were served at the same hours. Afterwards, while some went to read or write, in the multiple salons and boudoirs, the others climbed on to the deck to contemplate the monotonous waters which surrounded them on all sides. They extended sometimes like immense azure mirrors until the faraway horizons but other times, rose in tall waves which provoked some pitching and tossing or some swaying and inundated the deck, splashing the voyagers with salty water.

All in all, the crossing proceeded pleasantly. A cinema with some American films, brightened up the longest afternoons.

*
* *

At the end of a week of travel the "Fiacre de Paris" made a majestic entry into Hudson Bay into a panorama worthy of the counts of Ali Baba. The siren of the grand French ocean liner released its deepest moos, as if it wanted to convince the universe that it did not let itself be impressed at all by the incomparable power of the immense blocks of Manhattan, which stood in front of it to dizzying heights.

A tight crowd waited on the dock for the arrival of the voyagers. A horde of journalists surrounded the Marquis Bardzopolski, half-brother of the Princess Otwocka and of the Baroness Bartzel. He had at his side Lord Beechforest II, one of the greatest financiers on Wall Street, who had just succeeded his deceased father. In New York, everyone knew the two personages and one knew that they had come to welcome their relatives from Europe.

Despite his great age, the Marquis Edelfred Bardzopolski had always remained an aristocrat eminently elegant. He was also president – chief executive officer of the Northeast American Railroad Company, a situation that he had inherited from his widow, an American multi-millionaire. This arbiter of elegances was quite adopted by the American "high society" and her name figured with all its titles in the "Who's Who:" Marquis Edelfred Bardzopolski, CEO of the Philadelphia-Baltimore-Washington Railroads, former grand squire of His Majesty the Emperor of Russia, one of the last descendants of the Empress Auguste Viktoria. His influence imposed some of it even on the most democratic journalists although they did not know exactly in which country reigned this Empress Auguste Viktoria. After a short discussion, they concluded that that had to be in China, so much that the marquis had a certain oriental style.

The first to receive the assault of journalists and photographers was Ermelyne ; behind her came Widzislaw and Hippolyte, then the Bartzel children and Pozecki and bringing up the rear, Marjolyne who never hurried.

"You are some relatives of the Marquis Bardzopolski?" questioned the journalist.

"Yes, I am his sister," responded Ermelyne.

"And are the persons who follow you and all these children from your family?"

"Yes, of course."

"And how is it that none of you have the Chinese appearance?"

"The Chinese appearance! Why?"

"Are you not, like your brother, one of the last descendants of the Empress Auguste Viktoria?"

"Yes, but my great-grandmother was not Chinese, but Austrian."

"And where did you live before the world wars?"

"In Courland, sir."

"Courland... hold on... that must be Korea!"

"But no, sir, it is at the other end of the world; Courland is on the Baltic Sea and Korea is in the Far-East."

Some smiles appeared in the crowd, several broke out laughing. Ermelyne felt ill-at-ease, and Pozecki and Bartzel were frankly displeased.

"Why did you come to bust our chops with all these ascendancies?" murmured with an undertone Widzislaw to his brother-in-law, "we have more serious things to do in America! Find work, it is that which interests us."

Pozecki reflected, "All these foolish reminiscences of a

faraway country can only harm us. Once and for all, we need to turn this page and no longer speak of it," said he through his clenched teeth.

*

* *

Three immense American cars waited for the voyagers in front of the steps to the train station: an Oldsmobile belonging to the Marquis Bardzopolski and two Cadillacs from the garage of Lord Beechforest.

The marquis and his two sisters, whom he brought into his Philadelphia home, showed in the first car while the Bartzel and Pozecki piled in the two Cadillacs; in them, Lord Beechforest accompanied them all the way to his property in Green Hill, situated in Lancaster County.

For awhile, the cars followed a monotonous plain, which pulled away from the city of Philadelphia.

It is here that the two groups separate.

The marquis inhabits a very comfortable two-storied house. It was surrounded by churches, temples, chapels, Masonic lodges; Sundays one heard from all sides only the sounds of the bells large and small, carillons and little steeples in unison, what was often very harmonious. In this respect, Ermelyne was then satisfied.

Although close to the center of the city and a woodsy avenue, which linked to the grand museum, the quarter was only a construction site in full effervescence; they worked there, in effect on the demolition and the construction of numerous other residences. Throughout the day, one heard only the strident vrooms of drills and one saw only the immense mechanical steam shovels digging and scooping out the soil. A continual racket, a suffocating dust enveloped everything from morning to evening.

The vacant lot served as a hang-out for bands of adolescents of every race and of every color, who during the day, would insult you and during the night would not hesitate to sucker punch you. Also, Ermelyne was scared.

And yet, how splendid were these hot summer nights! It had to be the same hardly centuries ago when the Indians populated this savage land. Today, in one immense sky, the lights from the stars merged with those of the skyscrapers while all the land rang out with the song of the cicadas.

*
* *

The two small neighboring farms that Lord Beechforest had designated to the Pozeckis and the Bartzels, were dwellings with modest appearances. And yet, these "ranches" constructed in coarse wood from firs had every comfort; the same night as their arrival, both families could freshen up with hot water in large bathtubs; some provisions of meat, butter and eggs awaited them in the electric refrigerators, there was even a little bar with some whiskey and fresh water; finally, central heating unit with a thermostat, promised to distribute the desired temperature during the rigorous winters!

If it had been the unexpected comfort for a European, neither the magnificent "highways" always jammed that criss-crossed the entire district, they could have thought that it was somewhere in a countryside of Europe: broken with woods and isolated ranches, the fields and the prairies extended until the very blue line of the Alleghany Mountains on the horizon; a very great calm reigned everywhere, despite the faraway noise of the incessant flood of cars that flowed on the neighboring "highway."

The Bartzels and the Pozeckis, wives and husbands, rolled up their sleeves and without delay put themselves to arranging their homes and make their farms produce. The eldest of the children were sent to the neighboring schools. All were obligated to work flat out, to always save, often even to spend the entire nights on intellectual works. But the results were satisfying; not only, they could buy as property the farms, which in the beginning were rented to them, but Widzislaw succeeded even in once again taking up his former occupations as architect and the two wifes were admitted as teachers in the high schools of the region. Little by little, everyone was Americanized to the tips of their fingertips and their children spoke their maternal language with a very pronounced American accent.

*
* *

One of the first visits of Ermelyne was for Zinaida. The widow of Lord Beechforest I inhabited a charming cottage in a very Elizabethan style, situated on the Main Line in the vicinity of Philadelphia.

This neighborhood, one of the most elegant in all of America, kept absolutely intact the tradition of the XVIIIth century, at the time where Philadelphia was still the capital of the United States. The apparent modesty and the rustic lifestyle did not prevent that alone, the truly rich people could be permitted to construct there their residences.

The shade from century-old beech trees, birches, elms and oaks covered the house of Zinaida; very neat, this house climbed a grassy slope perfectly maintained in a bright green; on which the massifs of flowers added their richly colored textures.

From the other side of the railroad, which passed by, to the foot of the park, a tumultuous torrent rolled its troubled waters; its characteristic name of Schuylkill recalled the epoch where the Indians here crept out on their light canoes.

Zinaida came out of her beautiful cottage in order to welcome her old friend. She had changed a lot and walked with difficulty. Ermelyne stepped closer more nimbly because although the same age, she had kept more of her fluidity in her movements than Zinaida, dedicated for a long time to a sedentary and easier life.

A frank joy lit up Zinaida's face when she kissed Ermelyne, "How are you, dear friend?... for so many years we have not seen each other... both of us have lost our husbands since..."

"Yes, I just learned that... during this war, we were cut off from the world... without news," responded Ermelyne.

"It was necessary to know Kurt," continued Zinaida, "in order to appreciate him for his true worth. He seemed so hard, such a businessman, but deep down, he had a very good heart. Above all after the death of Barbara, he softened very much. And you know, Ermelyne, he had always the crucifix of Barbara next to his bed. He said nothing, but he looked at it often, most of all just before dying. I believed that this man, who long ago critiqued everything connected with religion, died as a believer. It seemed to me that he invoked the God of Barbara."

The two ladies entered into a very Old England salon, a

little cold and somber. On the shelves next to the portrait of Kurt, Ryffka and Barbara, Ermelyne noticed her own portrait, which represented her in the company of her husband. A fat black woman, undulated heavily from the haunches, placed on a table a very strong tea and a fruit cake that Ermelyne found delicious.

"I saw your son in New York," said Ermelyne interrupting a silence, "he came to pick up the Pozeckis and the Widzislaws in order to bring them to his properties in the country… He is very good with my children and I thank you for that, dear Zinaida."

"Vlady is my great support at this moment," pronounced Zinaida, "He often comes to see me with his wife and children. I would say even that I love better his way of working than that of his father. His social, economic and political opinions are much more humane and evolved. Do you know, Ermelyne, that he quit the Club of the Sons of Solomon in order to found a new club entitled 'the Sons of Abraham.' He is even one of the principal advisors in the White House. Evidently Vlady is very busy but he succeeded sometimes to escape from his occupations and come to land in a helicopter on the great lawn behind the house."

They still spoke for a long time about the two families, about people living or dead, about the children and their education. Around evening, the two ladies left profoundly satisfied of having met one another once again in such a mutual understanding. It seemed to Ermelyne that her friend had with age become much more natural.

CHAPTER III

THE CZERSKI FAMILY

Helped by some charitable friends and relatives, the Czerskis – after multiple pilgrimages in search of a stable job and a stable household – finally found a haven right in the heart of Paris, in the VIth arrondissement. Three small, ancient rooms barely equipped had to shelter the parents and their five children, whom they sent as soon as possible to different schools.

The Czerskis had then found an abode; there reigned a grand calm because their rooms were separated from the street by a large interior courtyard and the swarm of the capital as a consequence barely reached them. Only the trash cans dumped in the morning by the sanitation department could wake the inhabitants of the building.

Each morning also, the bell of the nearby chapel of nuns, called Amaldyne to Mass. Continuing the traditions of her pious mother, she went there each and every day and brought her children there on Sunday.

But the misery pursued this large family. Amaldyne was energetic and hard-working; every job was good provided that she served the needs of her husband and her children, mostly still very young.

Wladimir did everything possible in order to help his wife and contribute to the essential expenses. However, to the opposite of his cousins in America, the Pozecki and the Bartzels, he had neither the youth nor the energy any more, nor the habit of simple work. He was mostly an intellectual, a thinker and an artist, and it was more difficult for him to adapt to the hard life as a simple worker.

In spite of their grand material poverty and thanks to their sense of hospitality, to their kindness to their high culture, the Czerski formed quickly one of the principal homes of the Polish emigration after the second world war.

There was no one who appreciated the conversation of the former Prince Czerski, who from high in his armchair – reserved for him by his wife – expounded, punctuated by a distinguished gesture, well constructed phrases, full of originality and depth; Most of all. Amaldyne pleased her guests by the comprehension that she showed for all human misery and by a hospitality, which made her back down from no sacrifice.

What about the times Philibert, coming from his country parish, found here the family atmosphere where he relaxed the best! The naturalness, the gaiety, the cheerful spirit of his sister and her children, were for him a cure as any of the most beneficial. "You still have some luck at having a family so close in France," the people said to him in order to console him on his exodus from Poland.

The Czerski children grew up: handsome, natural, gay, active, intelligent. Nevertheless, the girls were more hardworking, more studious than the boys, who however had to succeed no less well afterwards.

An exuberant joy reigned in the three rooms when arrived their comrades, students, male and female, French and Polish, who in the opaque smoke of cigarettes, filled every apartment with their laughter and their jokes. The parents then benefited from it in order to withdraw to a neighboring cinema.

Despite the friendship, which surrounded him, the invitations that he received, the interesting and distinguished people that he met, Wladimir Czerski was bored.

"My place is not here, they gratify me very kindly, but it is only charity! I do not feel truly alive!" said he to his friends. He wanted to be useful again, he wanted to do something in his life! These few books that he had skillfully translated from Polish to French, were not enough for him. The honor to have during the annual sale signed his work sitting besides a French academician, was only a meager consolation for him.

"I think only of returning to Poland," he confided to his brother-in-law Philibert.

"And your wife and your children... do you want to bring them with you?" asked the abbot.

"Of course. We all are Polish. I would not want, in any case, only one of my daughters to marry a foreigner. I have absolutely nothing against the French. But it is our duty to remain Polish, otherwise, our tradition is going to be quickly lost in France."

"You judge for yourself," remarked Philibert, "for you, for me, for your wife, it is harder to forget Poland. But your infants, who are already more French than Polish, you do not have the right to prevent them from integrating into France and from marrying French citizens. Still if your entire family returned to Poland. But you perfectly well that it is impossible to impose on them the current communist regime. You would not even want that. Then better to let them peacefully adapt to the nation in which they are going to live…"

"For me," continued Czerski sadly, "the notion of Homeland is something religious: the soil on which one is born, the traditions in which one had been raised, are sacred. Every denial would seem to me treason."

"Your way of living, your patriotism," remarked Philibert, "are certainly very honorable, but I do not think that one can impose it as an absolute value. To be honest towards one's past is another thing, it is always a duty. But to live this past as you or I do it, is not an applicable rule for all. The past must be lived according to the present circumstances; however, these change, still more for the young than for others such as us.

The health of Wladimir declined moreover. He weakened and each day became more nervous and more irritable. A medical exam had discovered the cause of the pain: a cancer which was rapidly evolving.

He knew he was dying. To Philibert who had gone to see him some weeks before his death, he confided, "You know, Philibert, it is not necessary to fear death. Once, I already believed that I was going to part. It was a very gentle feeling, even pleasant."

Some weeks after this interview, he died in effect surrounded by his wife and his children and after having received the sacraments. Lying in the coffin, he seemed to breathe this peace of which he had spoken to Philibert.

They buried him, far from his country, in Thiais, close to Paris, in the anonymous quarter of the poor Polish emigrants. The magnificent weeping willows and the high poplars standing on the horizon recalled this place that all the cemeteries of the world resembled.

Amaldyne supported with dignity and courage the death of her husband that she loved and admired above everything else; she devoted herself entirely to her children and later to her grandchildren.

The eldest of the sons was prodigiously gifted but

rebellious in his purely theoretical studies; it is only afterwards that he showed his astonishing capacities for the commercial affaires where without a diploma, he succeeded in seeing himself entrusted with great responsibilities.

The youngest had the priestly vocation and although promised to a brilliant diplomatic career, preferred the ministry of souls and became a high-caliber educationalist.

It remained for the daughters to marry. The oldest found a Polish husband with a position in the bureaus of the United Nations in Geneva, where she followed her husband. The two others daughters chose Frenchmen for husbands, boys from good family listed in the "Bottin mondain."[1]

"Never would Wlodomir in his life have consented to giving his daughters to foreigners," said Amaldyne to her brother during one of the frequent visits that she paid him in his rustic rectory, "for Wlodimir, the word Homeland had a religious signification."

"I would very much admire Wlodimir for the nobility of his patriotism, but to speak frankly, I do not think that he was right. The same question was often posed to me in my Polish ministry in the countryside. The elders insisted obstinately that their children marry only amongst Poles. They often go so far as to look for the future wife in Poland. Not always because they have more confidence in the religious education of traditional morals of Poland, but because the future in-laws, who barely speak and understand French, sorely accept feeling like strangers in their future family. But this is not our case.

"Others such as us, people of the former generation, never succeeded in making us accepted by the French as full-fledged compatriots. At our ages, impregnated as we are by another culture, this one, in one way or another and despite all our efforts will always be perceptible. Our idiosyncrasy will be always be something a bit annoying to the French natives, and all the more, when they are less civilized.

"But if the generations, who follow us, do not run this risk, it would be, on the other hand, regrettable that they tend to cut their Polish roots and to broke from the traditions of their ancestors. The first shame would be for France herself, which can only build

---

[1] Bottin mondain: the most famous French society directory.

on the Polish cultural contribution. The more one respects his own traditions, the more respectable he is. Moreover, the fidelity to this Polish past does absolutely not impede a perfect integration into the French community. In order to cite only the most illustrious examples, neither Mr. Poniatowski nor Mr. Lipkowski, however eminent French Statesmen, have never – as far as I know – disavow their Polish origins."

The young Czerski girls married then effectively with some Frenchmen, excellent boys, moreover. As everywhere, it was not the idle life that awaited them. But they were at least right in some pleasant moments, full of charm and fluidity in a nation, which had become completely theirs. They brought to their French entourage this unwavering sense of a certain measure of life which gives to the existence a great firmness. This was the best heritage transmitted by their mother Amaldyne and through her by their grandmother Ermelyne.

CHAPTER IV

THE LAST YEARS OF ERMELYNE

Ermelyne had surpassed the hurdle of eighty years, but she had lost nothing of her vivacity. A terror for automobile drivers and for police officers, she zigzagged nimbly in the middle of the streets around City Hall while attaching the least importance to the lights and to one-way streets. Twice she had been knocked over by a car; the first time, she was in the right and was compensated, but at the time of her second accident, they judged that she was guilty and was not compensated. Ermelyne was contrite about it because she asserted while laughing that it was her only way of making a living. Her family only noted that she got off lightly.

All the stores, all the offices, were familiar to her. At each window, she had some friends; after having put stamps on her volume of correspondence and having sent the packages with gifts to the four corners of the world, she pulled out of her handbag, a pile of photographs, which represented her children and her grandchildren and showed them to the employee, who feigned a lot of interest in them. Ermelyne was in effect very proud of her numerous progeny.

The poor country church of Philibert had also benefited very much from the parcels from Ermelyne: chasubles, conopea,[1] cassocks – worn and outdated but of perfect quality – came at that moment to decorate the church of his parish to the joy of his old faithful sexton.

Separated for years by the entire immensity of the Atlantic Ocean, the mother and the son would have loved so much to see each other again. Alas! It was, for the moment, always impossible. None of them had the means to pay for the long voyage between Europe and America.

But one day Philibert received from his attorney in Paris excellent news: the favorable issue of the case for damages from the war that he had engaged against the current government of Germany; that permits him to set out on a faraway and costly journey.

Philibert decided to fly and left for Paris. It was the era

---

[1] Conopea: tabernacle curtain.

where General de Gaulle, coming back to power, strived to rebuild the prestige of his nation and to demonstrate that France no longer had the need of the American guardianship.

It was time! The American style had meanwhile invaded the capital; the gardens had become "squares," the restaurants, some "snack bars" or "grill-rooms;" they quenched their thirst by drinking a shot of red or a little white, which had been supplanted by "Coca-Cola;" the houses were called "buildings" and they looked no longer to improve their situation, but their "standing."

It existed already even a section of highway, which recalled those of America; it is true that it led for the moment only to the Orly Airport. The new airport was all new, beautiful, modern. Certainly, the plane, which must have brought Philibert was not yet a French "Concorde," but a "Boeing" of the purest American manufacturing.

*
* *

It was then by a magnificent evening in July that the "jet" of Philibert lifted off from Orly Airport, flying high above the immense Parisian agglomeration and sped away into the sky regaled in purple by the setting sun. Soon, the immense mirror of the oceans sprawled out far below on every horizon.

The sky began to darken, the American airline stewardesses served a light meal after which each of the passengers was ready to take some rest, deeply imbedded in his armchair. The plane advanced without turbulence and they could have believed that it remained in place. And yet, it flew at almost a thousand kilometers per hour.

Just in time to doze off and here is the sky that commences to clear up, then lights up all of a sudden in order to project on the layer of clouds floating above, all the colors of the rainbow. This fairyland lasts only several seconds and here is the "Boeing" which slows its speed and loses altitude. They are approaching the American continent suspended between the blue of the sky and that of the sea. Then distinctively appeared some houses and some roads, some fields and some trees. The plane was preparing to land at the Idlewild Airport.

It is with great joy that Philibert saw from afar the ascetic face of his first cousin Boryslaw Bartzel, who waited for him at the airport exit.

For some entire months, they had remained together in France, in the rectory of the abbey before the cousin had decided to leave for the United States in order to settle permanently.

After having abandoned the practice of his profession as architect, Boryslaw devoted his life to painting with pastels. He put into it his passion that characterized it in everything that he undertook.

From an astonishing erudition, knowing at the tip of his finger the Roman-French art, he was, for Philibert, a irreplaceable guide during their frequent trips into the Centre and Midi of France. Some pastel paintings by Boraslaw afterwards came to decorate the walls of the rectory of the abbey.

The two cousins knew each other since their childhood and some numerous memories linked them in friendship. Boryslaw brought his friend into the small apartment, very modest, that he occupied at the foot of the building of the Organization of the United Nations. In one miniscule room, Philibert, sitting on a narrow bed, swallowed an omelet while toasting their friendship to a very clear tea with lots of lemon. Afterwards, Boryslaw brought out some boxes from the armoire: his pastel paintings which represented different views from New York under the snow or in the shadows of a summer sun. Philibert found his painting very pretty.

*

* *

Barely in two hours, Philibert arrived by train in Philadelphia. His uncle, Edelfred Bardzopolski, had died in the mean time, during an excursion in Abyssinia, but his mother and his aunt lived always in the house of their deceased brother.

His mother had changed a lot since their last meeting after the war. On her side, although older, Marjolyne held up well. She found many things strange in this New World, but full of good sense and with her feet on the ground, she was accommodated to them by joking.

Ermelyne, on the other hand, felt a neat antipathy for all that she found simplistic, vulgar and superficial among the

Americans. "They are not complete men," she professed, "but half men." Her two consolations were the church situated just in face of her home, where she spent entire mornings, and her children and grandchildren who lived in the nearby county.

Philibert took his quarter at the home of a neighboring curate. The parish church was impeccably maintained, but its rich construction, brilliant and modern, was terribly standardized and impersonal.

On Sunday, it would fill up with a great crowd and many people, notably some young, took communion. Philibert was fascinated. "Do not let these beautiful appearances fool you," to him said the curate, "our religion is very superficial and mostly very conformist to the least tremor, all that will collapse like a house of cards!"

After his Mass, Philibert went to see his mother, close to whom he spends the entire morning. Ermelyne was crocheting non-stop while Philibert read to her a book. The afternoon, both went to town; most often they went into the stores in search of rare and special wool, of which Ermelyne needed for her work. Never was Philibert so bored, but in order to please his mother, he waited patiently.

However, he visited in that manner different quarters of the city and Philibert had the opportunity to be surprised by the contrasts that existed between the closest places; on the sides of splendid and luxurious marble buildings, the richest stores, they discovered a narrow street, bordered by rows of low red-brick houses, which exhaled the most primitive grime.

There are entire neighborhoods inhabited exclusively by Ukrainians or Poles, Blacks, Porto Ricans, Italians. Each nationality had its own clubs, its churches, its "saloons," which served specialties prepared in their own native style.

Sometimes, Ermelyne and his sons took the small train from the Main Line and went to see the Pozecki and Bartzel families. A great big American car waited for them always at the arrival to the station and they brought them towards the countryside where each of the two families possessed on its own a small villa modest yet very comfortable.

They were welcomed there in the former Polish manner: with delicious "zakuskis" with pâté or with ham – very much appreciated by Ermelyne, some "borscht,"[2] some Polish lamb chops. After the meal, sometimes they went off by car to visit Lancaster County and its forests that the early falls made blaze like a fire. On the way, they encountered the Amish with long beards with their wagons always pulled by horses, which recalled the laws of ecology.

*

* *

The mother and son also paid a visit to Lady Beechforest in her cottage along the tumultuous Schuylkill.

Zinaida rejoiced a lot at seeing the former "fiancé" of her daughter, today clothed as a respectable clergyman.

Always brimming with charity and projects, she exclaimed, "But it is a shame to leave Philibert to grow moldy in his French parish! Could one not prepare something in America for him? Like that, he would be closer to you, Ermelyne," said she speaking to her old friend. "Hold on! I have an idea! Vlady, my son wants to absolutely see Philibert. He will be at my home next week. Both of you, come. I am sure that he will give us good advice and powerful support. Count on him."

As agreed upon, Ermelyne and her son arrived at the scheduled rendezvous with Vlady Beechforest. The two old friends greeted each other very cordially. Zinaida having exposed to her son her plans and her projects for Philibert, the former exclaimed, "But yes! And I do not even believe that that would be difficult to organize. Philibert could very well teach at the University of Washington. Among the American professors, he would make a fine figure of a scholar! They are not very demanding among us. If you knew the level of some of our professors! With the baggage that he possesses, Philibert get along marvelously!"

It was then agreed between the two friends that they would go together to Washington the following week in the car of Beechforest, who had moreover some business to attend to at the White House.

Washington was very appealing to Philibert. The immense

---

[2] Borscht: beet soup.

panorama of the city seated on the banks of the Potomac, its general layout, its wide avenues, its elegant governmental buildings expressed something very open to the world.

They made some visits, they saw some important and interesting people, they encountered a group of representatives of the former Polish diplomatic corps, but – ultimately – nothing could be agreed upon. Philibert had therefore to leave again for Europe in order to get back to his parish and it is there that he learned the failure of the alluring project.

*
* *

Philibert came back again several times in America to see her mother. The health of this woman declined and she was growing old in the blink of an eye. Having always suffered for rheumatism, she was now crippled by it. She was no longer an elegant lady with a slender figure, but an completely old woman bent in two. She resembled an old witch and the children of the neighborhood, in seeing her pass by, would shout to her, "Old witch!" and throw stones at her. On the other hand, she wanted eat only mush and drank only hot water, Ermelyne realized the uselessness of her existence and the approach of her end. "I am like a hair in the soup," she said to Philibert, "I sense that I no longer have much time as that." It was said with a point of humor which, she never abandoned.

Seeing her in this state and not being able to leave her alone, her family found for her a hospital well equipped, with a chapel and run by nuns. Before going back to Europe, Philibert visited this facility and took away the best impression. And however, his mother was not happy there. She had certainly lost her status and fortune, but she was accustomed to certain respect, whose notion the Western Democracy had lost. Witness the little server who called her by her first name and treated her as a turbulent infant, who made Ermelyne cry bitterly.

However, she was not abandoned; her American family came to see her frequently, but as all were overloaded with work, they could not stay constantly near her, Ermelyne felt alone; she wrote to her son in France, "Do something for me to get out of here! I cannot take it anymore! I even have no longer any desire to pray!" The situation was desperate; at the end of her life, Ermelyne had lost all sense of decisiveness and when they proposed to her another solution, she backed off at the last moment.

But the day came when her heart wavered; they found her dead in her bed. Young, full of ardor, she had been ready to accept all the sacrifices of the hand of God and had essentially insisted in teaching to her children the sense of renunciation. Philibert had never forgotten the tears that still very small, he had poured after having offered his mother a small stuffed rabbit, which he adored and that she had never voluntarily returned to him! How many of her children had not suffered from having to always wait for the end of the meal, which went on until their mother had drank her seventh cup of tea because she would only ever permit an exceptionally anticipated close of the session! Herself, in her own life, which had been only a continuous defeat, had she not fully accepted without the least murmur, loss of her fortune, loss of her status, all that did not count for her. But here she is such that she must accept the greatest sacrifice, the one of Christ on the cross who had felt abandoned by his Father in Heaven. "Eli, Eli, lamma sabbacthani?" she should have also cried out in her last instants of life.

It did not seem that in her case, death had been a curse for Ermelyne. Reporting to Philibert the death of his mother, Widzislas Bartzel wrote to him, "In her coffin, she seemed fully peaceful and expressed a nobility and a grandeur that surpassed everything that we knew about her during her life.

Having received the news of the deceased, Philibert felt suddenly terribly alone. It was from his mother that he held the profoundest aspects that his religion had. He went from then on alone in life, but the message left by his mother in his soul never left him: the faith in God that his mother had taught him to love despite all the suffering and all the ordeals during the existence.

CHAPTER V

THE LAST WILL AND TESTAMENT OF ERMELYNE

Long years had flowed past since the death of Ermelyne, the matriarch of the Bartzel von Weyssensee tribe: from numerous ramifications because of her, this one extended now from Austria and Poland throughout Switzerland and France up to the United States of America.

Born into honors and wealth, Ermelyne had passed away into the extreme destitution and solitude, object of the indifference of her closest family circle, which could comprehend only that so poor an old woman could still claim respect due to a status that she no longer had.

During her entire existence, which had been in reality only a perpetual fall – since Austria, Courland, Poland, Germany and France until the United States – Ermelyne had always been supported by her religion, by her faith and her prayer; so well that at any moment, she had not felt the need to complain of these material upheavals. In this German language, which was the one of her childhood, in order to console Philibert in his ordeals, did she not say herself, "Wo die Not am grössten, da ist Gott am nachsten."[1]

But here she is all of a sudden towards the end of her life, feeling completely demoralized and discouraged; even prayer could no longer console her. Her sacrifice became total. It was a dark night. Like Jesus, her Master, she had to drink the chalice of bitterness until the sludge and like Him cry out to God her Father, "My Father, my Father, why have you abandoned me?" But is every Christian life not a life for Christ? And, is every Christian not another Christ? If Ermelyne had still lived, she – the tireless correspondent of the family – could have written some letters to her children, her grandchildren and great-grandchildren. They were around forty dispersed to the four corners of the world. She, who took such an interest in the global problems, could have exchanged her opinions on the great events of the era.

The aristocratic feudalism in which she had lived a long time, no longer represented only a faraway historic interest

---

[1] "The greater the misery, the closer God is."

reclothed in poetry, or even a sort of folklore good for the fools. The world of grand bourgeois and already the capitalism, which had succeeded it, was itself also, disappearing. It ceded its place to socializing capitalism, which was making the proletariat disappear with it, established a world of small bourgeois. But this socialism, limited to the borders of the rich nations, already suffered the assault of a new wave; under the push of the Third World, holder of the raw materials, the national socialism became a planetary socialism. The incessant whirlpools of the world already formed a new curve.

Always attentive to the entire world, the Catholics, the universals, were the first to understand the signification of this evolution and to perceive there the hand of God, perfectly complying to the eternal message of the Christian Revelation. For a long time, a religious, scholarly philosopher, Teilhard de Chardin, had discovered this synthetization of the world and had systematized it. But his way of presenting his ideas had seemed scandalously shocking to the old theologians and it is in this manner that later, the Vatican II Council adopted only the Teilhardian theses only by carefully avoiding expressly referring to their author and employing its formulas.

It was necessary to recognize the former Greek statism – under the push of the evolutionism of Darwin, of the relativism of Einstein and of the atomistic physics – was no longer in order. The world changed, its laws also, the harmony of the world was to find much less in the beginning than at the end of things. The perfection was more in the future than at the heart of the past. God was not only the Alpha, but also the Omega of the world.

It is through this light that we need to understand and explain the History of Humanity. It no longer existed from the social order established once and for all. The injustices and the illegalities between the men were no longer inescapable laws. The tolerance of Saint Augustine or of Saint Thomas for the servitude had to be understood like a correspondent in a given era, but not as an absolute and permanent law. Today it is the same for the nuclear bomb.

The French Revolution triggered first a great upheaval in the world. Three grand principles were proclaimed through it: Liberty, Equality, Fraternity. Although they had overturned and abolished a good number of just institutions, good and beautiful, that they had contributed to the assassination of the sacred and innocent persons of the royal family and made a mass of good people perish, it is nevertheless the revolutionaries, who were right.

The "Liberty" was the first to bloom. Each desired to liberate himself from the oppressive yoke of the Former Regime. By benefiting above all not the neediest but often the most dishonest and the least scrupulous. The great bourgeois capitalists take the place of the deposed nobles; they became rich as millionaires, then as billionaires. In principle, everyone was likewise free, but in fact, the inequality of the wealth contributed to the installation of the power of money and to the formation of a proletariat, whose status soon become worse than if it had been the one of the serfs.

The Liberty contributed to the development of a capitalist system like the dizzying rise of the advanced technology, but the second principle of the French Revolution, the Equality, was far from being recognized by the New Regime. Always increasing, the proletarian mass claimed an absolute equality and Marx brought a solid doctrine to it. Also revolutions more and more powerful began to pound down the domination of the capitalist system. The Great Russian Revolution of 1917 arrived and it is then that a powerful socialist State, which claimed the equality for all men, was established for the first time. Curiously however, they were not the socialist States, but rather those which belonged to the capitalist camp, which effectively put into application the ideal of Equality. It is in that manner that the system of the social Capitalism was born.

By adopting the democratic ideal and by applying it thanks to the social laws of the more and more daring, the social capitalism succeeded in establishing a quasi-general welfare, and with the same effort, the proletariat ceased to constitute a problem. In the rich nations, the proletarians disappeared almost totally. Nevertheless, those represented only a third of humanity. In the rest of the world's population, which one often called the Third World, the poverty had still increased more. Next to nations which abounded with food and luxury products, some millions of people continued to die of starvation, in Africa, in Asia, in Latin America, because socialism had not yet crossed the national barriers nor those of the races.

It still missed out on realizing the third rule of the Grand

Revolution, the "Fraternity," which alone would be capable of abolishing these borders. Still in this era, every attempt of no longer taking into consideration what separated the nations and the races was considered unforgivable, as a criminal treason against the National Ideal. The martyr of Martin Luther King was the most flagrant proof of it. And the exploitation of the Third World, of its virgin lands, which contained almost all the raw materials, continued, robbing the People of Color and enriching the Whites.

But here it is that for the first time, the eyes are opening amongst the people of the Third World; they began to become conscious of the fact that they possessed the riches under the soil, without which the most developed technology becomes sterile. And the Third World, with great cries, like this, it claimed its part, the first warning came from the Arab countries, which refused to deliver their petrol. The rich nations trembled; no matter how much money and factories of the world they had, without oil their wealth collapsed. Is it not then a planetary, economic system which is imposed? A system based on the fraternity of the human species?

Fraternity! What a grand word! She implies another thing still that the arithmetic calculation used by technology and commerce. The computers, even the most perfected, are no longer sufficient to make the world advance. It is necessary, for that, in addition, an unimaginable thing: the Love in humanity.

One had already realized that instead of bringing progress, the technology alone quite often only destroys Nature, the nursing mother of Man. One had not sufficiently had love for this Nature, one had not recognized nor respected its own law. As had already remarked Bergson, it is this law that makes it advance and conserve, not only through analyses but above all through the subscribed syntheses essentially at the bottom of the creation. Alone then the syntheses or the love can promote the evolution and to bring to it some satisfying solutions, the necessary syntheses for progress.

Love: law of Nature, but most of all, human law, it does not suggest only the necessary syntheses to the material progress but it alone is capable of abolishing the national or racist borders, which excessively taken into consideration, impeding the progression of humanity. Without destroying the reasonable and legitimate separations, without abolishing the former respectable structures, nor the best traditions of yesteryear, love overtakes them, surpasses them, encompasses them all and creates new syntheses in which Humanity can continue to survive, despite all that always separates and will always separate men from each other.

It is finally love which leads to the supreme synthesis, the Synthesis of syntheses, to the Suprapersonal God who constitutes, in order to understand the totality of things and to love them all, the Last Response in theory and in practice. Teilhard de Chardin, the greatest philosophy in our era, demonstrated it to us in his system.

But a God, who is only philosophical theory, will never know how to convince man. A God is not only abstract Thought, he is also Life. A God, who speaks only of love but who lived it in his latest consequences. Yet, nothing is more eloquent than God, who speaks from the Cross, a God suffering, abandoned, scorned, dying in the total destitution for love of mankind. Only the Christian God can convince us that the fraternity among men must be lived.

Sometimes, better than men, women understand the message of Divine Love. Such was the case of the mother of Teilhard de Chardin, such was also the mother of the mother of Philibert who said, "The only thing which will remain forever imperishable in our lives, the sole finery, which will be able to embellish us until our death, it is love!"

By her miserable end, becoming identified with Christ on the Cross, it is the message of this love that Ermelyne had bestowed to her children, grandchildren and great-grandchildren, that she loved so much, for whom she had lived until the end of her life. "Go, work in love in order to construct a better and happier world!" would she be able to write if she had lived.

CHAPTER VI

RENDEZVOUS AT THE HOTEL CRILLON

While the Abbot Philibert, after his Mass, was drinking his morning coffee, his housekeeper brought him the daily mail. Once, he discovered, among the newspapers, a very beautiful envelope carrying the emblem of the Hôtel Crillon in Paris.

"Oh, that is well depicted!" shouted the old damsel, while pointing out the insignia of the hotel drawn on the envelope.

After having opened it, Philibert tendered the envelope to his housekeeper," Take it, keep it, I do not need it," said he. Then he read the letter. It came from his former friend, Vlady Beechforest, who asked him to come to join him in Paris as soon as possible.

"I was in Paris with Kissinger on his way to the Middle east," it read there, "I am waiting for you at the Hôtel Crillon. I reserved an apartment for you. Vlady."

Philibert took the express train in the afternoon and arrived in Paris in the evening. When he got off at the Gare de Lyon, the warm atmosphere of a September night shrouded him.

He found a taxi easily enough and sank into the cab with his little suitcase. The car rolled along the Seine, which sparkled with lights of a starry sky, while the sidewalks on the right were blocked with a dense crowd, which came out and into the shadows was wedged an alley of lime blossoms.

After having passed by the walls of the Louvre inundated with white light projected by immense street lamps, the little taxi emerged on to the place de la Concorde, illuminated as in the middle of the day, with its obelisk standing in its center.

The car went around the plaza and stopped in front of the Hôtel Crillon, where in the blinding light, moved into a crowd of "grooms" dressed in red, with ladies and gentlemen in elegant summer outfits.

"Move it! Move it!" commanded, while approaching the taxi, a gendarme immediately shrouded in his uniform, "it is not the place for taxis."

Philibert lowered the glass and started to explain to the police officer that someone was waiting for him at the hotel.

Noticing this poor country curate seated next to a beat-up suitcase, the officer interpellated in an arrogant tone, "Who is waiting for you?"

"Lord Beechforest," responded the abbot, "member of the mission of the secretary Kissinger." The officer became at that moment quite affable, he hailed a "groom," who was in reach and commanded, "Go carry the suitcase into the hall of the hotel." Philibert spent all his time paying the chauffeur and got out slowly behind the "groom" and the suitcase.

In the hall, Philibert found a crowd of people, who belonged, from all evidence, to the highest society. On some canapés and in the deep armchair were seated some ladies with fine and long legs under their short dresses; they smoked and chatted with the gentlemen in smoking jackets, leaning on the side.

No one paid the least attention to the poor country parish priest with his grey, washed-out and dented suitcase. The abbot approached the desk. "What do you want, sir?" an imposing porter asked him while looking him over top to bottom through his half-closed eyelids.

"I must have a room here, which had been held for me by my friend, Lord Beechforest," responded Philibert tranquilly.

At the sound of this name, the face of the porter changed instantaneously. He became all smiles and affability, "But yes, in effect, Monsignor," said the superb porter emphasizing somewhat on the titles of the abbot, "His Lordship recommended to us to inform him as soon as you arrived. Excuse me, Monsignor…" and he took the receiver to telephone the upper floor. "Please wait a moment, take a seat among these armchairs, His Lordship is going to arrive in a second."

Philibert took a seat on the side of the elegant group, who were forming a circle seated in the armchairs. The members of this group considered his intrusion as an incongruity and regarded him with extreme disdain.

But here was the door of the grand elevator which opened up and left room for Lord Beechforest, who rushed in with open arms in order to greet his friend. The apparition of the Lord in the hall provoked an almost religious silence in the entire entourage.

The servants leaned over and at the heart of the elegant group from where Philibert had stood up in order to go ahead of his friend, they regarded him now with envy, almost humility.

"Who is this priest greeted with such respect by Beechforest?" asked a lady to her neighbor.

"I am taking you quickly to my place," said Vlady loudly to his friend, "Henry (it was the matter of Secretary Kissinger) just left for the Middle East barely an hour ago... we can use all the time we need." The journalists and correspondents present lifted their eyes.

Vlady and Philibert looked at each other. Since their last encounter, they had aged a lot. Their hair had whitened. But – as noticed Philibert – his friend had always kept his vivacity and his energy; it was a very handsome old man.

The elevator stopped and the two friends exited into a hallway richly wallpapered and discreetly silent. They entered into the apartment of the Lord. A high lamp distributed a softly filtered light on to a round table surrounded by deep armchairs.

Vlady pulled out a bottle of scotch and two crystal glasses from a cabinet. He filled them and presented one of them to Philibert, who meanwhile, sank lazily into the deep cushions of his seat.

Beechforest took a seat at his sides, "My mother," said he, "before her death asked me a lot to meet you again and to renew our former friendship. She spoke only of you and said how much she loved you and held you in esteem. 'The Bartzels,' she said, 'are people for whom I have the highest esteem.' It was inconceivable for me to pass through Paris without going to see you. I therefore said to Henry, 'Leave before me, I will join up with you in two days.' He will moreover be followed by my son Jimmy who is here with his wife Fatida, the very own niece of the Saudi King... Wait, there they are!"

In effect, the side door of the apartment opened discreetly and they heard a melodious voice of a young woman, "Can we enter, Papa?" Her Royal Highness Princess Fatida, spouse of Lord Beechforest III, appeared in the doorway, accompanied by her husband. With her magnificent black eyes, she resembled an oriental gazelle, and her young spouse could have been easily mistaken for Vlady when he was young. They very cordially greeted the friend of their father and afterwards took leave in order to catch the Boeing which waited for them at Orly.

"I am very happy for Jimmy, his wife is very nice indeed," said Vlady as soon as the door had closed behind them, "if you knew as he already knows how to replace me. I said to Henry that he would do his business much better than myself, so much more that he has at his sides his Fatida, a charming, fine and intelligent Arab.

"Before engaging in our direct conversations with the Middle East, we have decided, Kissinger and myself, to do a little detour in order to meet up with our President and to have a meeting with him," exclaimed Lord Beechforest slowly enjoying his alcohol.

"And how have you been received at the Elysée?" asked calmly Philibert, who was enjoying, after the fatigue of the trip, a fresh and heartwarming drink.

"Alas! Not very well. Mostly, the French since General de Gaulle have become the terrible children of Europe. They want always to act like lone knights and for us, it is consequently very difficult to constitute a common front with Europe in our negotiations with the oil-producing States."

"I understand. But it would be necessary still to know if your approach to the problem is truly the good one and if the French don't have some reason to distrust your commercial politics? Living in France for a long time, I have the impression that the French social politics made more progress in its planetary conceptions than yours, which did not reach to come out of the ruts of a national, impotent capitalism to resolve the problems of our era."

"Yes, I know," said a pensive Vlady, "yet from the living of my father, at the heart of our clubs, I advocated the development of a commercial politics more selfless than the one that we always follow. But my theses were considered only as reveries and utopias and never had I been truly followed. Yet here are the results; the poor countries, which one believed to be able to satisfy by alms, have become abruptly, thanks to the exploitation of their oil wealth, nations face-to-face from which we are those who are the buyers. The situation is reversed; it is no longer a gift that they demand, but a counter-party which they require, which through its scope risks to hinder our entire economy. It is the industrial ruin, the unemployment which threatens us presently."

"Is there not a test there," asked Philibert, "of the defectiveness of the capitalist system, at least of a certain capitalism, which sees only the interests of its own nation? The one, which does not understand starting today the planetary problems posed to us, which are confined to the sole interests of its country, prepares its own ruin. It no longer suffices from now on for a State to consider its economy to the measure of what its contractor can offer him immediately, but it will also be necessary that it foresees the own needs of the latter and that it accepts the ulterior reimbursement of the sums that it invested in this country. The national money exchanges will have to be replaced by international exchanges of needs and these are not always payable with money. The investments payable in money will have to give way to the investments payable 'in spe.'

"One thereby understands easily," continued Philibert, "that France which has some conceptions and even some laws more social than yours, hesitates to follow you blindly.

"All the more so that it believes to find on a land that to France, it seems to better understand than you. For, confess it, – oh, I do not question the priceless services that you rendered to Europeans! – despite your immense means, you never reached, by your fault or not, suitably resolving the problems of the Third World.

"Do not forget that vast territories of the Middle East and Northern Africa had for a long time been subjected to the influence of France and that they there still frequently speak French; all this added to the geographic proximity constitute many factors which call for an exceptionally close collaboration between France and the African world. On one hand, there exists next to the infinite riches, which the subsoil hides, an immense misery in the deserts of the Sahara and of Arabia. There is, on the other hand, our very advanced technology, that added to the one of the other European countries, could render these virgin lands farmable. Some very interesting exchanges could thereby develop in this respect.

"Everyone knows also that they are not only the Americans who would like in one way or another, to get their hands on these countries. The Russians have the same ambitions and they will not leave your hands free. The implantation of France and some other European countries in these territories would then constitute a situation less dangerous for the equilibrium in the world. In need of better, you should accept this conjuncture and let France and the other countries of Europe follow their own destinies."

"For my part," said Vlady yawning, "I would willingly

accord to the French free range, but I fear that all their efforts to ameliorate the fate of the concerned populations benefit ultimately only the emirs and other local kinglets. Your chances would not be better than ours."

"You are surely right… And however, it would already be so even if they succeeded in establishing in this country a powerful infrastructure, civilizing, cultural and technological, from which sooner or later, everyone benefits. Work of a long breath… But is it not time to go to sleep?"

The two friends stood up. Vlady opened a door and Philibert found himself in an apartment which was the exact replica of the one out of which he came: a large salon lit by a veiled green light, next to a bedroom with a great big bed, then some toiletries, a bathroom, some spacious armoires. All his businesses have already been impeccably organized in the placards and the drawers. After having recited his evening prayers, Philibert took a hot bath and laid down in his bed, whose sheets were of an impeccable cleanliness. Through the large, perfectly watertight French windows, he barely notices the noise of the big city, which resembled a murmur without end on ocean waves. Cradled by this faraway sound, Philibert soon fell asleep. He counted on only saying his Mass of the next afternoon. In effect, he had thus been agreed with the Confraternité sacerdotale where he had the custom of going to celebrate the Eucharistic sacrifice.

When Philibert woke up, his entire room was bathed in purple. It was already ten o'clock. Philibert opened the thick drapes of a Bordeaux color. The sun was already high in the sky.

After a hot bath, he dressed, said his morning prayers and went to knock on the door of his friend. "Enter!" heard he. All dressed, Vlady was at his work table and was writing.

"How is it going? Slept well?" said he to his friend holding out his left palm. "Wait for me a short moment. I just wrote a letter to Kissinger and I am finishing another to the President. We will take breakfast together. How do you want it, à la français ou à l'américaine?"

"A l'américaine," responded Philibert.

Vlady rang. A head waiter appeared. "Please serve us an American lunch," commanded the Lord. While Vlady still worked at his desk, they brought a copious lunch composed of "porridge," of "hot dogs," of "scramble eggs" with some crispy "bacon," some white bread with very fresh butter and some very strong coffee.

Vlady arose from his desk. He brought a magnificent ebony crucifix adorned with a Christ finely sculpted in ivory. "It is the crucifix of Barbara," said he, "it was hanging above the bed of my parents. I know how much you loved each other. I offer it to you."

Because of it, Philibert had tears in his eyes. "It is very nice of you," simply said he…

"What are we going to do today?" asked Vlady wedging his teeth into a delicious hot dog laid in a bun, "all day belongs to us. I leave just tomorrow morning."

"If we would go see my sister Amaldyne and my aunt Marjolyne," proposed Philibert, savoring with pleasure his scrambled eggs, "I need only to say my Mass in the afternoon."

"Your family is mine, your Mass is mine as well," responded Vlady, "we do everything together."

The two friends climbed down the staircase. They were greeted very low in the hall of the hotel. An impeccable domestic in a blue uniform rapidly came out from behind the counter and proposed, "Do his Lordship and Monsignor desire that I call you a taxi?"

"No need, dear friend," responded the Lord, "we want to have a stroll on foot. I would like to avoid any encounter with journalists," said he softly in the ear of his friend.

While leaving, they rubbed elbows with the same distinguished group of young men and young women, seated in the same place as yesterday evening. Philibert noticed that this time some more benevolent eyes followed his steps.

The two men were under the galleries of the Place de la Concorde. Philibert, small and puny, jogged next to his imposing friend. Both were dressed in somber grey. They resembled to two parish priests if only it is that Philibert solely carried a small cross on the inside of his jacket.

At the corner of the rue Royale, they took a taxi, which brought them to the foot of the Tour Montparnasse, where lived Amaldyne. She was alone in her modest apartment surrounded with low-cut dresses into which she tailored with assiduity.

At the sound of the buzzer, she opened the door and surprised and joyous, exclaimed, "I was not expecting you, Philibert!" – then noticing his companion – "But who is it that you brought us!"

They all kissed each other. Vlady deposed a very gallant kiss on the hand of Amaldyne. She was still a woman well preserved but no longer young.

"I was preparing some dresses for my two granddaughters, who just became engaged," explained she in seeing the two men throwing looks on to the salon now a workshop.

"How did that happen?" asked Philibert.

"Just simply. Both took some courses at the Sorbonne and they met their future husbands there: a Japanese student and a Hindu student. They were enchanted and were engaged. I would have been sorry if they had not been both good and fervent Catholics. The Japanese, a certain Prince Kamazaki (his father is only an enriched grocer), has a stupefying intelligence; the Hindu, descendant of the Maharajas Purda-Gutta, is so handsome and so charming that if I were younger, I would throw myself into his arms!"

All laughed. "And remember our escapades in Petrograd during the first world war? Of our strolls on the Nevski Prospekt?" asked a cheerful Vlady.

"And your juvenile love for my sister Cathalyne as well! The good old times of the young age!" sighed Amaldyne.

"You cannot stay for lunch with me?" proposed she always hospitable, "I am going to put away these rags and will prepare something light for you."

"But no, I beg you, Amaldyne," said Philibert, "we just had a copious lunch at the Hôtel Crillon, you cannot imagine what we could have swallowed. Vlad must leave tomorrow morning for Tel Aviv and we still have a pile of things to do together, I must say my Mass, and afterwards, we would like to go present our respects to Aunt Marjolyne."

"Then it will be for another time," said Amaldyne.

"It is we who are going to invite you," terminated Vlady.

From Amaldyne's home, the two partners took the path for the Confraternité sacerdotale.

They were welcomed at the counter by a young monk wearing a white smoking jacket, "You desire what, my fathers?"

"We come to say Mass," explained Philibert.

"Very well, go down into the cellars," said the brother, "but I doubt that you would find there an alb as grand for the other father."

"He will not say the Mass, he is not a priest, he came only to assist me… He is moreover only a Yuppie," said Philibert softly to the brother.

Vlady heard very well the last remark and gave a shove in the back of his friend. They started to laugh.

In the long tunnels, a row of altars were each waiting for its celebrant. Philibert chose one of them, as well as an alb adjusted to his size. Vlady lit two candles and started in the place of the choirboy at the bottom of the altar. Philibert said his Mass in French, language that his friend knew as well as himself.

After the Mass, the two men went into the grand Baroque chapel on the second floor and gave thanks kneeling in front of the open monstrance. A half-dozen nuns, dressed in all white, prayed next to them.

When they went out into the street, it was hot and they were very thirsty. They were sitting in straw chairs in front of a café at the corner of the Boulevard Raspail and ordered German beer. The fresh beverage seemed to them delicious, they slowly savored while watching pass by numerous dignified and distinguished adults as well as young girls and boys, who laughed and spoke loudly.

Philibert looked at this watch, "It is time," said he interrupting their pleasant siesta, "that we go see Aunt Marjolyne."

Vlady stood up with regret and said, "It hardly happens anymore to be able to relax and to unwind next to my good childhood friend! Shame, but all has an end."

The former Princess Marjolyne Otwocka occupied a miniscule room in an old-fashioned boarding house situated on the top floor of a tall building in the XVIIth arrondissement. They arrived there by an elevator, whose laborious and hesitant ascent made multiple creaking noises. After having reached a maze of poorly lit hallways, the two men knocked on the door.

Marjolyne has always remained a very grand lady, dignified and energetic. She could no longer see very well, but her viewpoint mixed with malicious humor and with kindness had lost nothing of its acuity.

She very affectionately received the two men, proposed a "drink" to them and pulled out a bottle that she hid under her bed for the guests.

"We come from Amaldyne's," said Philibert, "she was preparing the trousseau of her two granddaughters."

"In effect, I just learned by telephone," said the old lady, "but the most curious, it is only a letter from your other sister, Cathalyne, announcing the engagements of her two granddaughters Pozecki and Bartzel with a Black and a Chinese. It seems that the Black is very handsome and that the Chinese occupies a very important situation in business. Their names," now the princess consults the letter, "are Dr. Mumba-Lumba as the first and Chu-Chu Fi as the second."

"Are they at least baptized?" asked Philibert.

"Of course," responded his aunt, "and what will give you pleasure is that they have been led by the reading your books on Teilhard de Chardin!"

Philibert modestly bowed while Vlady watched him ironically.

After their visit to his aunt's, the two friends stopped at Place Péreire and ordered their dinner in an Italian restaurant. After the fatiguing walks of the day, the minestrone sprinkled with parmesan and the spaghetti spiced up with a meat sauce, seemed simply delicious to them.

"What are we going to do now?" asked Vlady while they came out of the restaurant.

"We are going to the cinema," decided Philibert. The film was long and it is only in the middle of the night that they returned to the hotel.

Having arrived in their apartments, Vlady pushed back the curtain, opened the French window and went out on he balcony accompanied by his friend. It was hot and delightful, and the immense city in front of them sparkled with innumerable lights, which moved in all directions.

"Here our day is finished," said with regret the Lord when they were sitting again in the deep armchairs of the salon, "tell me, Philibert, what you think of the future? Are you pessimist or optimist?"

"As you know – I have well noticed your smile at Aunt Marjolyne's – I am Teilhardian; that means that I believe in the spiral progress of things. Yet, the spiral does not exclude the cycles of returns, so dear to the Greek, neither the zigzags of the tragic clashes, which characterize, according to the Marxists, the progress of things. For those, it will always be the eternal monotony, for others, the tragedy of the fights and defeats. There are of course one and another in the unfolding of History, but the final progress, the resume of all, remains for me the spiral; although that would be imperceptible, the world always climbs! I am then reasonably optimistic because I believe in one sense in the definite orientation of the world in which we are living."

"Very reassuring," said Vlady, "I am going to repeat to Kissinger what you just said to me. He will hear it as soon as tomorrow evening. That is going to encourage him." On these words, the two men went each into his room to catch some sleep well earned at their age.

The next morning, each left in an opposite direction. Philibert had to return to his parish by train leaving from the Gare du Lyon while Lord Beechforest, accompanied by his secretary and his domestic, went to take the plane of the American embassy to arrive in Tel Aviv before evening.

It was agreed between the two friends that Lord Beechforest, before leaving for Orly, would drop off Philibert at the Gare de Lyon. They therefore took together the immense Cadillac of the Diplomatic Corps and could thus prolong their very short meetings to their liking.

"You are leaving for Tel Aviv," said Philibert absent-mindedly looking at the streets of Paris, "there you will encounter your numerous relations, there will be people that I have long ago seen at your grandmother's, some combatants in the ghetto, who will maybe remember me. Tell them how often I think of them and that I pray so that the Good God blesses them."

The car stopped in front of the platform of departures of the grand lines. Helped by the domestic of Lord, Philibert got out of the Cadillac carrying his small suitcase. "Goodbye, my old friend," Vlady shouted to him swallowing a tear that struggled to hide.

CHAPTER VII

AT THE VATICAN

Long decade drained away again. They were in the first half of the twenty-first century. All the contemporary of the Abbot Philibert Bartzel, as well as himself, were good and buried.

A great-great-grandson of the Baroness Ermelyne Bartzel, née Princess of Caramanlys, Msgr. Prince Eugene Czerski, undersecretary to the Secretary of State of the Holy See, examined an important dossier, which he had just brought from his morning audience with the Pope.

His Holiness Pope Theognosis 1st, a Chinese cardinal that they had just promoted to the papacy, had for a long time spoken that morning with his colleague.

"Dear Monsignor," said the Pope glancing through his Chinese eyes a pile of letters, "I am very satisfied with the correspondence that I just received..., look at all these missives, which come from five continents..., unanimously the governments of all the countries contacted me in order to ask to organize a planetary congress..., there is only one inconvenience; as for the place of the meeting, they eliminated a priori the cities and ask me to choose for them, with preference, a place in the countryside, which would not be touched by the pollution of the technological progress..."

The sharp and intelligent eyes of the old Chinese lifted up from the dossier and reflected an inspired look, "Oh, you know, Monsignor, it is not a politic role to which we aspire. But the fact that all the politicians of the world seem to show such a confidence in the See of the representative of Our Lord, filled me with a profound joy.

"There I find as a confirmation of what the Fathers from the first centuries of Christianity: Saint Ignatius of Antioch contacting Rome as 'the Church which presides over charity' or Saint Irenaeus from Lyon expressing the necessity for all the ecclesial communities to 'assembly around Rome.'

"All our current correspondents," and the Pope posed his finger on the papers spread out in front of him, "have, it seems, understood the role of Saint Peter in the world; in no way do they ask that we resolve their political, economic, commercial, social or technical problems, but they see the necessity of resolving them in the ambiance of a Catholic Church centered in Rome. If there exists a political mystique, it can be only universal, not Hitlerian, Jewish or in any other way, particularistic.

"In the capacity of head of the Roman Church," continued the Holy Father, "I do not want to put above the other Churches and beliefs from everywhere in the world. Each of them brings to us some richness, which we could be lacking. In order to speak only of Christians, I can only be inclined in front of the spiritual depths of the churches descended from Luther, in front of the magnificence of the liturgical mystique of the Orthodoxies, from which had so much benefited the Latin Church squeezed into its exaggerated legalism. Seems admirable to me also the mysticism of Buddha, the gnosis of the world, so simple and yet so just of Confucius, the law of the Mohammedans. All that earns our respect. Nevertheless, I think to sense that all the religions begin to understand that in order to give an efficient and practical evaluation to what they particularly carry, they need to not let themselves be governed by Us, but to profit from Our presence in the world. We are probably the only ones to help them evaluate what they believe just and good. And, we are ready to assume this role, which is the one of Servus Servorum Dei proclaimed by Pope Gregory the Great. 'Nihil hum anum mihi alienum est.' I was man, nothing, of which is human, must, I think, leave me indifferent. It is Our task to extend and to universalize. We are listening to all the voices of the world. Because it is not in vain that We are the Catholic and Universal Church. They accuse us of being a monarchical, autocratic, dictatorial society, but we are it only in the goal of assuring the triumph of charity in the world. We want to exercise no physical nor moral pressure on men, the conscience of each is for us sacred. Our task is to safeguard the charity between men and in God.

In the congress, which is announced, we are going to come across all opinions. It belongs to you, Monsignor, that I confide the task of organizing it. Find for them a place which suits everyone, where each participant will be happy and at ease. Yourself will assume no presidency, no dominant role, simply you will be their servant for everything, by facilitating their conversations and their meetings. Let them speak quite freely. I count on you…"

The young prelate, tall and blond, as all the Czerski princes, stood up, took under his arm an important dossier and after bowing before the Holy Father, disappeared behind a curtain and returned to his desk, "What rotten luck," he will sigh after having placed the papers on his desk, "all the work that this good Pope imposes on me!" He would rightly project, in this period of the dog days of summer, to take some vacation on the shores of the Adriatic. It was done with all these plans with all this work before him... a task for his vacation!

Despite the excellent air conditioning of his room, Msgr. Czerski, before restarting his work, felt a need for pure air; he thus opened the window of his seventh story, which looks fully over Saint Peter's Square.

Noon was hot, the square deserted, only many pigeons would fly above the fountains, from where distinctively climbed the murmur of waters. One group of lazy tourists loitered in front of the gate of the basilica.

"Let's begin then," reflected the young prelate by start to sort the mail, which the Holy Father had confided to him. The signatures came from every country in the world. Some names seemed known to him. He remembered, at that moment, that he possessed in his library, the memoirs of his great-great-uncle, the Abbot Philibert Bartzel, who had lived in the XXth century. He often consulted this work.

For example, this name of Myssiourkine, delegate from the Soviet Russia, did he not belong to the same family that the General Myssiourkine, who had been governor of the Baltic nations at the time of the Czarist occupation?

And this name of Wajdewis, delegate from the Baltic countries, would he not be of the lineage of Anton Wajdewis, of whom the memoirs of Uncle Philibert said he was a truly grand upstart? But are they responsible for the mistakes of their grandfathers?

And this Bartzel from Poland ? He is surely someone from the family. Maybe a great grandson of Widzislaw, who returned from America to his country of origin.

And this Prince Kamazaki of Japan? There was a Czerska married to a Kamazaki. He was not truly a prince. His father had been a simple grocer, but these people with a rare intelligence had made a fortune since.

Here is another descendant of a Czerska, the Maraharaja of Purda-Gutta, a true prince that one. And this Mumba-Lumba who comes from Africa. Would he not be a descendant of one of my great-great-aunts Pozecka?

Msgr. Czerski became reflective. How small the world is! All – Whites, Yellows, Blacks – we form in reality only one single grand human family.

"Wait," reflects the prelate, "these gentlemen ask that we choose for a place for their meeting a site well isolated, with preference in the soft, peaceful and picturesque countryside. I had just recalled that my uncle Philibert had given, in his memorabilia, an very engaging image of his parish… what was it called? Ah, yes: Bourg-sur-Landarge situated somewhere in the Center of France… This place could well suit our delegates…"

Thus he outlined a first plan for the organization of the congress and brought it to the Pope. Theognosis 1st was in agreement, all the more so, former brother from Taizé, it was agreeable to him that the congress would take place not far from the headquarters of his Order.

CHAPTER VIII

GRAND KERMESSE IN BOURG-SUR-LANDARGE

If they were the persons and the generations, which had succeeded each other, nothing for centuries had changed in Bourg-sur-Landarge. Far from the suffocating cities, polluting factories, blocked up highways, the old village always breathed the peaceful life of the country. They were always the same names and the same sites if the people had changed.

Looking over the same verdant prairies, ringed by the same forests of black firs, which covered the entire area of the department of the Loire until the bluish line of the Morvan, the small village had remained always immutable.

Here, a new pool glistened through the curtain of woods; elsewhere, the blue ribbon of a small tributary cut through vast prairies, from time to time, appeared the great tower of an old residence, but the monotony of this countryside slightly hilly was nowhere seriously perturbed.

Three times per day, as long ago, the Angelus ranged out from the tower of the small parish church, echoed to faraway, beyond the small castle and the old houses of the burg, until the heights behind the canal, up to the borders of the Forêt Verte, its calls to prayer.

*

* *

One glorious spring day, a small helicopter carrying the coat of arms of the Vatican, landed on the square before the church of Bourg-sur-Landarge. A young man, dressed as a clergyman, a small suitcase in hand, descended from the machine and headed towards the grill, which enclosed the garden of the rectory.

It was Msgr. Eugene Czerski. As agreed between the Vatican and bishop of the place, he had to live in the rectory of Bourg-sur-Landarge in order to devote himself to the preparation of the next planetary congress. He had already his key in his pocket because the young curate benefiting from the windfall of the unexpected replacement, had left to play football in Switzerland and had left his rectory empty.

"It is then here that lived my great-great-uncle, the Canon Philibert Bartzel," reflected the envoy of the Vatican opening, not without some difficulties, the door. In the foyer, he found in effect on the list of curates hanging on the wall, the name of his uncle, in the salon to the side was hung as well a huge portrait of Teilhard de Chardin, "And this as well comes from my uncle," meditated the young priest, "but this must be no stranger to my family," and he stared at a pretty screen with pastel paintings which represented the Roman churches of Auvergne, work of another uncle Bartzel.

The abbot Eugene was reheating his coffee in the kitchen when the ring of the doorbell rang at the door and that a small lady appeared on the doorway. She was thin, aged, dressed completely in black, a small silver cross was hanging on her ascetic chest. "I am Mademoiselle Terlaine," said she, "housekeeper of the Father Curates, I am at your disposal, Father Abbot."

"Your curate has left," said the young priest laughing, "he prefers maybe the sports in Switzerland to his pastoral occupations?"

"Each one has his business," prudently responded Miss Terlaine, "it is probably you who are going to replace him? What time do you want to say Mass? Also tell me the times of your meal."

"Listen, Mademoiselle," asked the young priest, "you will not know a place to park my helicopter?"

"Of course," responded Miss Terlaine, "just in front of you, look there under the hill, live the Très-Catholiques ladies, they will be delighted to loan you their garage." She quickly ran there and brought back the key.

"I am very grateful to you, Mademoiselle. Now I need to see my colleagues of the place, but I will come back for lunch.

"Really great, this young priest," thought the lady while scramming to prepare lunch.

Surrounded by a crowd of little children rushing from the neighboring homes, the abbot climbed into his helicopter and took off towards the administrative center of the canton. The priests were very welcoming and promised him all their cooperation.

He spoke also with the ladies of the Catholic Action whose meeting place was in the cantonal city. One of them was wife of the great solicitor, the other widow of a great industrialist. They were very up to date with everything and together they drew up heir plan for the reception and the activities of the congress.

"There will be almost a thousand delegates," began Msgr. Czerski, "it is necessary to house them, nourish them and facilitate their work; it is also necessary to assure them some relaxation."

"It doesn't matter," said the widow of the great industrialist, "we have excellent hotels and restaurants in our city: 'Aux Commerçants,' 'Aux Négociants,' 'Aux Capucines,' on the other side of the Loire.

"As for the central offices," added the spouse of the great solicitor, "your delegates will find the facilities very convenient, equipped with radios and television sets in the Supreme Castle of the Minimes, an old, historic residence, which overlooks our city and that we have acquired for our Works."

"For fun," thought the two ladies, "Bourg-sur-Landarge will have to be enough for us; the residence of Marquis des Hauteurs-Boisées could offer us very interesting hunting, the pretty manor of the count de Beau-Bourg would serve for our tea parties with music, the manor of the Chevalier des Vertes-Forêts is a good place for golf, one could organize there as well some scientific meetings on geology and archeology.

"And above all don't worry," said the good ladies, "we will take care of it. Several kilometers from here, there is still the sumptuous castle of the duchess of the Cross of Princes: ideal place for the conferences and mundane balls in an entourage of royal and serenissimo highnesses."

Content with the establishment of such a detailed plan, the young priest climbed back into his helicopter and arrived in time to have lunch with Miss Terlaine.

*

* *

The next day, he said his Mass in the adjacent church. The sole attendants were only Miss Terlaine and one of the Très Catholiques ladies.

Then, he paid some visits. The first was for the Marquis des Hauteurs-Boisées, who was also the mayor of the country. The marquis lived on the other side of the canal and had him stay for lunch. After the meal, they spoke of the planetary congress in the works.

What a beautiful park you have," shouted the priest, "these wide lawns surrounded by old oaks! This faraway escape on the houses of the villages extending on to the entire ridge on the opposite side! And all these forests on the horizon! It is truly splendid! I am just looking for an airport for the airplanes of the delegates... But no, your park seems too separated from the center..."

"It doesn't matter," responded very kindly the marquis, "but I have something which could make your business much better; look down there," and the marquis pointed out to the priest a great empty stretch on the banks of the canal; it is the former Champ des Lapins... enormous for the planes!" added he, eased by the thought of having thus separated from his manor an equally noisy neighborhood.

"In the capacity of mayor, you are going, is it not so, to receive the entire delegation?" asked Czerski.

"But of course. At the school of the Town Hall. Surrounded by all my advisors. We could also organize a hunting party. I have a pack of magnificent hounds, which is worth the one of Cheverny."

From the home of the marquis des Hauteurs-Boisées, the young priest took off towards Beau-Bourg Castle. It is the afternoon and the countesses received him with some tea and cakes.

The Beau-Bourgs were a family of artists and great travelers. The two ladies thereby accepted with enthusiasm the idea of organizing a musical and artistic soirée for the delegates of the Congress.

"A moonlit evening, the ramparts of the castle lit up by the outside lights, an orchestra playing softly behind the piles of flowers, all that could be only very romantic," said the Prince Czerski in order to summarize with a single phrase the expressionist side of that soirée.

Several hours remained for him still until night fall, he had thereby the time to pay a visit to the chaplain of les Vertes-Forêts, the knight of les Vertes-Forêts gave him a very cordial welcome. He led him through the salons of his residence showing him his beautiful library as well as a rich panoply of arms of former Resistance fighters; for one of his ancestors had been Companion of the Liberation at the end of the second world war.

It was agreed between them that one of the evenings of the

congress would be devoted to geology and archeology of the region.

The congress would take place in a week. In the mean time, Msgr. Czerski said the Mass each day, preached every Sunday, in a word, he replaced the curate. The people became accustomed to him and no longer called him anything other than "Father Curate."

One of his new parishioners proposed to him, "We would also like to have our meeting for the congress; we would love that it unfolds under the great walnut tree in the rectory garden; it will be necessary to invite our Msgr. Bishop and the priests; we are going to provide big tables and some champagne; we will do everything by ourselves." The idea pleased Father Curate ad interim.

The last visit of Msgr. Czerski was for Her Serenissima Highness the Duchess of the Cross of Princes. She lived in a vast and sumptuous castle in the middle of an shaded park. She accepted very willingly the idea of receiving at her home the delegates of the planetary congress. She organized a grand ball to which she would invite the fine flower of the European aristocracy.

Everything thus seemed ready to receive, to entertain and to facilitate the important works of the grand international congress.

*

* *

Came the D-Day of the congress.

From morning on, they were preparing to receive the delegates on the Place de la Mairie of the commune of Bourg-sur-Landarge.

The children were all there, the citizens formed groups, the notables were sitting in front of the bistro under immense red and blue parasols and ordered beer in order to pass the time before the inauguration of the festival. Even Mrs. Grocer, always on the job, stopped at each moment and pushed back the curtain of her French window which opened on the square. Immense cameras from the O.R.T.F.[1], hoisted on trucks, swept the square with their gigantic lenses.

One finally heard, coming from the Champ des Lapins, the

---

[1] O.R.T.F.: Office de Radiodiffusion Télévision Française.

siren's voice, which announced the departure of the delegates towards the Place de la Mairie.

A long parade of cars, accompanied by gendarmes shrouded in white and motorized, came out of the turn, and one after the other, these cars advanced slowly, each one decorated with its national flag.

At the threshold of the door of the town hall, appeared a group of gentlemen in black suits; it was the mayor surrounded by local notables, who came out to welcome the new comers.

The Marquis des Hauteurs-Boisées, slightly paunchy, carried around the waist his tricolor sash and had at his sides the town hall secretary, the municipal counsel, whose members belonged to the oldest families of the locality.

A little isolated, they recognized the Teacher and his spouse, as well as Msgr. Czerski, who was there, not only in his capacity as delegate of the Vatican, but also as the curate of the site. The priest was accompanied by the irreplaceable Miss Terlaine, who on this occasion, carried the most beautiful black outfit and some new shows of a neighbor and a friend.

The cameras of the O.R.T.F. turned their long lenses while Mr. Mayor and his counsel descended the steps of the building and carried themselves to the meeting of the delegates, who had left their cars and now advanced as a crowd towards the town hall.

The mayor stopped, pulled a paper out of his pocket and read a long discourse through which he wished the delegates a warm welcome and praised the benefits of nature, all while emphasizing the values of the agriculture and the forestry arts.

In the name of the delegates, Msgr. Czerski thanked in French the local authorities as well as the entire population for the hospitable welcome reserved for the planetary congress. For the most part, the delegates were people of color, but all civilized men, understood French.

After that, the town hall offered to the conventioneers a wine of honor and everyone left until the next meeting, which had to take place the next morning.

*

* *

During a week, they worked in the numerous rooms and

salons of the castle of the Minimes of the cantonal city. Some fruitful were signed between the countries of all the continents: exchange of oil against nuclear batteries for industrial usage, of rubber for potatoes, beef for coal… Everyone found almost his tally there. The most destitute were often the pole of attraction of the conventioneers.

Msgr. Czerski did not know much about industry nor about commerce, nor about the utilization of the raw materials, but he remained no less the active ingredient of the meetings. They loved him for his kindness and for his tireless good will. He found among the reunited delegates numerous contacts, some kinships and even some common points.

The Russian delegate, Myssiourkine, was good and well the descendant of an ancient prince-governor of Courland at the beginning of the XXth ; on his side, the count Bartzel, Polish delegate, was the descendant of Widzislaw Bartzel and through there, relative of the Czerski princes; the Prince Kamazaki, Japanese delegate, as well as the Maharaja Purda-Gutta descended likewise from a Czerska princess, while the Black, Mumba Lumba, and the Chinese Chu-Chu-Fi, had in the blood of the Bartzel in his veins.

The afternoons and the evenings were devoted to the excursions on the lakes and the mountains of the vicinity.

They passed a magnificent afternoon on the lawns of the park of the Marquis des Hauteurs-Boisées. Horses and dogs were brought, and after a polo party, the cavaliers surged into a gallop, the pack of hounds in the lead in the pursuit of a wild boar, who finally escaped them behind the Loire. The Prince Kamazaki, who had never mounted a horse, strained the foot, but Mumba-Lumba, who bragged about having climbed on antelopes, and Chu-Chu-Fi, who said to have done as much with the tigers, did not hurt themselves.

Very successful also was the musical soirée given in the Beau-Bourg Castle; in the environment of this ancient residence with its walls and its towers lit up with beams of invisible light, the music was truly an enchantress.

The evening at the castle of les Vertes-Forêts evoked the greatest interest among the specialists because the academician gave a long and knowledgeable conference.

Very brilliant was the great ball organized in the sumptuous residence of Her Serenissimo Highness the Duchess of the Cross of the Princes. They noticed that Purda-Gutta, Mumba-Lumba and Chu-Chu-Fi had much success among the damsels of the region. Most of all, Kamazaki – healed from his fall by the care of Miss Terlaine and her colleagues – showed himself a better dancer than a cavalier and drew long sustained applause.

"Wait, wait," said the duchess, who had at her sides the delegate of the Vatican, "it seems to me that there will be marriages between your continents!"

But the greatest success was the evening under the walnut tree of the rectory. Surrounding the bishop of the diocese, everyone without distinction of classes, of races or of nations, felt to belong to an even great family.

The congress was closed by a Mass celebrated by Msgr. Czerski, who pronounced also the words of goodbye; he thanked everyone for the warm welcome and wished for other reunions of the same genre.

"I believe that men," said he, "here did very good work. But if the peace had to be only a human work, it would not be durable. Because the Prince of Shadows always prowls, looking to blur the maps of men of good will. It is thereby necessary to pray for peace because it is also the work of God."

The Pope was very satisfied with the work of his delegate and named Msgr. Eugene Czerski financial protosecretary – he was until then only supra-financier. He then obtained the privilege of carrying from then on the cross on the chest, but without a ring or skullcap.

Commenting on the planetary reunion of Bourg-sur-Landarge, a professor at the Catholic University of Lublin wrote later, "Like that again, the synthesizing law of the negentropy won a victory over entropy; the static state of the world, lazy and selfish had to give way in front of utopia, the improbable; the material bowed and was illuminated by the spirit, and a revivable more unified universe extended on the earth…"

"The effort had been done but it did not suffice for a single one; we need to fight until the end of the world in order to maintain the victory of the Spirit over the material."

--THE END--

Titles from Dui Sun Jin Publishing

All titles available in soft cover on www.lulu.com at
http://stores.lulu.com/duisunjin

Adam Malik as Author:
Carte Orange, Carte Blanche
ISBN: 978-0-615-24578-2
Lulu ID #: 3386181

Your Own Private Coffin
ISBN: 978-0-615-24289-7
Lulu ID #: 3449289

Coming soon: Staring at the Sun From the Bottom of the Well

Aleksander Plater-Zyberk as Author, Translated by Adam Malik
The Last Barons of Weyssensee
ISBN: 978-0-615-25397-8
Lulu ID #:4097738

From a Castle in Courland to a Rectory in Nièvre
Souvenirs (1899-1950)
His Autobiography
Lulu ID #: 4231308

Count Tadeusz Czacki and his wife Countess Maria Czacka
History of the Count Czacki Family
Lulu ID#: 4231813

Compilation:
From a Castle in Courland to a Rectory in Nièvre by A. PLATER-
ZYBERK with History of the Count Czacki Family by T. Czacki
Lulu ID #: 4226471 (Softcover)
Lulu ID #: 4113348 (Hardcover with dust jacket)